T0323276

NEVER SHAKEN, NEVER STIRRED

NEVER SHAKEN, NEVER STIRRED

THE STORY OF ANN FLEMING AND LAURA, DUCHESS OF MARLBOROUGH

CHRISTOPHER REINDORP

Front cover image: Laura and Ann at a party at Warwick House, 1949.

Unless otherwise stated, all images are reproduced by kind permission
of the Morrison family.

First published 2023

The History Press
97 St George's Place, Cheltenham,
Gloucestershire, GL50 3QB
www.thehistorypress.co.uk

British Library Cataloguing in Publication Data.
A catalogue record for this book is available from the British Library.

ISBN 978 0 7509 9630 3

Typesetting and origination by The History Press
Printed and bound in Great Britain by TJ Books Limited, Padstow, Cornwall.

Trees for Life

CONTENTS

1

INTRODUCTION AND THE BEGINNING

From the moment of their birth at the beginning of the twentieth century, Ann and Laura Charteris were raised to be wives. Their only goal would be to marry, and to marry well. Which they both did. Repeatedly. When Ann married a peer, Laura married a viscount. When Ann subsequently married a press baron, Laura married a multimillionaire earl. When Ann finally married the man whom she believed to be the love of her life, Laura also married the man she professed as her great love – a publishing executive who was an ex-in-law of President and Mrs Kennedy. Following the executive's death, Laura bagged the 10th Duke of Marlborough, becoming a duchess and chatelaine of the mighty Blenheim Palace.

Ann and Laura would be defined by the men they married. But more than marrying often, and well, these sisters inadvertently created another legacy. A legacy that gives the women a rightful place in literary history.

Ann's third marriage was to a relatively impoverished journalist. While waiting for his impending marriage to Ann, this budding novelist sat down and wrote a spy thriller. Taking the name of a Caribbean ornithologist for his hero, he created a world of intrigue and villains. The novel was called *Casino Royale* and the character was, of course, James Bond. A character who would go on to become one of the most famous literary creations of all time, spawning the most successful film franchise in history.

As well as a welcome distraction from his upcoming marriage, Ian wrote for entirely practical reasons. He was marrying the 39-year-old Ann Rothermere, the ex-wife of the fabulously wealthy Viscount Rothermere. She had been accustomed to a certain standard of living, and the pressure was on for Ian to increase his income. 'She baited him to start writing,' Ann's niece, Sara Morrison, recalls.[1]

Ian started writing and huge success followed. Without his marriage, Ian may never have sat down at his typewriter. Without Ann Charteris, there may never have been James Bond.

But Ann's impact on the Bond novels goes beyond just being the catalyst for their writing. Alongside the character of Bond, Fleming also created one of the most internationally recognised female 'brands' of all time – the 'Bond Girl'. Fleming's fictional female creation is, in essence, his idea of the perfect woman. A beautiful woman who is socially adept, intelligent, well dressed, the perfect hostess, with more than a hint of iciness at her core. A woman irresistible to men.

A woman like his wife and her sister.

Both women were beautiful. Both sisters possessed a steely determination and hardness that drove them. And both women were irresistible to men. In the Charteris sisters, we have the type of women that Fleming loved. The type of women he sought to portray in his books. The type of women readers would fall in love with and want to make love to.

This is the story of Ann and Laura Charteris.

The Charteris Sisters: The Beginning

Ann and Laura Charteris came from a world of rarefied privilege. Born at the tail end of the Edwardian era, they were seemingly given all of life's advantages. Born to a father who was the son of a premier earl and a mother who was an heiress, the Charteris sisters were aristocratic and rich. In addition, both women would make their mark as beauties of their day, noted for their magnetism and charisma.

Ann and Laura were at the very epicentre of Britain's elite upper class. Through both their mother and father, they were related to many of the great, titled families of England. And those to whom they were not related to, the Charteris family called friends. 'You have to remember how *minute* the establishment was,' Laura's daughter, Sara Morrison, explains.[2] The aristocratic class that Ann and Laura were born into was an incredibly tight group of people which was near impossible to infiltrate. A small class of people who lived in grand houses, maintained staffs of hundreds and enjoyed lives of leisure. Men were not expected to have careers and women were expected to do little except make a suitable marriage.

Neither Ann nor Laura were ever expected to get an education or work. Beyond lessons from a governess in the schoolroom, and a brief flirtation with Cheltenham Ladies' College for Ann, neither woman received any sort of schooling. 'They were so badly educated,' Sara confirms.[3]

While both women were clearly bright, their lack of education affected them both. Their grammar and spelling would remain appalling for the rest of their lives. But emotionally, this lack of education influenced them differently. Ann would surround herself with the literati of the day, challenging and taxing herself. Laura preferred non-stimulating, and non-threatening, adoration. As Laura's granddaughter, Anabel Loyd recalls, 'Grandma was potentially bright. A quick brain, she didn't stretch herself. Ann went on educating herself.'[4]

For women like Laura and Ann, husbands would be the proxy for a career. Any power or status that women of that era and class could wield would come through the men they married. When bored or dissatisfied with their marriage, the only option would be for women to find a better, richer and more powerful husband. Instead of aiming for a promotion, women like Laura and Ann could only aim for a 'husband upgrade'.

But this was an era when divorce was controversial and difficult to obtain. Unusually, both Laura and Ann would go through divorces, accumulating three between them. In a world where leisure time was ample, marriages were arranged, and divorcées ran the risk of becoming social outcasts, extramarital affairs were routine. 'The upper classes turned a blind eye to extramarital affairs,' one historian recalls of the early twentieth century.[5] There was no shock or heartbreak over affairs. As well as accepting their husbands' mistresses, many wives enjoyed liaisons of their own, with their husbands choosing to live by the adage 'a gentleman never notices his wife's affairs'. In such a small, elite world, it was not untypical for husbands and wives to have lovers among their friends. While the affairs were not talked about publicly, the relationships would be common knowledge among their social circle.

Ann and Laura would happily and vigorously adopt this attitude. Both would later enjoy an impressive and energetic roster of extramarital affairs and accept that their husbands did the same. As Laura once said to her daughter, 'Sex means no more to me than cleaning my teeth.'[6]

But the way Laura and Ann approached sex, and their relationships with men, would eventually drive a wedge between the sisters. While Ann endeavoured to remain discreet about her romances, Laura relished the attention that came with being the focus of gossip. Having been close while growing up, their closeness would eventually descend into rivalry. 'They were certainly competitive over men, subconsciously if not consciously,' Sara concludes.[7] As Ann and Laura embarked on love affairs, their differing tastes would further divide the two sisters. As Sara explains, 'Ann disapproved of Laura's men. They were not heavyweight.'[8] While Ann became increasingly attracted to power and the political elite, Laura wanted adoration. As Clarissa Eden, a friend to both sisters, would later say, 'Ann brought the energy to politics which Laura brought to sex.'[9]

Sex appeal is difficult to put into words but both Charteris women had the most raw, compelling and captivating sex appeal. One of her four mothers-in-law would describe Laura as 'sex on legs'.[10] A bishop who met Ann later in life recalled being 'speechless sitting next to her. Her appeal, it was mesmeric.'[11] Their friend, the garden designer and writer Lanning Roper, succinctly described the allure of the sisters: 'They had the most magnetic sexuality I have ever encountered.'[12]

But with their collective seven husbands between them, as well as myriad love affairs, there was something other than sex, or even the quest for power and status, driving Laura and Ann. They both lived their lives at a million miles an hour. Theirs was a life of perceived privilege but both women were haunted by their childhoods. 'They really had no upbringing at all,' Laura's daughter recalls.[13]

When their mother died in 1925, Ann was 12 and Laura was 10. Their father, Guy, was bereft: 'I never had much heart, but all the heart I had died with her.'[14] The 12-year-old Ann was taken to provide comfort to her shattered father, irrespective of her own, confused feelings. From then on, Ann and Laura and their siblings were shuffled between relations and grandparents, with no proper home to call their own. For both of them, early marriages would provide an escape and the solidity of homes of their own. But 'the blinding horror of their mother dying young' and their subsequent rackety upbringing would inevitably haunt them, driving them to behave in different ways.[15] 'My mother concealed her feelings. Ann wallowed in hers,' Sara remembers.[16]

Ann would spend her life travelling and socialising and had an abhorrence of boredom. As Sara says of Ann, 'Her boredom threshold was subterranean.'[17] While Laura would not achieve the reputation of a society hostess like her sister, she also had her own motivations: 'Aunt Ann's fear of boredom was almost as great as my mother's fear of not being adored.'[18]

Her unhappy childhood drove Laura to recreate her life as something akin to a fairy tale. Each of her lovers and relationships would take on a gilt and glow, with men falling instantly and passionately at her feet. And when these relationships floundered, Laura would run. As her daughter confirms, 'My mother ran away from anything to do with unhappiness.'[19]

2

CHILDHOOD

In the same month that suffragette Emily Davison threw herself in front of King George V's horse, Anmer, during the Epsom Derby, Ann Geraldine Mary Charteris was born at her family home, 26 Catherine Street, Westminster. The eldest child of Guy and Frances Charteris, Ann was born in the early evening of Thursday, 19 June 1913.

Situated near Buckingham Palace, 26 Catherine Street had been built for Ann's parents by her wealthy grandparents, Francis and Anne Tennant, after Guy and Frances' marriage on 23 July 1912. The house, a solid and imposing townhouse spanning five floors, on the corner of Catherine Place, is considered enormous by the standards of today. But in 1913, the house would have been thought modest, albeit in one of the smartest areas of town. Despite a cook and several housemaids, the Charterises had no butler or housekeeper, leading Laura to reflect later, 'Compared to our relations who had a full staff, we felt quite poor.'[1]

Ann's father, the Honourable Guy Charteris, was the second son of the 11th Earl of Wemyss. The title had been created in the peerage of Scotland in 1633 for John Wemyss, a Scottish landowner. Over time, the Earls of Wemyss became powerful, intermarrying with other dynastic families and acquiring land and estates across England and Scotland. These included Gosford House in East Lothian; Neidpath Castle overlooking the River Tweed in the Scottish borders; Stanway House in Gloucestershire; and Elcho Castle in Perthshire, leading to the heirs to the Earl of Wemyss being known by the courtesy title of Viscount Elcho.

The title passed through the generations until David, Lord Elcho, son of the 5th Earl, was implicated in the Jacobite uprising of 1745. As a punishment, all of David's property and titles were confiscated by George II in 1746. Recklessly, David ignored the king and assumed the title of the

6th Earl of Wemyss after his father's death in 1756. David died in 1787 and was succeeded by his younger brother, Francis, who assumed the title of the 7th Earl of Wemyss, despite not being legally entitled to do so. He also changed the family name to Charteris, in return for being the sole heir to a wealthy maternal uncle. His was succeeded by his grandson, another Francis, who became the 8th Earl of Wemyss.

With the name change came a run of good luck for the Charteris family. In 1810, a second cousin, the 4th Duke of Queensbury, died without heirs. While the dukedom went to another relation, the 3rd Duke of Buccleuch, another family title, the Earldom of March, came to the Charteris family and Francis became the 4th Earl of March. In 1821, Francis was created Baron Wemyss of Wemyss in the County of Fife, in the Peerage of the United Kingdom. Finally, in 1826, Francis obtained a reversal of the confiscation of the family titles of 1756 and legally became the 8th Earl of Wemyss, restoring full legitimacy to the Charteris family.

By 1914, when Ann and Laura's grandfather, Hugo, inherited the title, the Charteris land and estates had been depleted. But the family were still in possession of the mighty Gosford House in Scotland and the imposing Stanway House in Gloucestershire. When Ann was born in 1913, her great-grandfather, the 10th Earl of Wemyss was still alive. While he and his wife – another Ann, the second daughter of the 1st Earl of Lichfield – lived at the main family home of Gosford House, his son lived at Stanway. It would be Stanway that Ann, and later Laura, would view as the family home.

The family business, such as it was, was politics. In 1883, Hugo succeeded his father as the Conservative MP for Haddingtonshire, before losing his seat in the 1885 general election. But he was re-elected as MP for Ipswich in 1886 and remained so until 1895, also serving as Lord Lieutenant of Haddingtonshire from 1918 to 1937.

The same year that he first entered Parliament, Hugo had married Mary Constance Wyndham – a granddaughter of the 1st Baron Leconfield. Mary and her two sisters became the society darlings of their day, immortalised in an 1899 portrait by John Singer Sargent, which still hangs in the Metropolitan Museum of Art today. Mary and her siblings were founding members of a Victorian social group which was made up of other well-born intellectuals and politicians. Nicknamed 'the Souls' by Lord Charles Beresford, the group was established in response to the Irish Home Rule debate. Tired of a lack of honest discussion, the Wyndhams founded a salon where people could have open, spirited political debate without fear of recrimination.

The young Lord and Lady Elcho managed to produce seven children, although the parentage of all the offspring is uncertain. Wemyss family legend has it that when Mary was in Egypt with her paramour, the poet Wilfrid Blunt, she discovered she was pregnant. In a bid to maintain respectability, she made plans to return to England and wired her husband, who was enjoying an affair with the Duchess of Leinster. On receiving the news, Hugo replied by telegram, 'Do not worry, I too am having a baby.'[2]

As was typical of their class and background, Hugo and Mary both enjoyed extramarital affairs – a penchant later shared by their granddaughters. The earl would eventually have a long-term affair with Lady Angela Forbes, daughter of the 4th Earl of Rosslyn, while his wife enjoyed a string of affairs with several men – most notably, the future prime minister, Arthur Balfour.

Lord and Lady Elcho's eldest son, another Hugo, married a daughter of the 8th Duke of Rutland. Their eldest daughter, Cynthia, who later became a noted writer and biographer, married the son of British Prime Minister H.H. Asquith. And their youngest daughter married the 2nd Earl of Plymouth. Thus, the Charteris family seem to be related to the majority of the British aristocracy.

While their father's side of the family had breeding, Ann and Laura's mother, Frances Lucy Tennant, came from money. Also hailing from Scotland, the Tennant family wealth came from the industrialist Charles Tennant, Frances Tennant's great-great-grandfather. Born the ninth of a staggering sixteen children to a farm labourer, Charles served an apprenticeship to a handloom weaver. But he quickly became frustrated with the slow and costly process of bleaching wool. The antediluvian practice involved soaking the wool in stale urine before leaving the material stretched across 'bleaching fields' to whiten in the sun.

Sensing an opportunity, Charles purchased several bleaching fields and experimented with different formulas for bleaching. He eventually hit on the winning combination of chlorine and lime, which he patented on 23 January 1798. The new bleaching process was adopted around the world, making Charles the most successful industrialist of his era and earning him a fortune. Establishing Charles Tennant & Company, Charles expanded his company to include metals, minerals, explosives and even railways. By the time he died in 1838, Charles was one of the richest men in the world.

His son, John, took the reins of the company before being succeeded by his eldest son, Charles. Despite being hugely wealthy, the Tennant family were still viewed as 'trade' in the harsh world of Victorian aristocracy. While overseeing his family business, the younger Charles set about using his ample cash to transform the Tennant family from 'arriviste' to 'establishment' in one generation. First, he purchased land and commissioned architect David Bryce to build a house reflective of the Tennant family's status and power.

The result was The Glen, a massive castellated baronial-style house in the Scottish Borders. Second, Charles entered politics, serving as MP for Glasgow from 1879 to 1880 and for Peebles and Selkirk from 1880 to 1886, earning himself a baronetcy in 1885.

Charles married twice, first to Emma Winsloe, with whom he had eight children, including Ann's grandfather, Francis. After Emma's death, Charles married Marguerite Miles, with whom he had a further four children. Charles firmly established the Tennants as a political dynasty with two of his sons following him into politics. Even his daughter, Margot, by his first wife, became the second wife of future Prime Minister H.H. Asquith. Charles died in 1906 and was succeeded in the baronetcy by his eldest son, Edward, who became MP for Salisbury. Two years before Ann was born, Edward was raised to the peerage as Baron Glenconner of The Glen in the County of Peebles in 1911.

Ann and Laura's mother, Frances Tennant, was born in 1887 to Anne and Francis Tennant. As the granddaughter of Sir Charles Tennant, 1st Baronet, Frances had a privileged upbringing. She grew up between homes in Morayshire in Scotland and Romney in Kent, where her parents later bought Lympne Castle. In 1912, she married the son of the Earl of Wemyss, Guy Charteris.

Born in 1886, Guy had attended Eton and Trinity College, Cambridge. As a second son with no estate to inherit, unusually, Guy went out to work. His career seems to have made little impact on his family life as all of his children remained mystified by their father's work. As Laura recalled in her memoirs, 'I believe he had some kind of work at a place called the "Investment Registry", but I would say he was an inefficient and uninterested man of business.'[3]

When war was declared, Guy joined the Shropshire Infantry, later transferring to the Scots Guards in order to go to the front. He attained the rank of captain and fought in the Somme in 1916 before being invalided out of the army. After the war, Guy returned to work for the Investment Registry, a now-defunct government department which monitored government assets and investments. But this was work in the very loosest sense of the word. There was much leisure time in which Guy could indulge his real passion – ornithology – a love which he passed onto his eldest daughter.

The marriage between Guy and Frances may not have matched the grand unions of their siblings: Frances' sister, Kathleen, married the Marquess of Granby, who later became the 9th Duke of Rutland, while Guy's brother, Hugo, married the Marquess of Granby's sister, Lady Violet Manners.

But the union between the second son of Earl of Wemyss and the eldest daughter of a strand of the wealthy Tennant family was an entirely and suitable match. As the first of a new generation of Charteris children, Ann was born into the very highest echelon of British society – a rank that she would be aware of for the rest of her life.

Two years after the birth of Ann, on 10 August 1915, Frances Charteris gave birth to a second daughter, Frances Laura. Confusingly, the record of her birth at Somerset House lists the baby as Jean Charteris. This mistake can potentially be explained by the fact that Laura was a strapping 12lb when she was born – nearly killing her mother in the process.[4] Doctors battled to save Frances' life, which may explain why Guy Charteris chose a wholly inappropriate name for his second child.

The two eldest daughters of Frances and Guy Charteris were quite different in character. Ann was more bookish, with a serious outlook on life, spending her time writing poetry and reading books.[5] Meanwhile, Laura happily admitted to viewing life as more of a joke. She was more outdoorsy than her older sister, with a passion for animals. She enjoyed country pursuits like riding, shooting and playing golf with her Tennant grandparents in Scotland.

On 10 February 1919, the Charteris family swelled with the birth of another daughter, Mary Rose Charteris, an event that seems to have made little mark on the lives of Ann and Laura. Finally, on 11 December 1922, a much longed-for boy was born and named Hugo, Guy's brother, who had been killed in action in Egypt in 1916. Typical of all younger brothers everywhere, Hugo was adored by his siblings, who treated him like their very own living doll.

Initially, the Charteris children had a happy, carefree childhood. Laura recalls roller skating along a traffic-free Catherine Place with visits to St James's Park. The nursery floor at 26 Catherine Street was ruled by the aptly named Nanny Oger. Both Laura and Hugo recall Nanny Oger as unkind – she once kicked Hugo across the nursery floor while he was sitting on a china potty.[6] Such behaviour might seem shocking from someone who was *in loco parentis*, but Oger may have been pushed to her limits by the four spirited Charteris children, whose pranks included putting frogs and worms in the beds of their nanny and governesses.

There were divisions within the schoolroom which threw the children's different characteristics into relief. 'Hugo always said that Mary Rose was a victim of her two sisters,' Sara Morrison recalls.[7] While Ann took a more tolerant attitude towards her youngest sister, which would continue into adulthood, Laura terrorised Mary Rose. 'For certain Laura bullied her,' Sara confirms.[8] Even Laura herself is brutal in her recollections of her late sister in her memoirs: 'My younger sister I never liked much.'[9] The discord in the schoolroom became such a problem that Mary Rose was separated from her siblings and dispatched to stay with a rotation of relatives for much of her childhood, the excuse being that the smog in London was not good for Mary Rose's health.

For Ann and Laura, their happy childhood came to a brutal end in 1925. Throughout the autumn, Frances Charteris was frequently unwell. During the last weekend of October, she travelled to Stanway to stay with her Wemyss in-laws, leaving the children in London. When she returned, she entered a nursing home on Park Lane to undergo a gynaecological procedure.

On the evening of 4 November, she was visited by three of her children – Ann, Laura and Hugo (Mary Rose was on yet another extended visit to her Asquith cousins). On the afternoon of 5 November, Ann and Laura were told by their governess, Mlle Angerhoff, that their mother had died. In an era when the disease of cancer was thought of as base and unmentionable, Frances had died of cervical cancer. Ann was taken to Guy's study to provide comfort to her grief-stricken father while Laura and Hugo were left in the school room, mournfully watching the fireworks of bonfire night.

The Charteris children did not attend their mother's funeral, which took place in Aberlady Parish Church in East Lothian in Scotland (a memory which rankled Ann and later affected her own decision to allow her youngest son to attend his father's funeral). Following the funeral, life changed beyond all recognition for the Charteris children. Without Frances, Guy felt unable to cope with his children and the Catherine Street house was sold. He moved to 24 Oxford Square, near Hyde Park, where the Charteris children would spend only brief, intermittent spells. From 1925 onwards, Ann and Laura had no real home, constantly moving between the homes of their grandparents and relations.

Stanway House in Gloucestershire was the closest thing to a real home for the children. After the death of the 10th Earl of Wemyss in 1914, Hugo and Mary Charteris had chosen to keep Stanway as their primary residence, paying annual visits to Gosford House in East Lothian. Built of the local stone, which Ann and Laura would forever refer to as 'golden', Stanway is a rambling, gabled manor house.[10] With a gatehouse and façade designed by Inigo Jones, the house lies in the heart of the Cotswolds, dominated by vast, leaded windows looking out to a magnificent lake and rolling parkland.

At Stanway, Ann preferred to spend time indoors, reading and talking with her grandmother, Mary, always known to the children as 'Grumps'. Laura became the apple of her grandfather's eye, with the pair playing endless card games and riding together. Despite their separate lives, the Earl and Countess of Wemyss endeavoured to provide a happy home for their grandchildren. Their Charteris cousins – David, who became the 12th Earl of Wemyss in 1937 and Martin, later Lord Charteris and Private Secretary to Queen Elizabeth II – were frequent visitors and playmates, as were the children of Guy's sister, Cynthia Asquith.[11]

Another frequent visitor to Stanway was the novelist and playwright, J.M. Barrie. In 1926, the year after their mother's death, Barrie wrote a play for the Charteris children called 'The Wheel'. Barrie drilled the children in rehearsals, making sure they were word perfect for the performance.

The play starts with the discovery of a magic wheel in the nursery at Stanway. Ann is the first child brave enough to step through the magic wheel, followed eventually by her siblings and cousins. The children are transported to their futures, as imagined by Barrie. Prophetically, Ann uttered the line, 'I shall be snapped up by a nobleman in my first season.' Laura introduced herself as 'Name Laura – Profession Vamp', a surprisingly prescient prediction of her future.[12]

Tragically, Barrie also convinced 8-year-old Mary Rose that she could fly. She believed him and jumped from the roof of a barn. 'She had a terrible fall at Stanway,' her niece remembers.[13] Her actions and subsequent injuries further convinced the adults that she was imbalanced and should be separated from her siblings.

The Charteris children also spent time with their Tennant grandparents in Scotland. The Tennants split their time between Hyndford House, a surprisingly suburban Victorian house just along the coast from Gosford House, and a grander residence, Innes House in Morayshire. Here, days were crammed with brisk, outdoorsy activities such as golf, tennis, picnics, fishing, swimming and riding. While Laura seemed to thrive in this environment, Ann preferred the more sedate, academic life at Stanway. Her time at Innes was spent in the solitary pursuit of reading poetry in the library.

Whatever Laura or Ann's preferences for grandparents or houses, Anne Tennant was the grandmother who fulfilled the practicalities of the Charteris children's lives, arranging dentist and medical appointments, buying clothing for the children and making a concerted effort to help Mary Rose. She also recognised that Ann was increasingly bored and needed stimulation.

As a result, Ann was dispatched to Cheltenham Ladies' College. This was a highly unusual step for a girl of Ann's background. While boarding school for boys was a requisite, girls did not commonly have a formal education much beyond a governess and a spell at a finishing school. Unfortunately, Ann loathed Cheltenham Ladies' College, resenting the curtailments on her freedom, and she begged to be removed. After one disastrous term, Ann's father and Cheltenham Ladies' College decided mutually that Ann would be better off elsewhere.

3

TEENAGE YEARS

As Ann and Laura became teenagers, they began to appreciate the power that they were able to exert over men. Neither Ann nor Laura were classically beautiful, but sex appeal is mysteriously inherent and surpasses a lack of physical perfection. In her memoirs, Laura recalls her first experimentation with flirting. At the age of 12, her teenage cousins, Martin Charteris and Michael Asquith, claim Laura 'bitched them up' – a rather crass way of saying that Laura was leading them on, testing her burgeoning sex appeal on her hapless cousins.[1]

In 1930, Ann turned 16 and was judged too old for a governess. In April, she travelled to Paris to be 'finished', where she was enrolled at the Villa Marie Antoinette in Versailles. Intended to prepare young women to 'come out' in society, lessons focused on social graces and deportment. Girls would be taught how to run a household and manage staff, as well as activities thought appropriate for upper-class women, such as drawing and painting.

The lessons at the finishing school were not of primary importance to Ann, who was more interested in the experiences that such a vibrant city had to offer. She thrived in Paris, enjoying the sights, sounds and culture of a new city. But many of the skills which defined her as a hostess for the rest of her life were gleaned from her education in Versailles. While she learned the art of entertaining at the feet of her Wemyss grandmother, the basics, such as management of household staff, were learned at Versailles.

Another rite of passage took place during her time in Paris when Ann fell in love for the first time. At a dance, Ann met a 6ft 6in Frenchman called Jean in the autumn of 1930. Their conversation revolved around the remarkably unromantic subject of the fall of the French Cabinet. Nonetheless, when Ann fell asleep on the journey home, she woke to find her hand being held. Sadly, the romance was short-lived as Ann had only one more week left in Paris. But in the great romantic fashion, Jean surprised Ann with three pink carnations at the Gare du Nord as she boarded the train for London. His parting words epitomise the power that Ann was to hold over men for the rest of her life, '*Au revoir, Enchantereuse.*'[2]

Ann returned for Christmas 1930 at Stanway before she and Aunt Violet 'Letty' Benson made plans for Ann's season in London. The antediluvian process of 'coming out' was a rite of passage for all well-born young women up until the latter part of the twentieth century. The season involved a round of balls, cocktail parties and events – the most important of which was the court presentation. Primarily social, the season was intended to provide girls with an opportunity to meet other girls of the same background, in order to create an appropriate social group. The secondary aim was for the girls to find a suitable husband.

Families would decant to their London houses for the season, which began in late May and lasted until early September. Each girl would have their own 'coming out' party, consisting of a ball or cocktail party in a private house or one of the big London hotels. While some families were happy to splash the cash and host ostentatious parties, daughters of more economical families would share their coming out party with a friend or relation. Bearing in mind the cost involved in doing a season – a house in London, myriad outfits for the debutante, a party – and given the economic climate of the 1930s, when many aristocratic families were reeling from the Great Depression, small wonder that these families looked for ways to make a saving.

The rules during the season were strict and the girls were never unchaperoned. Mothers would attend every party with their daughters, sitting in gilt chairs which lined the ballrooms of London, While the more outrageous daughters might slip away from a ballroom to attend a forbidden nightclub with a beau, the stern presence of a chaperone made licentious behaviour almost impossible.[3]

Presentation to the king and queen at Buckingham Palace was the focal point of the season, the ceremony conferring respectability on each debutante. Intended to remain exclusive to the upper echelons of British society, debutantes had to meet certain criteria in order to be presented. Girls could only be presented by women who had been presented themselves, and could only attend wearing long, white gowns with a train. On their hands would be white gloves to their elbow and in their hair would be three ostrich feathers. A string of pearls around the neck of the debutante was permitted, but other jewellery was frowned upon.[4]

Ann was presented at court by her Aunt Letty, the former Lady Violet Manners. Having five sons but no daughters, Aunt Letty happily undertook the role of chaperone for both Ann and Laura during their respective seasons. Ann moved between the London houses of her relations during the season, staying with both sets of grandparents, as well as her father in Oxford Square. Her other Tennant aunt, Kathleen, the Duchess of Rutland, always known as 'Kakoo', gave Ann her traditional 'coming out' party. Ann wore a white dress decorated with silver and green flowers, which she loved, according to her diary of the season. But her happiness was marred by a spot on her nose which infuriatingly kept shining through her make-up.[5]

Nevertheless, Ann was a hit with the young men, known as 'debs delights', during her season. With her dark hair and grey-green eyes, Ann was beginning to show a hint of the allure she would later develop. While she had no particular beau during her first season, her diary for 1931 does list her favourite men, which included both Lord Shane O'Neill and Maurice Bridgeman, the younger son of the former Home Secretary William Bridgeman, the 1st Viscount Bridgeman.[6]

Attractive, despite a rapidly receding hairline, with a mature and confident manner, the 29-year-old Maurice made quite an impression on the now 18-year-old Ann. In September 1931, he drove Ann to a weekend house party given by her aunt, Lady Mary Strickland, at Apperley Court, in Gloucestershire. During the journey Maurice proposed. The proposal was a curious mixture of romance and practicality. Maurice told Ann that he adored her and wished to marry her. He also talked through his financial situation so that Ann would understand how much money she would have as Mrs Maurice Bridgeman. Ann does not seem to have been put off by this level-headed approach to marriage. In her diary, she described Bridgeman as a 'sensible unromantic man'.[7] While the offer was tempting, Ann refused his proposal, telling him to wait three years and then ask again. She was determined to see who else was out there.

4

FIRST MARRIAGES

It was during her second season in May 1932 that Shane O'Neill became a serious suitor for Ann. At 25 years old, he was five years older than Ann. He was tall, good-looking, extremely popular with both men and women, rich and titled.

Shane O'Neill was born on 6 February 1907 to Arthur and Lady Annabel O'Neill. His father was the second but only surviving son of Edward O'Neill, 2nd Baron O'Neill. In 1902, Arthur had married Lady Annabel Crewe-Milnes, daughter of the 1st Marquess of Crewe. The couple settled in Ireland and Arthur was elected to the House of Commons for Mid-Antrim in January 1910, succeeding his uncle, Robert O'Neill. The couple had five children, of whom Shane was the third child and eldest son. When war was declared, Arthur O'Neill joined the Life Guards and was sent to the front. On 6 November 1914, he was killed on Klein Zillebeke Ridge, earning the dubious accolade of being the first MP to be killed in the conflict. Shane was 7 years old when his father died, becoming heir to his grandfather, the 2nd Baron O'Neill.

The O'Neill family was one of the most prominent families in Ireland and Shane was able to claim descent from Niall Glundub, a tenth-century king of Ailech, an area in modern-day Northern Ireland. In 1868, Baron O'Neill of Shane's Castle was created as a title in the Peerage of the United Kingdom for William O'Neill. He was succeeded by his eldest son, Edward, who represented County Antrim in the House of Commons from 1863 to 1880. After the death of his eldest son, William, in 1882, Edward's second son, Arthur became his heir apparent. When Arthur was killed in 1914, Shane became the heir.

Shane grew up between Ireland and England, spending time at his grandparents' home, Shane's Castle in County Antrim. At the age of 15, Shane's mother, Annabel, suddenly remarried Major James Hamilton Dodds after twelve years of widowhood. A son, James, was born shortly afterwards, followed by another son, Quentin, in 1926. Shane was fifteen years older than his oldest half-brother and seventeen years older than his youngest half-brother. Inevitably, he felt excluded from his mother's second family and, much like Ann, spent his childhood shuffling between relations.[1]

After Eton and Sandhurst Military Academy, Shane entered the 8th Kings Royal Irish Hussars. On 19 November 1928, Shane's grandfather, Edward, 2nd Baron O'Neill died at the age of 89. The new Lord O'Neill promptly resigned his commission, leaving the army with the rank of lieutenant, and joined the board of the Gillet Brothers Discount Company.

While Ann's diary shows that Shane was one of her particular friends during her first season, the pair were in no way romantic. Enjoying his post-army freedom, Shane was enjoying the social world and the ease with which he could attract women.[2]

While Ann and Shane kept in touch and saw each other at occasional house parties during the winter of 1931, by the time the season proper began in 1932, Shane seemed to get serious. With a demanding and lucrative job in the city, the 25-year-old Shane clearly felt it was time to settle down. Ann also found herself increasingly drawn to the handsome peer. At a dance in May, Ann overheard Shane ask a girl if she would like to sit out the next dance with him on the stairs. Not wanting to ruin her dress, the girl refused. Ann, clearly seeing an opportunity, said, 'I don't mind ruining my dress', and promptly sat down.[3]

In June 1932 Shane proposed to Ann and she accepted. The match seemed to be made in society heaven. He was rich, good-looking and from good Anglo-Irish stock. She was pretty, entertaining and from an equally old and respectable family. Lord O'Neill's mother, now Lady Annabel Dodds, was pleased with the match. However, she immediately began to irritate her future daughter-in-law by mispronouncing 'Charteris' as two syllables, rhyming the surname with 'Tartars'.[4]

Ann was only 18 when she became engaged and 19 when she married. She had barely spent a year out of the school room and was now committing her life to a man. But this was a time when people married young, irrespective of naivete and immaturity. And Ann was as naive as they came. Despite having had many admirers, Ann knew little of sex or relationships. Laura gleefully records in her memoirs how Ann, at the age of 16, went out with a young man who was staying with the vicar at Stanway. When the man kissed her goodnight, Ann came screaming into their bedroom, worried that she was pregnant.[5]

Nor did the fact that Ann and Shane were vastly different personalities seem to occur to either the young couple or anybody around them. Being slightly older, with an army career under his belt, Shane had at least some experience of life. He was confident and serious, with a forceful personality. He was ready to settle down and continue to build his career in the city. Ann was immature, fun-loving and believed life would change little for her after her marriage. She saw her future as primarily social while Shane wanted quiet evenings and early nights. Hindsight might suggest that the odds were stacked against Ann and Shane, but the wedding was set for October and plans forged ahead.

Tuesday, 6 October 1932 dawned grey and rainy. As the guests entered St Margaret's, Westminster, the conversation was focused on the forth-coming general election, which had been announced that morning by Prime Minister Ramsay MacDonald. Despite large-scale unemployment and pov-erty across the UK, the wedding of Ann and Shane was an extravaganza. Crowds surrounded the church as the ceremony, dubbed the 'wedding of the year' by the press, took place.

Ann wore a white satin gown with long sleeves and a demurely high neckline, with just a single string of pearls around her neck. The dress was starkly simple, reflecting the change from the elaborate wedding dresses of the 1920s. The gown had a 10ft-long train, carried by two page boys, and a veil patterned with small flowers. In her hands she carried a bouquet of white roses and freesias from Stanway. As Ann and her father arrived at St Margaret's, the crowds of onlookers roared with pleasure. The impact of Ann's arrival was intensified by the presence of ten bridesmaids following her up the aisle, all wearing Grecian-style headdresses and carrying bouquets of red roses. Shane wore a dark morning suit, his light hair slicked back.[6]

Leaving St Margaret's, Shane looked happy but solid and serious, with a beaming Ann on his arm. She looked very young and almost bird-like, with her slender frame dwarfed by her train. Despite the dress and the accoutre-ments of the wedding, Ann looked plain and gawky, displaying none of the allure she was to exude later.

At the wedding party following the celebration, Laura, who was a brides-maid, was introduced to a fellow guest, David Long, the Viscount Long of Wraxall. The 17-year-old Laura was not impressed with his opening gambit: 'You must have an inferiority complex, having such a pretty sister.' Unbeknownst to David Long, he hit a very sore point as Laura was jealous of all the attention her sister was receiving. As she stalked furiously away from David Long, little did Laura know that she had just met the man she would later marry.[7]

The newly married O'Neills started their life together in fashionable Montagu Square, just north off Oxford Street. They began to entertain, holding small dinner and drinks parties for friends and business associates of Shane's, with Ann slowly growing in confidence in her role as hostess. The couple were rich by the standards of the day and lived well. But Ann quickly became bored of her new husband. While she enjoyed gossip, parties and entertaining, Shane was serious. 'He had no humour,' Sara Morrison recalls.[8]

But socially, the young O'Neills were a triumph. With the birth of their first child, Raymond, on 1 September 1933, Lord and Lady O'Neill appeared to be a young couple who had everything. But any hopes that a baby would discourage Ann from endless socialising were quickly dashed. She loved her child but, having received a scant parental upbringing herself, she did not let a baby interfere with her social life. Similarly, Shane, who had been raised by a distant mother, was not overly present. Typical of their class and generation, the O'Neills quickly relegated the baby to a nursery and the care of a nanny, leaving the couple free to explore their increasingly diverse interests.

In 1933, Laura was ready to be presented and enjoy a London season for herself. Again, Aunt Letty was pressed into action. Laura was overcome by the grandeur of her presentation at Buckingham Palace and found herself fighting back tears. As she made her curtsey, accompanied by Aunt Letty, she later recalled detecting a twinkle in King George's eye.

Like Ann before her, Laura was a hit during the season. And much like her sister, Laura was more popular with the debs' delights than the debs themselves. Laura, at 17, was more aware of her own sexuality than Ann had been. There was something very knowing about the young Laura. She was more classically beautiful than her sister, with dark hair and eyes. She also already had the sex appeal which Ann would only develop later. While this appeal may not have been the fully formed sexual magnetism that people recall of Laura later in life, this pull was enough to intrigue the men and irritate the women. As one of her acquaintances remembers, 'She loved men … she was a different person if a man walked into the room.'[9]

During her season, Laura was taken up by legendary society hostess Emerald Cunard, who would also later become friends with Ann. Born Maud Burke in San Francisco in 1872, she grew up in New York, before marrying Sir Bache Cunard, the grandson of the founder of the Cunard shipping line. Sir Bache was twenty-one years older than his wife and while he adored her, the couple had little in common.

While Sir Bache stayed at their country home, Neville Holt Hall in Leicestershire, Maud remained in London and rebranded herself as 'Emerald'. Emerald was a consummate hostess, with people clamouring to be at her table. It was not just her audacious mixing of guests that provoked comment and conversation. Emerald enjoyed discussion bordering on conflict around her table. She would frequently be provocative to rouse a reaction from a guest, making her parties wild and exciting. Later, when Ann became a noted hostess, much she had learned from Emerald could be seen at her own table. 'She definitely enjoyed conflict,' Anabel Loyd claims of her great-aunt. 'She was naturally iconoclastic.'[10]

At her first lunch at the Cunard townhouse in Mayfair, Laura was surrounded by politicians and academics. She recalled feeling intimidated but tried to keep up conversation with the men seated on her right and on her left. Towards the end of the meal, Lady Cunard bitchily decided to put Laura on the spot. Firing down the table, the terrifying *grande dame* of London society said, 'I think it is time we heard something from little Laura Charteris.'[11] Laura panicked and told a wildly indiscreet story about her grandfather and his current mistress, Lady Angela Forbes, leaving her hostess open mouthed at such frankness.

Laura's favourite beau during the season was David Spence-Colby, the son of Captain Cecil Spence-Jones. But David Long was also keen to make up for his faux pas at the O'Neill wedding and began to chase Laura. The two Davids were both amateur steeplechasers and when David Spence-Colby was thrown off his horse and tragically died, their mutual grief naturally brought Laura and David Long closer together.

They began to see more of each other and his thoughts began to turn to marriage. While David's thoughts were romantic, Laura viewed marriage in entirely practical terms. As her daughter recollects, 'Marriage meant an escape from Stanway and Aunt Letty ... and a home of her own.'[12] And besides, David Long was a highly eligible bachelor. 'My father was the first competition that she won. The point was the catch. It was a triumph for each of them,' Sara concludes.[13]

The Long viscountcy was created in May 1921 for David's grandfather Walter Long, who was a leading Conservative politician. He served as Secretary of State for the Colonies and First Lord of the Admiralty. Following Arthur Balfour's resignation as Conservative leader in 1911, Long was widely tipped to be leader of the Conservative Party. However, when a leadership contest threatened to divide the Conservative Party, Long and his fellow contender, Austen Chamberlain, sportingly withdrew in favour of Bonar Law.

David was born Walter Francis David Long on 14 September 1911 to Brigadier General Walter Long, son of the 1st Viscount Long, and his wife, Sibell Vanden Bempde-Johnstone. When David was 6 years old, his father was killed in action in Hebuterne, France, on 28 January 1917. King George V was so overcome by the death of such a promising young general that he took the unusual step of sending a telegram to Viscount Long expressing his sympathy. With his father's death, the 6-year-old David became heir to his grandfather, inheriting the viscountcy at the age of 14.

But, following his father's death, tensions developed between David's mother and his grandfather. The Long family owned two grand properties. South Wraxall Manor was a rambling Tudor manor house, just north of Bradford-on-Avon which had been in the family since the fifteenth century. A Long ancestor, Sir Walter Long, had been a friend of Sir Walter Raleigh, and South Wraxall Manor is believed to be the first place in England where tobacco was smoked. However, the 1st Viscount Long preferred to reside at another family property in Wiltshire – Rood Ashton House in the village of West Ashton. The enormous house consisted of eleven principal bedrooms and thirty-five secondary bedrooms and was considered a grander home than South Wraxall Manor.

The tension between Lord Long and his daughter-in-law, Sibell, came from his love of Rood Ashton House. Following the death of his son, Lord Long wanted the young David to spend time at the house, which he would eventually inherit. Lord Long hoped that Rood Ashton House, rather than South Wraxall Manor, would be the boy's eventual home. However, Sibell Long refused to allow her son to spend time with his grandfather. A situation exacerbated by her marriage in 1921 to Major, later Lord, Ralph Glyn and a move to Yorkshire where David grew up. The new Mrs Glyn further alienated her ex-father-in-law by sending young David to Eton when previously all Long boys had attended Harrow.[14]

The estrangement meant that, despite being his heir, David was not close to his grandfather. As Lord Long had feared, the young David had little affection for Rood Ashton House. After Lord Long died, the house was sold, ending nearly 300 years of family ownership.

After Eton, David went to Sandhurst and joined the Coldstream Guards. From his base in Windsor, David was still able to enjoy the social events of the season and formed a friendship with Shane O'Neill, who had been a few years ahead of him at Eton. The friendship resulted in an invitation to Shane's wedding to Ann and his first meeting with Laura.

After proposing marriage to Laura, David met with Guy Charteris. Concerned that Laura, at 17, and David, who was 21, were too young, Guy suggested that the couple delay their engagement for six months. 'The trouble was both were frightfully spoiled,' Sara recalls. 'My grandmother later described them as "children colliding".'[15] The couple refused to be separated, their respective families capitulated, and the wedding was set.

Laura looked beautiful when she married David Long at St Margaret's Westminster on 14 November 1933. As the wedding date came so soon after

Remembrance Day on 11 November, David and Laura had to walk past a field of memorial poppies outside the church – a poignant backdrop to their wedding. Laura wore a simple, shimmering satin dress in off-white, with a flowing veil of tulle. David wore a dark morning suit, top hat and carried a rolled-up umbrella, looking more like a merchant banker en route to the city than a groom on his wedding day. Press photographs from the wedding day show David looking happy and proud, a great beam of a smile plastered across his face. As he leaves the church with his new wife on his arm, Laura looks preoccupied and uneasy.

In a kitschy twist, Laura dressed the five bridesmaids and five page boys in Charles Dickens-inspired costumes. She was escorted down the aisle by a phalanx of miniature Victorians, the boys in Oliver Twist suits, the girls dressed as pint-sized Nancys.[16] Following the wedding reception, the new Viscount and Viscountess Long spent their wedding night at a friend's house in London ('a bit of a flop,' as Laura remembered),[17] followed by a few nights at the Ritz in Paris.

Shortly after their wedding, the Longs departed for New Zealand where David had accepted a job as aide-de-camp (ADC) to Lord Bledisloe, the Governor of New Zealand. Almost as soon as the six-week boat journey began, the couple realised their incompatibility. Having barely spent any time alone together during their courtship, the couple had not appreciated that they were polar opposites. The racy, excitable Laura clashed with the more conservative David. While Laura enjoyed socialising with their fellow passengers, who included the noted decorator, Elise de Wolfe, and the politician Victor Cazalet, David wanted the journey to be more of a honeymoon, with the couple spending time alone together. Their increasing fractiousness was not helped by Laura feeling unwell. Advised by Ann before her wedding to see the noted gynaecologist, Cedric Lane-Roberts, Laura had had a crippplingly embarrassing interview, during which she had been advised on how to use the Dutch cap – an early but haphazard diaphragm.

Thinking that she was protected from pregnancy, Laura believed that she was only suffering from seasickness. As the boat travelled towards the equator and the heat intensified, she became increasingly lethargic. Finally, as the ship arrived in Colombo, David forced his wife to seek medical help and a local doctor confirmed her condition, despite Laura's protestations about her Dutch cap.[18] Still feeling unwell on arrival in New Zealand, Lady Bledisloe, the wife of the governor general, immediately dispatched Laura to a doctor. Again, her condition was confirmed, much to the horror of Lady Bledisloe, who did not want a baby to be born at Government House.

The Bledisloes were a popular couple in New Zealand. Lord Bledisloe had been an MP until his retirement in 1928, after which Prime Minister Ramsay MacDonald had asked him to be the fourth Governor General of New Zealand in 1930. The first Lady Bledisloe had died in May 1926 and on 16 April 1928, he married the Hon. Alina Cooper-Smith – the daughter of the 1st Baron Glantawe, a Welsh industrialist. During his term as governor general, Lord Bledisloe had taken the unusual step of cutting his own wages, as well as those of his staff, in sympathy with New Zealand citizens struggling during the Great Depression. He had also forged a better appreciation of Maori culture among New Zealanders, even referring to ancient Maori leaders as 'king' when addressing them.[19] Lady Bledisloe had made her own reputation as an engaging and somewhat eccentric hostess at Government House.

While David and Lord Bledisloe established a good working relationship, the relationship between Laura and the governor general's wife was distinctly frigid. Unfairly incurring the ire of Lady Bledisloe due to her pregnancy, Laura failed to ingratiate herself with either the governor general or his wife. During her first formal dinner at Government House, Laura committed the cardinal sin of sitting on the floor after dinner, when the ladies retired to the informality of the drawing room. The next morning, she was summoned to Lady Bledisloe's bedroom for an absolute blasting. She was reprimanded for her behaviour, as well as the infinitely more shocking act of wearing red nail varnish. Laura was furious, and from then on referred to the Bledisloes as 'The Bloody Slows', although Lord Bledisloe would later stand as godparent to Laura and David's daughter.[20]

Miserable in New Zealand, Laura resented the expectation that she would act as lady-in-waiting to the governor general's wife. She was bored by life in Wellington and was increasingly unwell as her pregnancy progressed. 'She felt so ill all the time,' her daughter remembers her mother's recollection of her time in New Zealand.[21]

Barely 18, Laura wanted fun and glamour. Instead, she was pregnant, lonely and forced to spend her time attending rather dry official events. She began to write desperate letters to her Wemyss grandfather, imploring him to come and take her back to England.

In response to his beloved granddaughter's pleas, the 11th Earl made plans to travel to New Zealand, arriving in May 1934 in the company of his mistress, Lady Angela Forbes. Lord Wemyss immediately informed the Bledisloes that Laura would be returning to England with him.

There was no great love lost between Laura and the Bledisloes, but David had thrived in his role as ADC and was reluctant to resign after only a few months in the job. Realising that staying in New Zealand would cost him his marriage, David reluctantly decided to return to the UK. The decision was bolstered by Lord Wemyss promising David that he would find him a lucrative job in the city. Already worried about supporting a wife and child on a military salary, as well as the cost of upkeep on the remaining Long estate, South Wraxall Manor, David agreed to resign and return to England.

The entourage left Wellington in June 1934 on RMS *Rangitata*. Travelling back to England via Panama, Laura spent time with fellow passenger George Bernard Shaw. Despite travelling with his wife, Charlotte, Bernard Shaw made repeated passes at the heavily pregnant Laura.[22]

The Longs arrived back in England in early July 1934. David's mother, Lady Glyn, had rented them a temporary house close to her own home in Manchester Square. On 8 August 1934, Laura tripped over her white Pekinese, Rene, triggering contractions. On Thursday, 9 August, Laura gave birth to a daughter. Like Laura herself, the baby was big – weighing a healthy 9lbs. In her memoirs, Laura claims that both her gynaecologist, Cedric Lane-Roberts, and her husband, David, 'passed out with exhaustion'.[23] The idea of a leading gynaecologist collapsing through tiredness due to a completely average labour length seems a tad dramatic. Laura's description of her daughter's birth is probably rooted in her love of embellishment. As Hugo Vickers ruefully recalls, 'Laura could exaggerate.'[24]

Regardless of who collapsed and for what reason, Antoinette Sara Frances Sibell Long was born the day before her mother's nineteenth birthday on 10 August 1934. The baby, who would always be known as Sara, was viewed by Laura as a doll with which to play rather than a daughter whom she had to raise. She enjoyed dressing her and taking her for walks, but the main responsibilities of practical mothering fell to the nursery maid, Susan.

In September 1934, the Longs moved to Gloucester Place in Marylebone. Today, Gloucester Place is a thundering thoroughfare, but in 1934 the street was quiet, popular with young families due to the proximity of Regent's Park to the north and Hyde Park to the south. Despite having a real home for the first time in her life and enjoying the process of decorating and staffing her new house, Laura quickly became bored. Her prematurely adult life seemed to yawn ahead of her with nothing more exciting than household management and the odd dinner party to organise.

Neither Laura nor David seem to have made any effort to make their marriage work, and both went out of their way to avoid each other. 'I never saw them together,' Sara remembers.[25] Laura had quickly recovered her pre-baby figure and enjoyed the male attention she received during her daily walks with her baby daughter in Regent's Park. She had always had confidence in her looks but her newly independent, adult status seems to have given her an enhanced poise. Bored with her life and her husband, like many women of her generation and class, Laura began to indulge in affairs.

She assembled an impressive pack of beaux. One was a good friend of her husband, Owen 'Bobby' Roberts, the grandson of railroad tycoon Marshall Owen Roberts. Roberts was a pilot, who frequently took Laura for trips in his plane. Another boyfriend was Francis 'Frankie' More O'Ferrall, a good-looking Irishman who trained horses. Yet another beau was John Spencer-Churchill, then the Marquess of Blandford and heir to the Dukedom of Marlborough.[26]

By the summer of 1935, barely eighteen months since their wedding, the Long marriage began to seriously disintegrate. After a row, Laura temporarily left Gloucester Place, staying with Ann at a house she had rented for the summer in Sandwich. There was a brief reconciliation when David became ill during the summer and he and Laura decided to travel to the spa town of Vichy in France. The politician Duff Cooper and his wife, Lady Diana, were also staying in the French town. Lady Diana Cooper was the sister of Laura and Ann's aunt, Violet 'Letty' Benson. Her husband, Duff, was a noted lothario, who 'pinched every passing bottom', as Laura's daughter remembers.[27] Predictably, he took an immediate shine to Laura, who was flattered.

On their return, David and Laura admitted defeat and decided to separate after a year and a half of marriage. David stayed at Gloucester Place, while Laura returned to her father's house at 24 Oxford Square, where the top floor was made into a nursery for Sara and her nanny. Neither the Long nor Charteris families seem to have been surprised by the breakdown of David and Laura's marriage.

Despite being terrified of telling her adored grandfather, Hugo was understanding and even arranged a meeting for Laura to discuss the separation with David's mother, Lady Glyn. Expecting the blasting of a lifetime, Laura was happily surprised when Lady Glyn was sympathetic and understanding, concluding that David and Laura had been too young to marry. She even suggested the practical solution of an official separation, which was duly agreed by Laura and David. Lady Glyn continued to take a maternal view of her former daughter-in-law for the remainder of her life. As Sara remembers, 'Laura remained an important part of her life.'[28]

Technically free from her marriage, Laura could now live as she chose. But this was a time when separation was frowned upon by British society, and divorcées were practically social pariahs. In an effort to escape the gossip, Laura left London, staying firstly at Haddon Hall in Derbyshire with her Aunt Kakoo, before sitting out the winter between her Wemyss and Tennant grandparents while her small daughter was 'parked with relatives'.[29]

5

ANN MEETS IAN ...
AND ESMOND

Ann was also experiencing an emotional upheaval. As her sister began to explore relationships with men other than her husband, Ann met the man who would become the great love of her life.

The first meeting between Ann O'Neill and Ian Fleming could not, by any stretch of the imagination, be described as a *coup de foudre*. In fact, there was no indication that this inauspicious encounter would eventually lead to the defining relationship of both of their lives. The November weekend in 1934 when both were guests at the same house party was particularly cold, and the introduction between the pair seems to have been equally chilly.

Bizarrely, despite none of the Charteris family being in residence at the time, the meeting took place at Stanway. Whenever Ann's grandparents stayed at their Scottish home, Gosford House, for a long period of time, their Gloucestershire home would be rented out. During the winter of 1934, the tenants were banker Gilbert Russell and his beautiful young wife, Maud. From banking circles, Gilbert knew Ann's new husband, Shane, while Maud had befriended a fellow banker's wife – Eve Fleming. Through this friendship, Maud met Eve's dashing and glamorous son, Ian, a journalist with the news agency Reuters.[1]

Throughout 1933 and 1934, Ian was a regular guest at the various country homes leased by Gilbert and Maud Russell. While tongues wagged about the relationship between the banker's wife and the young journalist, the understanding and kindly Gilbert quietly and deliberately turned a blind eye.

One freezing weekend in November 1934, Ian arrived for a weekend at Stanway.[2] His fellow guests were Shane and Ann O'Neill. Despite Ian's penchant for pretty girls, Ian barely noticed Ann, assuming she was just a daughter of the house.

Despite the unpromising start, a few months later Ann and Ian would meet again. This time their eyes met across a glittering swimming pool on a warm, spring day in 1935 in Le Touquet, France. The few short months between their first and second meetings had seen significant changes for both Ann and Ian.

Determined to make some money, Ian had left journalism. First, he tried banking after Gilbert Russell magnanimously found him a position in Cull & Company, the merchant banking firm he had founded in 1917. Initially, Ian enjoyed banking, which allowed him both the time and the money for his main passion – the pursuit of women. But by early 1935, he was bored and unwisely decided to take an unsuccessful stab at stockbroking. Despite these career changes, Ian still found the energy to move from woman to woman with staggering and unchivalrous speed. Charming, attractive and funny, Ian Fleming was rapidly establishing a reputation as an eligible man about town.

Ann had also begun to establish her own reputation as hostess and party-giver, taking advice from Maud Russell, as well as legendary society hostess Sibyl Colefax. Always beautiful and spirited, the rather naive schoolgirl began to grow in confidence, showing for the first time a certain hardness to her character. As her friend, Nancy Hare, described Ann, 'When young, she couldn't understand why people took their emotions so seriously.'[3]

Ann had also discovered a passion for power, and in particular, men with power. For the rest of her life, power would be the ultimate aphrodisiac and, sadly, her husband was lacking in what Ann most wanted. As Shane's sister, Mary 'Midi' Gascoigne later said, 'Ann would have left Shane anyway because he wasn't powerful.'[4]

While Ian may not have had power, he had magnetism with a vital and engaging personality. 'He had a manner of speaking and behaviour which was attractive. It was attention-catching. And he had a very good voice,' his niece recalls.[5]

Having left Cull & Company, Ian took a motoring holiday through Europe before undertaking his new role with stockbroking firm, Rowe & Pitman. Ian planned to drive to the South of France before looping back to play in a golfing tournament in Le Touquet over the Easter weekend. While driving south, he made a detour to Geneva to visit his old friend Martin Hill, and his Irish wife, Diana, always known as 'Didy'. Finding Didy alone, Ian asked her to join him on his motoring tour, during which the pair embarked on a short-lived affair. Arriving in Le Touquet in time for the golfing tournament, Ian rather ungallantly dumped Didy with the words, 'I wish you could stay but I wouldn't want you hanging around.'[6]

Having put Didy on the train to Geneva, Ian enjoyed a few days of golf
– a sport which he was mad for all of his life – and enjoyed a sunny Easter
weekend. While relaxing by the swimming pool he saw the familiar face of
Ann O'Neill. Having said goodbye to Didy, Ian was on the lookout for the
next sexual challenge. The young and wantonly appealing Lady O'Neill
provided just that challenge. But this passion was not to be. At least, not yet.

Ann was staying at Le Touquet with her friends John and Nancy Hare.
Nancy was the daughter of the 2nd Viscount Cowdray and a childhood
friend of Ann's. John was the younger son of the 4th Earl of Listowel and a
Conservative politician. Enjoying lunch in the sunshine, Ann caught sight
of the 27-year-old Ian sitting by the swimming pool, describing him for
the first time in her diaries as a 'handsome moody creature'.[7] But despite
the obvious charge between the pair, Ann and Ian did not speak. She did
not seem to recognise the man she had met a few months earlier at Stanway,
while Ian, mysteriously and very unusually, did not make a play for Ann or
even remind her of their acquaintanceship.

But fate stepped in the following month when Ian became a member of
White's Club in St James's. Here he met Shane O'Neill, who was already
an active member of the club. Shane took a shine to Ian, with both men
sharing a love of sports. He began to ask Ian back to Montagu Square for
regular games of bridge, where his wife found herself increasingly attracted
to his new friend. As Ian Fleming's biographer, Andrew Lycett, concludes,
'He [Ian] had a number of girlfriends and she [Ann] became one of them.'[8]

But alongside her growing interest in the enigmatic Fleming, Ann was
becoming increasingly enamoured of a truly powerful man. In 1936, she
met the dynamic and 'devastatingly good-looking' Esmond Harmsworth,
the scion of the newspaper-owning Rothermere family.[9]

Born on 29 May 1898, Esmond was the youngest child of the 1st Viscount
Rothermere, Harold Harmsworth. Alongside his brother, Alfred – later
Lord Northcliffe – Harold founded the *Daily Mail* in 1896 and the *Daily
Mirror* in 1903. Knighted in 1910 and ennobled as Baron Rothermere of
Hemsted in 1914, by 1921, Harmsworth owned the *Daily Mirror*, the *Sunday
Pictorial*, *The Daily Record*, *The Evening News* and the *Sunday Mail*, as well as
shared ownership of Associated Newspapers with his brother. Following
the death of his brother in 1922, Harold acquired controlling interest in
Associated Newspapers, and in 1923 bought the Hulton newspaper chain –
making him the most powerful newspaper magnate of that time.

On 4 July 1893, Harold married Lilian Share. The couple had three
children, Harold (always known by his middle name of Vyvyan), Vere and
Esmond. As the youngest son, Esmond was never intended to take on the

family business or inherit the viscountcy and was very much in the shadows of his brothers.

Despite the trappings of wealth and status, Esmond's childhood was not happy. At Eton, he struggled in the wake of his high-achieving older brother Vyvyan, who was an academic and sporting star. Esmond was also deeply affected by the breakdown of his parents' marriage just as he entered his teens. To an introverted boy, the gossip and innuendo surrounding the collapse of the Harmsworths' marriage cut deep, as did the sudden absence of his mother, leaving Esmond in the sole charge of a devoted but domineering father. Esmond was also embarrassed by his father's blatant displays of wealth, which seemed vulgar and gauche, setting the young Esmond apart from the more established and subtle families of his Eton contemporaries. While Esmond was bright like his brothers and a keen sportsman, he suffered routinely from ill health, earning him the reputation of being frail and sickly – a death knell in the tough environment of a British boarding school, where strength is frequently the only currency.

Esmond's school days were also overshadowed by the First World War and the horrifying fatalities on the front. On 13 November 1916, tragedy struck the Harmsworth family when Vere was killed during the first day of the Battle of the Ancre. In 1917, Vyvyan, who was serving with the 2nd Battalion Irish Guards, was seriously wounded in France. While Esmond wanted to serve his country and immediately joined the Royal Marine Artillery on leaving school, his father had other ideas. Having endured the death of one son and the injury of another, Lord Rothermere used his political influence to ensure that his youngest son would not see action – a move which rankled Esmond.

When Vyvyan died from his injuries on 12 February 1918, Esmond was suddenly in the unexpected position of being the only son and heir. His bewilderment at finding himself centre stage was compounded by Vyvyan posthumously being awarded the Military Cross for bravery. When the war came to an end in November 1918, Esmond was left with a deep sense of shame that he had not served in the trenches, nor been awarded any medals. For many years afterwards, he would avoid formal occasions where medals were required to be worn.[10]

As the only remaining son of Lord Harmsworth, as well as the only remaining heir to the childless Lord Northcliffe, Esmond had little say over his own life. He was pressured to run for Parliament in the 1919 Isle of Thanet by-election, which had been precipitated by the death of the incumbent MP. With a Conservative–Liberal coalition elected immediately after the Armistice, radical tax rates were being discussed to generate much-needed cash for a near-bankrupt Britain. By having Esmond on the Conservative benches, his father and uncle hoped to sway government policy away from higher tax rates.

Esmond ran a cleverly orchestrated campaign against the Liberal candidate, William J. West. He advocated for an 'anti-waste' agenda. Following the massive public expenditure during the First World War, Esmond advocated the avoidance of 'wasting money'.[11] He promised to generate wealth through job creation rather than higher taxes. As the Harmsworths owned two of the largest corporations in Britain and would benefit from corporate tax cuts, Esmond's motives were far from altruistic.

Esmond scraped in as MP for the Isle of Thanet with a majority of just 2,653 on 15 November 1919. At 21 years old, he was the youngest Member of Parliament, earning the traditional nickname of 'Baby of the House'. He was almost immediately handed the plum role of ADC to the Prime Minister David Lloyd George during the Paris Peace Conference.

Esmond received this accolade not because of his intellectual ability or diplomatic skills but purely because of his name. Lloyd George had hung onto the premiership in the 1918 general election as leader of the coalition government. But his predecessor, H.H. Asquith, continued to battle for the leadership of the Liberals, who were rapidly losing public support. Lloyd George needed favourable press and hoped to gain favour with the Harmsworth family by employing Esmond.[12]

Despite his relative inexperience, Esmond impressed the prime minister and many of his government colleagues at the peace conference. Gradually, he grew in confidence, eventually winning three consecutive general elections, gaining a reputation as a solid and reliable backbencher.

Esmond's popularity in his constituency was helped by his wife, Margaret, who exuded charm and impressed locals with her seemingly staggering memory. Unbeknown to voters, Margaret, who was always known as Peggy, had come up with the vote-winning question designed to make each constituent feel special. Realising that the sea air inevitably caused aches and pains, Peggy would ask each constituent, 'Are you feeling better now?'[13] The delighted local would then assume that the minister's wife had remembered their previous ailment from an earlier meeting, before joyfully regaling her with their current health woes.

As well as an outgoing and energetic personality, Peggy was beautiful. Blonde with exquisite bone structure, she always seemed to be smiling. Born Margaret Redhead, she was the daughter of a businessman who died in 1909, leaving 10-year-old Peggy and her mother, Jane, extremely hard up. Jane then befriended the older Lord Rothermere. Through her mother, the young Peggy met the three Harmsworth boys and the four children became playmates.

Despite having known Esmond since they were both children, the pretty and vivacious Peggy was not a popular choice of bride among Esmond's family. Lord Rothermere, having transformed his family from arriviste to establishment, hoped that his only remaining son would make a far grander marriage. Peggy was also a Roman Catholic, whereas the Harmsworth dynasty was solid Church of England. None of the Harmsworth family chose to attend the wedding on 12 January 1920 at St John's Church, Bromley, except for Esmond's uncle, St John Harmsworth – the founder of the Perrier water company.[14]

But Peggy was irresistible. Over time, she gradually won her father-in-law round with her vivacious charm and prettiness. She also produced three children in quick succession – Lorna in 1920, Esme in 1922 and the longed-for son, Vere, in 1925.

Initially, the family lived at Hill Lodge in Kensington, before moving to the massive and impressive Warwick House in St James's. Warwick House had been bought as a blatant show of wealth and status – a palace for a princely family. Huge and rambling, the house was said to be so big that if a soufflé were served, the staff had to form an athletic relay, passing the plates speedily from basement kitchens to the dining room before the soufflé deflated.

Further encouraged by his father to flaunt the Harmsworth wealth, Esmond purchased the eye-wateringly beautiful Mereworth Castle in Kent in 1927. Originally the home of the Earls of Westmoreland, Mereworth Castle was built in the 1720s. Designed by Colen Campbell, the house is an almost exact replica of Palladio's Villa Rotonda near Venice. With two massive wings, imposing porticos on four sides of the house and topped with a dome, the house features ornate interior plasterwork by Giovanni Bagutti and fresco paintings by Francesco Sleter. Mereworth was the perfect showpiece for the young Harmsworth family, complete with beautiful grounds and extensive stables to house Esmond and Peggy's collection of horses.[15]

Both Warwick House and Mereworth were run on an incredibly impressive scale – even for the decadent era of the 1920s. Both houses were staffed with myriad butlers and servants, with twenty gardeners employed at Mereworth. 'My word it was grand,' a former guest breathlessly remembers.[16]

In 1929, Esmond did not seek re-election as MP for the Isle of Thanet, instead choosing to focus solely on the Harmsworth newspapers. From 1929 to 1937, he served an apprenticeship, learning about newspapers from the top down. Gradually, Lord Rothermere began to relinquish control but the handover was not always smooth sailing. Rothermere held on tight to his beloved *Daily Mail*.

With no experience of journalism and little knowledge of the business of newspapers, Esmond frequently dithered over decisions. This left him susceptible to influence from his father, as well as senior members of staff. Esmond was also prone to blame editors and journalists for dwindling readership, rather than other more systemic factors.

When Esmond was made chairman of Associated Newspapers in 1932, *The Evening News* was still selling nearly 2 million copies. But many *Daily Mail* readers were instead choosing to buy Lord Beaverbrook's *Daily Express*, whose readership overtook that of the *Daily Mail* in the 1930s. In a panicky response, Esmond rapidly changed editors. But this did nothing to shore up readership. The abandonment of the *Daily Mail* by so many readers had little to do with the editorial and more to do with the political stance of the proprietor. Lord Rothermere was an early and enthusiastic supporter of the Nazi Party, as well as the sinister Blackshirts movement and its bombastic leader, Sir Oswald Mosley.

Readership continued to dwindle as Lord Rothermere went so far to decree that nothing negative should appear in his newspapers about either Hitler or Mussolini. As other newspapers, such as the *Express*, began to predict the likelihood of war and reported some of the shocking events in Nazi Germany, the *Daily Mail* seemed out of touch. Rather than confront his father about his political views, Esmond continued to change editorial staff, earning himself a reputation as a harsh chairman who viewed journalists as dispensable. By the time Lord Rothermere officially retired to Monaco in 1937, Esmond needed to make some drastic changes.

Esmond's personal, as well as professional life, was under serious strain as he and Peggy found that they were fundamentally unsuited. Esmond, who could often seem cold and patrician, was at odds with his bubbly, outgoing wife. With his business and parliamentary activities, Esmond preferred to be in London. Peggy, who had a huge love of the country and was an expert horsewoman, preferred to spend her time at Mereworth. Alone in London, Esmond began to pursue other women, while Peggy began an affair with the dashing Prince Aly Khan, the son of the Aga Khan, the leader of the Nizari Ismaili Muslims.[17]

In 1930, Peggy moved out of Warwick House, taking the children to live at Claridge's. While this marked the beginning of an official separation, the couple were not to divorce until 1938. Unusually, during the separation, Esmond was given custody of the children, who were now aged 10, 8 and 5. When the divorce was finalised in 1938, Esmond was officially granted custody, with Peggy having the children for two months of the year. She was also given a large settlement and a country home, Athelhampton Hall, near Dorchester.[18]

During the eight-year separation, Esmond had continued to pursue other women, leading Peggy to cite a number of co-respondents in the divorce proceedings. The might of the Harmsworth family ensured that the divorce was kept out of the papers, but gossip around London suggested that a staggering twenty-eight women had been named by Peggy as co-respondents.[19]

It was during this extended period of separation in August 1936 that Esmond had taken a holiday to the fashionable resort of Lake Wörthersee in Austria. On the banks of the beautiful lake, during a hot, sunny summer, Ann and Esmond were introduced for the first time. Naturally, Ann would have been aware of the Harmsworth wealth and power. But she would always maintain that physical attraction was what first drew her to Esmond. 'He was very good looking,' recollects Sara Morrison.[20] But as well as being handsome, the 38-year-old Esmond was powerful and rich – an irresistible combination to Ann. 'She moved in on Esmond,' her niece said. 'She viewed him as a fascinating citadel to storm. And she never failed to make tracks for whatever was on offer.'[21]

The timing was perfect. Ann was 23 years old and had blossomed from a naive, gawky newly-wed to an interesting beauty with a reputation as a budding hostess. Having had her second child, a daughter, Fionn, on 9 March 1936, Ann felt she had done her duty to her staid husband and was now looking to have some fun. The relationship started as a summer fling and potentially should have been left in Austria. But Ann was hooked. 'She enjoyed the fruits of her hunt,' her niece recalls.[22]

When Esmond asked to see Ann when they were both back in London, she happily agreed. From the beginning the affair was the talk of the town. While Esmond continued to be discreet, Ann almost flaunted her new relationship. The couple were frequently at the same parties or events, with many hostesses colluding in the affair for fear of incurring the wrath of the mighty Harmsworth press. Already popular in London, now as the mistress of one of the country's richest and most powerful men, Ann was hugely in demand.

For two years the relationship between Ann and Esmond continued. Even after the Harmsworths received their decree absolute and Peggy married Captain Thomas Hussey, neither Ann nor Esmond made a move to change the dynamic of their affair. By 1938, while Esmond remained her primary admirer, Ann regarded Ian Fleming as 'the best antidote' whenever Esmond was unavailable.[23]

Ann and Ian were always vague in their correspondence about the start of their sexual affair. This is unusual, given Ann's typical frankness and complete lack of discretion throughout her other correspondence and diaries. But whatever the state of play between the couple, by the summer of 1938, Ian had made up his mind to pursue Ann in earnest.

Making yet another of his beloved motoring tours across Europe, Ian travelled to Kitzbühel in Austria. Whether by design or by coincidence, Ann also happened to be staying in Austria that summer – in Carinthia, an area over 200 miles from him. After a few days in Kitzbühel, Ian drove across Austria to where Ann was staying on the Wörthersee as a guest of Jimmy Foster, cousin of the novelist and *bon vivant*, Lord Berners. One fellow guest during the summer of 1938 was 'Nin' Ryan, daughter of German-born New York financier, Otto Khan. Ryan always believed that Ian travelled to Wörthersee for one reason alone – to see Ann.[24]

The closest Ann ever came to admitting to the start of the affair with Ian is when she accepted an invitation to dine alone with him at his flat in Ebury Street in early 1939. Somewhat surprisingly, given his reputation as a party-loving bachelor with an eye for the ladies, Ian had only moved out of his mother's London house in his late twenties. Eschewing a smart mansion flat, he had chosen rooms in a converted Nonconformist school in Belgravia.

Built in a Greek revival style, with a façade dominated by ionic columns supporting a vast portico, Ian had moved into 22B Ebury Street in 1936.[25] The flat amounted to the majority of the upper part of the chapel-like interior, with a small bathroom and kitchen and a vast drawing room and impressive bedroom. Painted grey with stylish concealed lighting, the flat had no windows, only skylights, significantly adding to the sepulchral feel. A rumour which persists to this day is that the bedroom contained nothing except a vast bed on a raised dais. While this arrangement may seem suited to Ian's vigorous amorous adventures, the rumour may be attributed to the previous tenant, Sir Oswald Mosley, who had an equally impressive reputation as a lothario.

Ann arrived for the dinner, only to be told by Ian that he had a migraine. He gave her a book to read and told her to stay quiet for an hour while he got ready. Ann was understandably peeved, later noting in her diary, 'Considering the slightness of our acquaintance, very odd behaviour.'[26] While most women would have made for the door following such a blatant and pitiful attempt at power play, Ann seems to have been drawn to Ian's arrogance. As she herself admitted in her diary in 1931, she was irresistibly attracted to 'cads and bounders'.[27] She meekly complied with Ian's demands and waited until he was ready for her.

Ann and Ian had met their match in each other. Both had liberal and fairly callous attitudes towards their love affairs. Both could be described as somewhat cruel in their opinions of others. Both were intelligent and witty. And both had the most incredible sexual charisma. For Ian, Ann was the quick, glamorous and steely type of woman he so enjoyed, while Ann was a woman used to getting her own way: Anabel Loyd, her great-niece, recalls, 'When she said jump, you jumped.'[28] In Ian, she had found a man who was strong enough to dominate her. And so began a sporadic sexual relationship.

LAURA MEETS ERIC ... AND RANDOLPH

Having endured six months' exile as a recently separated woman, Laura arrived back in London in the autumn of 1935, returning to live at Guy Charteris' house on Spanish Place. Aged 21, Laura was determined to forget her marriage and start having some fun. She was not yet divorced but received an allowance from David for Sara and herself. Nevertheless, Laura felt poor. Out of boredom as much as financial necessity, Laura took a job at the dressmaker, Madame Fernande, in Queen Street, Mayfair.

Having always had a love of fashion, Laura relished working for Madame Fernande. The job provided her with an income as well as heavily discounted outfits for her myriad social engagements.[1] The work was undemanding, leaving plenty of time for her social life, as well as her roster of male admirers, known as 'the seals' (nicknamed by one of her boyfriends, Frankie More O'Ferrall, because they lined up for Laura like 'performing seals').[2] The seals were an eligible group and included John, always known as Bert, heir to the Dukedom of Marlborough. While Laura gadded about with her seals, gossip reverberated through London drawing rooms about Ann and Esmond, fuelling the budding rivalry between the sisters.

When Laura travelled to Belvoir Castle in the autumn of 1936 to stay with her aunt, she was delighted to discover that her fellow guest was William Ward, the 3rd Earl of Dudley. Like Esmond, the Earl of Dudley, who was always known as Eric, was older, handsome and very rich. He was also single, having been widowed six years before. Here was a man to rival her sister's paramour and Laura went to work. 'She may have chased Eric a bit,' her daughter admits.[3]

Eric Dudley was a complicated character. Born on 2 January 1894 to the 2nd Earl of Dudley and his wife Rachel, he was born just as the Dudley fortunes began a downward slide. The earldom had been created for Eric's grandfather, William Ward. Despite never having held political office, William received his earldom in return for his philanthropy, which included financing the restoration of Worcester Cathedral in 1859. The Dudleys had owned steel and coal mines in the Midlands since the seventeenth century, making the family one of the richest in England.

The family seat had been Dudley Castle until it was damaged during the English Civil War, after which the Dudleys made their home at Himley Hall in Staffordshire. In 1837, Eric's grandfather bought Witley Court in Worcestershire. Purchased from the 4th Baron Foley, Witley Court was a sprawling mansion which had been remodelled by noted architect John Nash in 1805. During a major reconstruction, the house was extended and remodelled in the Palladian style, with two enormous and imposing porticoes added to the north and south fronts. Eric's grandfather, the 1st Earl, carried out further renovation work to the house. Having used the architect Samuel Daukes to remodel Dudley House on Park Lane, Lord Dudley employed Daukes to remodel Witley in the Italianate style. The overall effect of Witley was magnificent, imposing and enormous – suitably reflecting the power and position of the newly ennobled Ward family.[4]

Eric's father, the 2nd Earl of Dudley, inherited the title as well as 30,000 acres of mineral deposits in Staffordshire and Worcestershire including 200 coal and iron mines. He served with the Queen's Own Worcestershire Hussars during the Second Boer War before pursuing a political career, sitting on the Conservative benches in the House of Lords.

Having worked as Parliamentary Secretary to the Board of Trade from 1895 to 1902, William was made a Privy Councillor. On 16 August 1902, William was installed as the Lord Lieutenant of Ireland before Prime Minister Henry Campbell-Bannerman offered William the post of Governor General of Australia, which he formally undertook on 9 September 1908. In Australia, as in Ireland, Lord Dudley lived extravagantly, insisting on the formality of the vice regal style. He maintained two official residences – one in Sydney and one in Melbourne – and travelled around Australia on a private steam yacht, all of which was funded from his own pocket.[5]

Having achieved remarkably little during his time in Australia, William returned to Britain on 31 July 1911 to run the Dudley estates. But the cost of living so lavishly while abroad, as well as the upkeep of two huge estates and a palatial London residence, had vastly diminished the Dudley funds. Witley was sold in 1920 to a carpet manufacturer and the family returned to Himley permanently. But, as coal and steel prices fell during the 1920s, Lord Dudley began to sell off land to stay afloat.

When Rachel died tragically by drowning while in Ireland in 1920, William went completely off the rails. Continuing to sell land and family property to fund his lavish lifestyle, he married the actress Gertie Millar.

When William died on 29 June 1932, the family still owned Himley Hall and Dudley House in Mayfair, but the family assets had been hugely depleted by the Wall Street Crash and the effects of the Great Depression.[6] When Eric became the 3rd Earl Dudley, inheriting the family property and estates, the Dudleys were on the brink of collapse and the new earl was determined to resurrect the family fortunes.

Born at Witley Court, Eric grew up in grandeur between the colossal family homes. While a pupil at Eton, Eric began to become aware of the steady depletion of the family fortune and heard snide gossip about his father's lack of political accomplishments, which all combined to make Eric an angry but determined young man.

While he was single-minded and hard-working, Eric played as hard as he worked. While at Oxford he was fined 2s 6d for drunkenly playing bicycle polo on Merton Street alongside Prince Paul of Serbia and Lord Cranborne.[7] He was also a keen sportsman, enjoying any sport that had an element of danger. An accomplished horseman, he was an enthusiastic steeplechaser, competing in amateur events across the country.

In 1912 Eric joined the Worcestershire Yeomanry, transferring to the 10th Hussars at the outbreak of the First World War. Promoted to lieutenant in 1915 and ending the war as a captain, Eric was awarded the Military Cross for bravery.

Following the war, he threw himself into the family business. The British economy was in tatters with prices for coal and steel at an all-time low, exacerbated by a shortage of manpower due to the huge fatalities on the battlefields. The future looked bleak for the Dudley family. In a by-election in 1921, Eric was elected to represent the constituency of Hornsey as a Unionist candidate – a seat he held until the 1924 election when he stood down.

Following the Wall Street Crash of 1929 and determined to protect his holdings in the Midlands, which were being ravaged by the Labour Government of the day through excessive taxation, Eric, now Viscount Ednam, made a remarkably canny move. He was elected as Conservative Member for Wednesbury – a constituency in the Black Country, where many of the Dudley mines were situated. An astute politician, Eric worked to protect the Dudley assets as well as serving as Parliamentary Private Secretary to the Undersecretary of State for India, Lord Winterton. When his father died on 29 June 1932 at the age of 65, Eric resigned from being an MP and took his seat in the House of Lords as the 3rd Earl of Dudley.

In 1919, Eric had married Rosemary Leveson-Gower, the youngest daughter of the 4th Duke of Sutherland. Rosemary was one of the great beauties of her day and had fallen passionately in love with Edward, Prince of Wales while working as a nurse during the First World War. After a short, unsatisfactory romance with the future Edward VIII, Rosemary had become engaged to Eric – a close friend of the prince.[8]

Eric and Rosemary married on 8 March 1919 and a year later, their eldest son, William, was born. In the early 1920s, the Ednams' happy marriage was rocked by the stillbirth of a baby daughter who they named Mary Rose. Although the Ednams went on to have two more sons – John in 1922 and Peter in 1926.[9]

During the beginning of their marriage, the Ednams seem to have been very much in love. And when Eric's father moved to France, Eric and Rosemary moved into Himley Hall with their sons. But as the 1920s progressed, and the couple began to spend more time apart, the marriage began to suffer. Eric had an affair with the socialite Venetia Montagu, and is widely believed to have fathered her baby, Judith (who became a great friend of Ann's).[10] Rosemary was rumoured to have reignited her romance with the Prince of Wales.

But then tragedy struck in December 1929 when the Ednams' second son, John, was killed while riding his bicycle near the family's Cheyne Walk house in Chelsea. Losing control of his bicycle, he was hit by a lorry and died a few hours later.[11] Rosemary and Eric were devastated, and their mutual grief seemed to bring them closer together. But their rapprochement was to be short-lived.

Tragedy struck the family again the following summer when Eric and Rosemary decided to take a holiday at his stepmother's villa in France. During the holiday, Eric caught typhoid fever. Returning to Himley ahead of her husband, Rosemary boarded a flight from Le Touquet to Croydon on 21 July 1930. Flying over Kent, the plane encountered a storm. Battered by wind and heavy rain, the plane broke up over Meopham, killing everybody on board.[12]

Eric was grief-stricken and he threw himself into work. He successfully built up the Dudley assets, rebuilding the family fortune as trade began to improve during the 1930s. He diversified into other minerals and exported Dudley steel around the world, becoming one of the first industrialists to recognise the American market as a potential buyer for British steel.

Eric also threw himself into his social life. He had an affair with Lady Bridget Paget, as well as rekindling a romance with a former flame, the glamorous, American-born Josephine 'Foxy' Gwynne, who had recently separated from her first husband. Eric also began a serious romance with Freda Dudley Ward, arguably the most famous of Edward VIII's girlfriends.

Following her flagrant and enduring relationship with the Prince of Wales, Freda and her husband, William, had divorced in 1931. Eric and Freda talked of marriage and Eric proposed. However, following the death of George V, the new king came for a weekend at Himley with his mistress, Wallis Simpson. Acting as hostess, Freda Dudley Ward was obviously uncomfortable with the closeness of her potential husband and her former lover. Following the weekend at Himley, Freda finally refused Eric's proposal. In an embittered mood following Freda's rejection, Eric travelled down to Belvoir Castle to stay with the Duke and Duchess of Rutland. At Belvoir, he found the recently separated Lady Long. An eligible, lonely, older man and an available, sexy, younger woman – the die was cast.

In her memoirs, Laura recollects meeting the Earl of Dudley at Belvoir and falling in love with him 'almost at once'.[13] Eric had incredible presence. He was good-looking, sophisticated and rich. And, irresistibly, he was touched with sadness. No wonder that Laura felt herself so drawn to the Earl of Dudley. He was equally taken with Laura and before leaving Belvoir, he asked her to dinner. A few days later, Eric and Laura had dinner at the Embassy Club in Mayfair, followed by dancing at the 400 Club in Leicester Square. Laura mistily recalled the romantic evening, delighting in the jealous looks of other women as she danced with the eligible earl.

Initially, Eric did not take the relationship seriously, regarding Laura as a harmless fling and continuing to romance other women. In retaliation, Laura continued to see her seals. She clearly enjoyed the attention she received from these men, but the relationships and flirtations were all part of a less-than-subtle effort to capture the bigger prize of Eric. As she herself tellingly admitted, 'I probably behaved fairly outrageously on occasions but, looking back, I am pretty sure Eric would not have wanted me for his own if I had behaved differently.'[14]

Another relationship which Laura formed during the 1930s was with Barbara Wallace, the daughter of the architect, Edwin Lutyens, and the second wife of the multimillionaire industrialist and politician, Euan Wallace. Laura was not the type of woman who placed much importance in friendship with other women. Nor did she encourage female friendships, preferring the company of men. 'She adored men. She barely tolerated women,' an acquaintance recalls.[15] But the relationship with Barbara 'Barbie' Wallace, who later married Herbert Agar, is noteworthy because she became one of the few women whom Laura viewed with any warmth.

Laura was a frequent visitor to Barbara and Euan Wallace's Scottish home, Kildonan House in south Ayrshire. The solid and unattractive building had been designed by Euan's first wife in 1913 with luxury and illicit shenanigans in mind. Every guest room had a bathroom, almost unheard of in country houses at that time. And many of the bedrooms had secret, interconnecting doors as the first Mrs Wallace had been a passionate and committed nymphomaniac.[16]

After one such visit, the shenanigans did not take place in the house, instead occurring on the night train as Laura returned from Ayrshire to London. Duff Cooper and Count Paul Munster, the husband of a cousin of Eric Dudley's, who matched Cooper in the bottom-pinching stakes, both happened to be travelling on the same train. Finding that her berth was situated directly between the berths of the two men, Laura spent a hilarious night in fits of giggles as first one man, then the other, knocked tentatively on her door, hoping for something more than just bottom pinching. Both men were unsuccessful and Laura slept alone that night.[17]

Another successful and enduring relationship for Laura began during the 1930s when she met Randolph Churchill in 1938. True to form, Laura explains that from their meeting, 'I know it to be true that he loved me deeply.'[18]

While Laura's arrogance may be breathtaking, her statement, this time, is completely true. Randolph was a volcanic character, deeply flawed and prone to frequent but short-lived passions for women. But his love for Laura lasted throughout his life. As Randolph himself said, in a letter to Laura in 1943, 'I shall always love you.'[19]

Three years older than Laura, Randolph was born in 1911, the only son and second child of Winston and Clementine Churchill. He had shown little promise at Eton, receiving regular beatings for insubordination. From a young age, Randolph was precocious and demonstrated a hatred of authority and discipline. In January 1929, he went to Christ Church, Oxford, where he showed little academic flair and began to develop a dependency on alcohol which would blight him for the rest of his life.

Dropping out of Oxford in October 1930, Randolph embarked on a lecture tour of the United States before beginning a career as a journalist with the Rothermere press. On 6 February 1935, Randolph stood as an Independent Conservative candidate in the Wavertree by-election in Liverpool. Despite not getting elected, Randolph had split the Conservative vote, giving the Labour Party an easy win. Continuing his disastrous political campaign, Randolph stood as a Conservative candidate for West Toxteth in November 1935, where he was so unwelcome that locals threw bananas at him, before he stood in the 1936 Ross and Cromarty by-election, in which he was defeated by the National Labour candidate.[20]

By the time he met Laura in early 1938, he was working as a journalist, embittered by his political failures and drinking heavily. The pair met at a cocktail party in Mayfair. Randolph was bored and was preparing to leave when he was introduced to Laura. Instantly drawn to her vivacity and sexiness, Randolph suggested that the pair leave the party and have drinks at the Cavendish Hotel off Regent Street. Looked after by the legendary owner of the hotel, Rosa Lewis, who had once been cook to the Churchill family, Laura and Randolph drank champagne until the early hours with 'much popping of champagne corks'.[21]

The idea that two good-looking, broad-minded people finished a champagne-fuelled evening with nothing more than a handshake seems pretty unlikely. But this is what seems to have happened. The relationship between Randolph and Laura may have been intense but remained platonic. 'I don't think she ever slept with Randolph,' says Laura's daughter. 'I don't think the fling was ever consummated.'[22]

The friendship for Laura and Randolph was enduring, and the lack of a sexual relationship may explain the longevity. As Sara Morrison concludes, 'Of all the hangers on, Randolph was not one she played along with. He was too big a fish to partially fry.'[23]

Randolph Churchill was a hugely complicated man. Today, Winston Churchill is remembered for his admirable leadership during the Second World War. But during Randolph's growing up years, his father was a divisive and controversial character. Elected to Parliament in 1901 as a Conservative, Churchill was soon at odds with his party about economic protectionism. As the Liberal Party grew in popularity, Churchill crossed the floor and joined them. The move made Churchill hugely unpopular. His defection was viewed as serving his personal ambition as the Liberals looked set to win the next election.

In 1911 Churchill was promoted to First Lord of the Admiralty. However, during the First World War he was held responsible for the disastrous 1915 campaigns in the Dardanelles and at Gallipoli. When Prime Minister H.H. Asquith reluctantly agreed to form an all-party coalition government for the duration of the war, the Conservatives demanded that Churchill be removed from his role as First Lord of the Admiralty.

Following the First World War, Churchill held various positions, such as Secretary of State for War and Air and Secretary of State for the Colonies, but in the November 1922 election, he lost his seat. Having rejoined the Conservatives, Churchill was elected as MP for Epping in 1924, and served as Chancellor of the Exchequer from 1924 to 1929. But the years from 1929 to 1939 were wilderness years for Churchill as he remained on the backbenches, an unpopular figure due to his track record during the First World War, as well as his controversial criticism of Germany in the 1930s.[24]

Winston was a dynamo but an applause junky. While he demonstrably loved his son, Winston always came first. Randolph's mother, Clementine, was also very loving of her children. But they came second to her husband, who demanded the vast majority of her time and attention.[25]

Randolph was achingly good-looking, with thick, blonde hair and piercing eyes, and was also capable of great charm. But he could also behave appallingly, making him the scourge of ballrooms across London. 'I remember seeing a footman reeling back after he threw food in his face,' Sara recalls.[26] Randolph would frequently get paralytically drunk and pick fights. As Laura herself recalled, 'For so long he was like an enormous bonfire – flames licking out in all directions ... Randolph revelled in argument, promoting it whenever possible ... His dynamic and irrepressible personality made many enemies.'[27]

Randolph made a disastrous and spontaneous marriage to Pamela Digby on 4 October 1939, having proposed to her on their first meeting. Like many people in wartime marriages, motivated by the impending risk of death on the battlefield, Randolph was desperate to have a son. Pamela was the eldest daughter of the 11th Baron Digby. After the collapse of her marriage to Randolph, she would go on to have a staggeringly prolific reputation with men. She would later become the mistress of Gianni Agnelli, Baron Elie de Rothschild and Prince Aly Khan, before marrying the Hollywood agent Leland Hayward and later, the billionaire industrialist Averell Harriman.

Despite his marriage to Pamela, Randolph continued to pursue Laura, writing passionate love letters from all over the world as he served with the 4th Hussars. In 1942 from the Central Hotel in Glasgow, Randolph wrote, 'If you should decide that you want and could make a happy and useful life with me [...] you can count on me in every way.' Writing to Laura a year later, in 1943, he says, simply, 'I really have nothing to say except I love you.'[28]

As her divorce from David Long finally looked set to materialise in early 1943, Randolph became desperate, rightly suspecting that Laura would marry Eric. He even asked a mutual friend, the journalist Virginia Cowles, to plead his case. Cowles wrote to Laura:

Randolph is in Algiers and you are very much on his mind. He thinks of nothing else [...] Do think seriously before taking the plunge with the

Earl. Life with him [Randolph], I am sure, would be far more glamorous and exciting.[29]

When Laura wrote to Randolph, explaining her decision to marry, he disconsolately replied from Cairo, 'Any letter from you will always bring me joy; but this one has made me very gloomy [...] I have no right to challenge the wisdom of your decision', ending with the plaintive, 'All my devoted love now and always.'[30]

Randolph's protestations of love continued for the remainder of the war. Even after Laura's marriage to Eric, he wrote to her from Chequers in 1944, 'I love you, I love you, I love you.'[31] But later, the relationship between him and Laura evolved into an intense, protective friendship. Following the breakdown of his second marriage, and the years leading up to his death, Randolph would be a frequent house guest of Laura, spending every Christmas at her home in Buckinghamshire, as well as holidaying with her in Barbados.[32]

7

THE WAR

As the 1930s drew to a close, the clouds of war began to gather in Europe. Neither Ann nor Laura had any memory of the First World War, but the men that they were sleeping with in 1939 had both been scarred by their different experiences of the Great War. Eric Dudley had fought in the trenches and refused to speak about his experiences while Esmond Harmsworth remained deeply ashamed of not seeing action.

The Second World War was a pivotal time for both sisters. Like so many of their generation, their lives would be changed beyond all recognition. Against the traumatic backdrop of a horrific war, both women had passionate love affairs and suffered devastating losses of friends, lovers and even husbands.

Laura, despite being sharp as a tack, seems to have been oblivious to the impending war. She had read of the troubles in mainland Europe and seen the rise of Hitler and the Nazi Party in Germany. Like all Britons, she had breathed a sigh of relief when the Sudetenland was conceded to Germany on 30 September 1938, and Prime Minister Neville Chamberlain declared, 'Peace for our time.'[1]

In August 1939, Laura travelled to Cannes where Eric had taken a house for the summer. While Eric seemed concerned at the rapidly unfolding events in Germany, Laura continued to be her capricious self. Despite being on holiday with Eric, she accepted an invitation from his friends, Commander and Mrs Buist, to accompany them on a plane trip. The trip was to be a whistle-stop tour of Europe.

Eric was understandably irritated by Laura's decision to join the Buists and fly around Europe.[2] Not only was he wary of the international situation, which could develop into war at any moment, he was also jealous. The plane was to be piloted by Arthur Forbes, the hugely rich heir to the earldom of Granard. Twenty years younger than Eric, Forbes was the same age as Laura, and handsome into the bargain.

The group left Nice in August, flying to Venice, Budapest, Bucharest and Constanta on the Black Sea. As the plane flew into Constanta, the wheels jammed, which meant that Forbes had to do a 'pancake' landing – hitting the runway with the base of the plane, rather than the wheels. As an expert pilot, Forbes successfully landed the plane, before telling his passengers to disembark quickly, in case the fuselage caught fire.

Shaken by the landing, the Buists decided to head straight back to England. Laura decided to wait in Constanta until she could get a flight to Rome, from where she hoped to be able to travel back to Nice. The war was now clearly imminent and for the first time Laura began to panic. Abandoning her plans to fly to Rome, she went to Constanta train station, hoping to catch a train to Cannes, despite the abandonment of normal time-tables. While waiting, Laura watched a cattle train pull into the station. To her horror, she saw hundreds of weary, malnourished Jews disembarking in order to empty overloaded buckets of human excrement before being manhandled back onto the trains by the guards. The sight would remain seared on Laura's memory for the rest of her life; the first time that she fully comprehended the seriousness of the impending war.[3]

Eventually Laura was able to catch a train back to Cannes, where she was met by a furious but relieved Eric. The pair joined the mass exodus of tourists desperately trying to return home before war was declared. Eric and Laura made for Calais, where they managed to get on a boat crossing the Channel, arriving back in London just as Britain and France declared war on Germany on 3 September 1939.

Guy Charteris was planning to pack up the house on Oxford Square and decamp to the country for the duration of the war. Eric was planning on returning to Himley. He had been appointed Regional Commissioner for the Midlands – a big responsibility as the Midlands was an industrial area, vital to the war effort, and would later be heavily targeted by the German Luftwaffe. Laura was unsure of what to do, until Eric suggested that she join him permanently at Himley, which would be safer than remaining in London. Eric did not have to ask Laura twice. The very next day, she packed up her things and left for the Midlands. As Laura and Eric remained unmarried, Eric also asked his sister, Lady Alexandra 'Patsy' Ward, to move into Himley in order to add a veneer of respectability.[4]

Despite the relative safeness of Himley Hall, Laura did not take her young daughter. (She did, however, take her dog and her maid, Biddlecombe.) Initially, after her parents' separation, Sara had remained at Oxford Square with her nanny, where David visited regularly, 'Every day at 5 p.m. … my father would turn up,' Sara remembers.[5] When David took up residency of

South Wraxall Manor after the last tenant died in 1936, Sara and her nanny were permanently installed in Wiltshire with her father, allowing Laura to lead a totally responsibility-free existence. 'She had a lack of maternal everything,' her daughter recalls.[6] When David rejoined the Coldstream Guards, Sara was dispatched to the Cotswolds to stay with her cousin-in-law, Didy Asquith.

★ ★ ★

Ann O'Neill was in London when war was declared. Like her sister, initially she did not take the prospect of war too seriously, boasting to friends that she relished the threat of bombs. But Ann's trivialisation of the war was just a defence mechanism utilised as an act of self-protection, her fear coming across as a cool hardness.

Ann seemed typically calm during a lunch with Anthony Winn at the Ritz, the day after war was declared. Winn later wrote to a friend that Ann seemed 'quite unaffected by Armageddon, which was all to the good'.[7] But privately, Ann was scared. Following lunch, she went to Fortnum & Mason, where she joined a queue of people purchasing tinned food. On arriving home to Montagu Square with her provisions, she received a telephone call from Shane. Seemingly unaware of Ann's burgeoning relationship with Ian Fleming, Shane told his wife that he would be bringing him back to their home that evening, warning Ann not to laugh at Ian's new uniform. Following the declaration of war, Ian had quickly joined the Royal Naval Volunteer Reserve. He had been made a lieutenant in the Special Branch and Ian was sensitive about the startling blue uniform. Ann managed to avoid laughing but later referred to Ian as looking like a 'chocolate soldier' – a nickname that unfortunately stuck.[8]

The Charteris sisters were together on the evening of 4 September 1939, when Laura arrived at Montagu Square to say goodbye before her departure for Himley. Ann did not approve of her sister's lover and was not pleased that Laura was uprooting her life to live with Eric, a man whom she would come to despise. But her attention was soon focused elsewhere. As a former soldier, Shane O'Neill had immediately joined the North Irish Horse, Royal Armoured Corps and travelled to Belfast to begin training. He was granted an emergency commission on 20 September 1939 as second lieutenant. In October 1939, he was granted the acting rank of captain, before being promoted again in December 1939 to lieutenant colonel.

Life remained largely unchanged for Ann during the 'phoney war', except for the absence of her husband. However, with the German invasion of

France on 10 May 1940 and the German *Blitzkrieg* beginning in September 1940, Ann decided to pack up the Montagu Square house and move into the Dorchester Hotel on Park Lane, which Esmond was also using as his London base.

The Dorchester became the hubbub of social activity for London during the war. Many rich patrons took up residency there in the mistaken belief that the building was impervious to bombing as it had been constructed from concrete.[9] Society figures flocked to the hotel, including Lady Cunard, Diana and Duff Cooper, Mrs Ronnie Grenville and Pamela Churchill.

Fearing the impending bombing campaign and urged by Shane to remove Raymond and Fionn from London, Ann also leased Lane End, a cottage in the small village of Buscot, in Oxfordshire.[10] The house was near her sister-in-law Midi Gascoigne and her two children, as well as her friend, Lady Margaret Douglas-Home and her three children. Laura's daughter Sara would also later swell the ranks of children at Lane End, with Laura making occasional, fleeting visits.[11]

But the real motivating factor was that Esmond had temporarily leased nearby Buscot Park. At the beginning of the war, both of Esmond's homes had been requisitioned. Warwick House was taken over by the Red Cross, while Mereworth Castle was requisitioned by the RAF. Later, Esmond rented a small country house on the edge of Windsor Great Park called Lovel Dene. Esmond would conduct his newspaper business by telephone from this house and would be joined by Ann whenever she could get away.

In the spring of 1940, before the Blitz began in earnest, a bomb fell near Lovel Dene. Ann was woken by the blast which blew out all the windows in the house. Terrified, she saw flames in a nearby wood and was initially told that Esmond had been buried by rubble when a ceiling collapsed. Luckily, Esmond was unhurt and only covered in plaster from the downed ceiling.[12]

★ ★ ★

Another romance which seems to have been hastened by the war was between Mary Rose Charteris and Roderic Thesiger. Like her sisters, Mary Rose was pretty, with dark eyes and the neat Charteris nose. But her face was more rounded and less elfin than Ann's and she also lacked the confidence and allure which her sisters seemed to exude so effortlessly. Mary Rose did not have the toughness, nor did she develop the toughness, that her sisters adopted in order to survive their upbringing.

Like her sisters, Mary Rose had been presented, but she had been a reluctant debutante during her 1937 season and did not receive the same level of male attention as her sisters. Laura later bitchily recalled that Mary Rose married the first man who showed any interest in her.[13]

The man in question was the handsome and intelligent, Roderic Thesiger, whom Mary Rose met at the beginning of the war. Roddy, as he was always known, was an extraordinary mix of dashing, hardy soldier and softly spoken, intellectual art lover. 'He was absolutely enchanting. He could not have been nicer. Top class,' Sara recalls.[14]

Born in Addis Ababa in 1915, Roddy was born the youngest of three sons of Wilfred Thesiger, the British Minister to Ethiopia and his wife, Kathleen. Educated at Eton and Christ Church, Oxford, Roddy became an early student of the Courtauld Institute before finding work as an assistant at the Tate Gallery. When war was declared, he immediately signed up and was commissioned into the Welsh Guards.

On the surface, Roddy seemed like a good match for Mary Rose. As well as being from a good family – his grandfather had been the 2nd Lord Chelmsford, while his uncle had been Viceroy of India – he was kind and intelligent, sharing an interest in art and culture with Mary Rose. Following the war, Roddy forged a career as a noted art dealer, specialising in old masters and becoming an adviser to Sotheby's auction house.[15]

With Roddy about to depart on active service, he proposed marriage to Mary Rose. Like so many wartime marriages the courtship was rushed, with little consideration given to whether the couple had anything in common, let alone being in love. Like her sisters, one of the main attractions of marriage for Mary Rose was independence and a home of her own.

Roddy and Mary Rose married on 21 September 1940. The wedding was not a grand affair like the first weddings of Ann and Laura. The couple married in a quiet ceremony at St Peter's, Vere Street, and had a brief honeymoon on the south coast before Roddy had to rejoin his regiment.[16] Independent for the first time, away from the watchful eyes of relatives and worried about her husband, Mary Rose began to drink heavily, succumbing to alcoholism, which would plague her for the rest of her life.

★ ★ ★

Ann was able to make intermittent trips across to Ireland to see Shane during his training. She delighted in the abundance of meat and cream, smuggling extra rations back to England for family and friends. Ann had just returned from one such trip when she heard the news that Esmond's father was ill. Lord Rothermere, embittered by the breakdown of appeasement, had travelled to Canada at the beginning of the war. He joined his granddaughter,

Esme, in New York in October 1940, where he became seriously unwell and was advised to travel to a warmer climate to recuperate. He sailed to St George's, Bermuda, with his granddaughter, arriving in Hamilton on 3 November 1940, where he immediately suffered a relapse and was admitted to the King Edward VII Memorial Hospital. He remained in hospital for several weeks before dying in the early hours of 26 November 1940. He was 72 and diabetic, but the cause of death was diagnosed as 'dropsy' or oedema – the swelling of body tissue caused by excess water retention.[17]

Despite being one of the richest men of his generation, Lord Rothermere had spent his final years splashing his cash. He had bought houses and art, gambled heavily at Monte Carlo casino, invested in the stock market, gambled on currencies and given away large sums of money to family members and old girlfriends. Following his death, Esmond was left with a complicated financial mess. Heavy taxes were levied on the estate, and Esmond had to pay out several large legacies dictated in the late Lord Rothermere's will. He later confided to a friend that a whopping £34 million had to be found to sort the tangled Rothermere estate.[18] The death of his father also threw up a complicated emotional situation for Esmond. He was now the 2nd Viscount Rothermere. He was also now in sole charge of the *Daily Mail* and General Trust and Associated Newspapers. And, without the risk of incurring his father's wrath, and divorced from his wife, Esmond could now marry Ann.

When Ian returned from a covert trip to the United States in an attempt to encourage America to join the war, he had dinner with Ann at a restaurant on Jermyn Street. By now, Shane was fighting in northern Africa, and Ann asked Ian whether she should divorce her husband in order to marry Esmond. The new Lord Rothermere had a lot to offer – a title, money and power. As the wife of press baron, Ann would have access to the powerful people she so adored. Ian's response was remarkably blunt and unhelpful. If she wanted to marry Rothermere she should do so, he said.[19]

On New Year's Eve in 1940, both Esmond and Ian were guests at a party held by Ann. She used her winnings from a bridge game to hire a suite at the Dorchester and invited her inner circle of Loelia, Duchess of Westminster; Duff and Diana Cooper; and Oliver and Maureen Stanley. Determined to make her party go with a bang, Ann plied her guests with champagne and asked one of the pipers playing in the lobby of the Dorchester to pipe in the suite, nearly deafening her guests.[20]

As the new year began, Ann decided that she had had enough of the status quo. Determined to marry Esmond, she offered him an ultimatum. Either he marry her or she would never see him again. Esmond dithered momentarily before agreeing that Ann must divorce Shane and marry him.

The draconian divorce laws of the time meant that no divorce could be granted without proof of adultery. In the spring of 1941, Ann and Esmond travelled to a Bournemouth Hotel for a staged discovery by a maid of the couple '*in flagrante*'.[21] This would provide Shane with the evidence to divorce his wife. Ian, who was on leave at the time, accompanied the pair to Bournemouth.

The case felt apart when the maid, who had previously given evidence in a well-publicised divorce case, said she had no recollection of finding Esmond and Ann in bed. Ann furiously accused Esmond of changing his mind and bribing the maid. She even went so far as to accuse Esmond of dragging his heels in the hope that Shane would be killed in action, leaving Ann free to marry without a messy divorce.[22] Relations subsequently cooled between Esmond and Ann after this escapade – she remained married to Shane and Esmond remained single.

★ ★ ★

Like her sister, when Laura arrived at Himley Hall at the beginning of the war, she was caught between two men and found herself in the odd position of being the pseudo-lady of the manor. She was the mistress of the earl but not his wife.

Himley Hall is a vast Georgian house, evenly proportioned, with a middle block and two large wings. Built of a soft, rusticated red stone, the hall was constructed in the early eighteenth century, replacing an earlier, medieval moated mansion. Surrounded by 180 acres of parkland designed by Capability Brown, the house looks down to an imposing lake which is filled by interconnecting cascading waterfalls. A long, sweeping drive leads up to the main entrance of the hall – an imposing entrance to a grand house.

The Ward family had originally left Himley in the 1830s because of the house's proximity to the Black Country and the all-encompassing dust from the nearby mines. But when Eric took up residency, he had significantly modernised the house. One wing, which was formerly the servants' quarters, was renovated to include a swimming pool – almost unheard of in England at that time – and a squash court. Eric's first wife, Rosemary, had had the swimming pool painted with Venetian scenes and even installed a cocktail bar in the gallery.[23]

Laura's move to Himley marked a huge change in her life. As she admits in her memoirs, 'Perhaps for the first time in my life my thoughts were wholly serious.'[24] She was determined to be useful and decided to train as a nurse.

Despite having no qualifications, Laura began her training at the Dudley Road Hospital in Birmingham. The hospital was situated in Ladywood – one of the poorest areas of Birmingham – and her training in one of the most poverty-stricken areas of the country was a baptism of fire for Laura.

She brought her own individual verve to the role of nurse. Laura was unhappy with the unflattering nurse's uniform, so she employed a professional dressmaker to make alterations. She was also unhappy being known as plain 'Nurse Long', which the matron had insisted upon. Laura quickly let it be known that she was a viscountess, which resulted in Laura being known as 'Nurse Lady Long'. She was also saved from living in the nursing accommodation by gaining special dispensation to return to Himley every evening.[25]

To begin with, Laura was shocked by the injuries and illnesses that she had to deal with. Her first training placement was in the casualty department of the hospital, where Laura saw the horrific emergencies coming in. One of her first cases left a lasting impression. A young woman had resorted to an illegal backstreet abortionist and the injuries caused by the knitting needles used had led to septicaemia, from which the woman died.[26]

But she overcame the trauma and became a diligent, caring nurse. Oddly, she thrived doing the many menial tasks required of a nurse such as cleaning and bedmaking – the first time in her life that she had ever had to do such work. When Laura's daughter later met the former Mayor of Birmingham, Arthur Hillman, he remembered Laura: 'He told me that she was a good nurse.'[27]

The kindness and dedication which Laura displayed as a nurse seems slightly at odds with the more frivolous aspect of her character. But nursing may have provided Laura with some of the power that she craved. As a friend archly explains, 'She was able to be kind in certain circumstances. She could be kind when she was dominant. Absolutely in control.'[28]

Laura was still training in 1940 when the German *Blitzkrieg* began, with industrial areas such as Birmingham and Coventry becoming key targets. The Luftwaffe attacked Coventry on the night of 14 November 1940. Codenamed Operation *Mondscheinsonate* (Moonlight Sonata) by the Nazis, the raid was intended to obliterate every single factory in Coventry and cripple British industry. In total, 515 German bombers dropped hundreds of tonnes of explosives and thousands of incendiary devices, destroying 4,300 homes and damaging two-thirds of all the buildings in Coventry, including the cathedral; 568 people were killed and 863 were seriously injured.[29]

On duty at Dudley Road, Laura was immediately seconded to Coventry to deal with the injured. The site was biblical in its horror. The famous cathedral was engulfed in flames and bodies lay scattered in the streets.

Laura and her fellow nurses worked through the night as casualties poured into the hospital.

Despite these horrors, Laura loved being a nurse. When her training period came to an official end, she was outraged to discover that she would not be able to receive accreditation as a State Registered Nurse due to a lack of an educational qualification. Laura cleverly and determinedly sidestepped this setback. She chose to officially continue her training and unofficially act as a qualified nurse on the wards of the Dudley Road Hospital until the end of 1942.[30]

Alongside her nursing, Laura was also acting as chatelaine of Himley and gradually 'morphing into a Countess'.[31] As Regional Commissioner, Eric was expected to play host to guests visiting Birmingham and Laura acted as his hostess. The roster of guests included the Home Secretary Herbert Morrison, Sir John Anderson, General Montgomery, Charles de Gaulle, John F. Kennedy and the Duke of Kent, who visited a few weeks before he was killed in an air crash.

Laura also decided to send for her daughter, who was installed with a nanny – Nanny Lee – on the top floor of Himley. Here, Sara had an 'endless stream of governesses', until one visitor behaved inappropriately.[32] 'One went off in a strait jacket after Malcolm Sargent made a pass at her,' Sara remembers.[33] Shortly afterwards, she was dispatched to a school in nearby Stourbridge, making the daily journey by pony and trap.

In early 1943, Laura had to return to London to finalise her divorce from David Long. An oversight by their lawyer meant that despite their formal agreement of separation signed in 1935, the Longs would not be able to seek a divorce without proof of adultery. Laura had been living openly with Eric Dudley and David Long had pursued relationships with other women, but apparently this was insufficient. As Regional Commissioner, Eric was reluctant to be cited for infidelity in case his reputation was affected. Magnanimously, David agreed to provide the evidence of adultery, allowing Laura to become the Countess of Dudley without a blemish on her character.[34]

In order not to jeopardise the divorce proceedings by arousing the suspicion of the hawk-eyed king's proctor (the judiciary responsible for granting divorces), Laura left Himley and moved into the Dorchester Hotel, where her sister was staying. During her London stay, Laura obtained work as a private nurse until she had a run in with a patient. While giving an elderly man a bed bath, Laura recalled how the patient 'was delighted to get a huge erection'.[35] She doused the man with a glass of water in a bid to cool his ardour. The man, rather unfairly, complained, resulting in Laura being struck off the private nursing register.

Eventually, in late January 1943, Laura, accompanied by Ann, went to the High Court to obtain her decree nisi. David was serving abroad and did not attend the court but the evidence he supplied was accepted. The judge delivered a sonorous, lecturing judgement but granted the decree nisi.[36]

On 23 February 1943, Laura and Eric were married at Caxton Hall, followed by a blessing afterwards at Holy Trinity Brompton in Knightsbridge.[37] The marriage of the earl and his 28-year-old bride was celebrated at a reception held in the drawing room of 5 Belgrave Square, the home belonging to Henry 'Chips' Channon and his wife, Lady Honour.[38]

Having spent their wedding night at Claridge's, the Dudleys returned to Himley on 24 February. That night, Laura was due to give a speech at Dudley Town Hall as the new Countess of Dudley. The mayor, Arthur Hillman, would be introducing her and Laura would respond, marking her formal entrance into public life.

Laura took to the role of countess like the proverbial duck to water. As the wife of the largest landowner in the Midlands, Laura rejoiced in the nickname of 'Queen of the Midlands'.[39] But alongside her official role, Laura was determined to devise a way to return to nursing. Unusually, Himley Hall had not been requisitioned and remained a private home. Laura quickly convinced a reluctant Eric to turn over part of Himley to the Red Cross.

With Laura in charge, Himley became a Red Cross Hospital, catering to patients who had suffered burns and were awaiting plastic surgery. The majority of the patients had been operated on by Archibald McIndoe, the pioneering plastic surgeon. As many of the patients had to undergo several different operations, such as nose, ear and even eyelids reconstuctions, many stayed for extended periods.[40]

Again surrounded by the truly vulnerable, Laura demonstrated an admirably caring side. She instituted a rigid regime of rehabilitation, both physical and emotional. She would not allow the men to retreat into themselves because of their disfiguring injuries. Realising that a child would cheer these men and help them to contemplate life outside of a hospital, Laura urged her daughter to chat and play with the men during their stay. The young Sara adored the men and delighted in their encouragement of her increasingly wild behaviour. 'I was encouraged to let my pony walk on the beds and to steal Mummy's cigarettes in return for sweets … I adored Himley. It was a very happy part of my childhood.'[41]

Laura also used her natural talents with the men. Despite their awful injuries, she would flirt with the soldiers, bolstering their confidence. As her daughter concludes, 'For those soldiers, Himley during the war was the most therapeutic thing around.'[42]

Laura also proved an accomplished fundraiser and hit upon the idea of throwing a fete in the grounds of Himley. She enlisted the help of the Mayor of Dudley, Arthur Hillman, who was enthusiastic about the idea.[43] Eric, on the other hand, was not keen. As Laura later recalled in her divorce petition from Eric, 'My husband was very rude to members of the committee and criticised the organisation.'[44]

Despite Eric's opposition, Laura organised attractions such as whippet racing and a gymkhana. Showing a remarkable flair for PR, she also persuaded professional sportsmen, such as golfer Henry Cotton and American tennis professional Jack Kramer, to give lessons. Laura even used her remarkable charm to persuade a local regiment of paratroopers to do a practice jump over Himley on the day of the fete. No one, it seems, could refuse the Countess of Dudley.

The fete took place on 28 August 1944 and was opened by Clementine Churchill. She was joined on stage by Laura, Field Marshall Sir Philip Chetwode and a very disgruntled Eric. In her memoirs, Laura recalls over 100,000 people attending the fete, which is entirely possible. She also claims that the fete raised £40,000, which is less believable.[45]

But tragedy was never far away during wartime. One of Eric's responsibilities as Regional Commissioner was to meet the regular hospital trains which transported the wounded around the country. On the night of 23 September, Eric was tired and he asked Laura to meet one of the trains at a station near Wolverhampton. Laura went in her full Red Cross uniform and waited with a stream of ambulances for the hospital train to arrive. The train pulled into the station to disgorge the injured.

The scene was horrific. Many of the injured had received only basic medical care, while others had received hurried amputations on the battlefields of France. Injured men begged to be allowed to die and others held cotton wool and swabbing to burns and wounds. Greeting an officer whom she vaguely recognised, Laura asked him if there was anything that she could do. The distraught man, not knowing who Laura was, revealed that his senior officer, David Long, had been killed by a sniper earlier that day. Surrounded by the injured, Laura realised with horror that her ex-husband was dead.[46]

Laura returned to Himley to tell her young daughter of her father's death. At 10 years old, Sara was the same age as Laura had been when her own mother had died. But she did not draw on her own experiences of childhood grief. Sara recalls her mother sitting at her dressing table and looking out of the window as she explained that her father was dead: 'She always ran away from anything to do with unhappiness.'[47] The little girl was so distraught by the death of her father that she did not speak for three weeks.[48]

★ ★ ★

Ann received the news of her own husband's death in a more traditional but no less shattering way. When Ian was granted some leave at the end of October 1944, he and Ann decided to spend a few days with Esmond at Lovel Dene.[49] Extending an invitation to Ian would suggest that either Esmond was oblivious to a sexual relationship between his mistress and another man or, more likely, Ann and Ian had reverted to friendship at this stage.

On the afternoon of Wednesday, 25 October, she received a telegram telling her that Shane had been killed in Italy the day before. Ann was shattered by the news. Almost immediately, she suffered intense guilt for her blatant infidelity, saying to Ian, 'Death is the best revenge.'[50]

Despite being in Esmond's house, Ian was the man to whom Ann turned. And Ian was the one who arranged for Fionn to be brought over from Buscot and Raymond to be collected from his prep school, Ludgrove.

Now that Shane was dead, there was no reason for Ann not to marry Esmond. But no engagement was forthcoming. Esmond was still dragging his heels.

8

POST-WAR

With the announcement of Victory in Europe, Ann and Laura celebrated along with the whole of Europe. Laura and Eric were staying at the Dorchester and the earl insisted that Sara be brought to London by his chauffeur, Wheeler. While Laura and Eric celebrated in their suite, Sara was taken by Peter Ward to see the crowds outside Buckingham Palace. 'The only time Peter was friendly,' she remembers wryly.[1]

Ann and Esmond spent VE day together, having finally decided to marry. Ian had been increasingly absent from London as he travelled around the world as part of his role with the Admiralty. With the announcement of Victory in Europe on 8 May 1945, Ian's work in the notorious Room 39 began to wind down and he began to look to post-war life.

Having attended the 1942 Anglo–American Intelligence Summit in Jamaica alongside Ivar Bryce, Ian had fallen in love with the island. He had vowed to return after the war and build a house on Jamaica so that he would never again have to endure a cold British winter.[2] With the war at an end, he began to draw up architectural plans for a house, intending to return to the island during the winter of 1945.

On 27 June 1945, Ian dined with Ann to discuss his post-war career. She derailed the conversation by announcing that she would be marrying Esmond the following day. After the meal, Ann and Ian walked round and round St James's Park talking. Ann later admitted that if Ian 'had suggested marriage I would have accepted'.[3] But this statement was made much later, after Ann and Ian had married, and may have more to do with romantic hindsight than fact.

During the war, the relationship between Ann and Ian had been sporadic, but Ian was not about to suggest marriage. He had been devasted by the death of a girlfriend, Muriel Wright, in the Blitz and would berate himself for not being kinder to her while she was alive. As Andrew Lycett concludes, 'Ian was incapable of marriage at that stage for one reason or another.'[4] And Esmond was not the sort of man who would marry a woman who was involved with someone else. 'He was not that sort of fool,' Sara recalls. 'I like to think that he [Ian] was not her lover when she married Esmond.'[5]

On 28 June, Ann and Esmond finally married and Ann's life now entered its most impressive, extravagant and seemingly enviable phase. As wartime restrictions were still in place, a far-flung honeymoon was off the cards. The new Viscount and Viscountess Rothermere headed to Margate for a few days before returning to Lovel Dene in Windsor.[6] But there was the pressing question of where the couple were going to live more permanently. Ann had visited Mereworth Castle in the past and loved the grandeur of the house, but Mereworth had been the Rothermere family home, where Peggy Harmsworth had lived and raised her children.

There were practical as well as emotional reasons as to why the Rothermeres did not take up residence at Mereworth. On 5 July 1945, a Labour Government swept into power in Britain and change was in the air. The new government promised to smash pre-war imparity. In the new Britain, everyone would be equal. Edifices like Mereworth would be discouraged and despised as relics of an outdated class system.

Britain was also flat broke after the war. The easiest way for Britain to return to a financial even keel would be to tax the rich. If punitive taxes came into effect, Esmond feared that he would simply not have the money to run Mereworth. He sold the Mereworth estate to Peter Beatty, the younger son of Lord Beatty, a noted racehorse breeder and trainer, who had inherited a fortune from his grandfather, the American supermarket magnate Marshall Field.[7]

Ann and Esmond did, however, decide to keep Warwick House in St James's. Big enough to rival any country house, Warwick House would become their main home for their entire marriage and would remain Esmond's home for the next fifty years.

Mixing her style and elan with her new husband's money and power, gradually Ann made Warwick House the focal point of London society, mixing together writers, artists, journalists and politicians. But the task of refurbishment and redecoration was daunting, even if Ann had the Rothermere millions to do as she pleased. The home was bigger than any house she had previously run. Across seven floors, the house had four main reception rooms, a ballroom, eight principal bedroom suites, a maze of basement kitchens and a warren of servants' rooms. Originally built in 1770 by Scottish architect, Sir William Chambers as a showpiece, Ann was determined to resurrect Warwick House as a grand London salon.[8]

After five years occupancy by the Red Cross, Warwick House was in a sorry state. The massive basement kitchens had been neglected and many of the large entertaining rooms had been divided into smaller offices with the use of cheap plywood. With little thought given to conservation during the war, the beautiful decoration in the main rooms – painted panels, cornicing, frescoes and crimson velvet curtains made out of a Delhi Durbar tent – had all been damaged or destroyed.[9] Seeking advice from friends such as noted decorator Sibyl Colefax, Ann set to work creating a stylish, comfortable and elegant home, a skill which she would exercise on other houses throughout her life.

The renovation and refurbishment would take two years, with the Rothermeres finally moving in during the summer of 1947. In the meantime, Ann and Esmond and her two children lived in the marginally less grand surroundings of Montagu Square, which Ann had inherited as Shane's widow following his death in 1944.[10]

The Rothermeres were also in need of a country home and leased a succession of houses outside of London. The summer after the war, Esmond and Ann leased Bailiffscourt, Lord Moyne's eccentric house in Littlehampton, near Bognor Regis, where guests were unable to swim in the sea because of the mines. Later, they also intermittently rented South Wraxall Manor from the trustees of Ann's young niece, Sara, who had inherited the house following the death of her father in 1944.

As well as houses, there were children to consider. Raymond and Fionn O'Neill were 12 and 9 when their mother married Esmond Rothermere. Their new stepfather remained a remote figure to the children. 'He didn't like children. He was a distant and lofty figure,' Ann's niece remembers.[11] Soon after Ann married Esmond, Raymond was dispatched to Eton while Fionn remained in London and attended the Francis Holland Day School.

Ann was not an altogether popular figure in the lives of her stepchildren. At 31, Ann was closer in age to her stepchildren than her 47-year-old husband. Esmond's eldest daughter, Lorna, was 25 and married, as was Esmond's second daughter, Esme, who was 23. Vere, Esmond's only son and youngest child, was 20 years old when his father remarried.

Ann initially made overtures to build a relationship with Esmond's son and daughters but animosity soon developed. She found his children dull and referred to Lorna, and her husband, Neil Cooper-Key, as 'the Cooper-Cows' or 'The Cooper-Coos'.[12] However, Ann's animosity may have been fuelled by resentment. Ann was only five years older than Lorna and seven years older than Esme, making them almost the same generation. Lorna and Esme were both breathtakingly beautiful. Both had been Debutante of the Year during their respective seasons, and both girls had scant regard for economy, having been born very rich. While the daughters resented their new stepmother, suspecting that she had married Esmond for money and position, Ann resented the girls for effortlessly having everything that she wanted.

With her marriage, Ann began to establish herself as the paramount hostess in London. Having been well off while married to Shane, Ann was now in the super-rich league. Her friends noticed that, while her entertaining had never been shabby, once she married Esmond, the champagne and caviar really flowed. Not only did marriage to a press baron give Ann access to the powerful people she adored but these same powerful people were lining up to ingratiate themselves with the new Lady Rothermere.

During the early years of their marriage, the Rothermeres appeared to be a successful couple, despite the near-constant presence of Ian. When the Rothermeres took up full-time residence in Montagu Square, Ian rented a flat in nearby 5 Montagu Place. In the afternoons, when Ann was walking with her children in Hyde Park, Ian would just 'happen' to be out for a walk and would join Ann and the children. The continuing friendship resulted in London wags nicknaming Ian 'Lady Rothermere's fan'.[13] But as Christmas 1945 approached, Ian left Ann, and the UK, for an extended trip to Jamaica to oversee the building of his house on a plot of land he had purchased near Oracabessa.

Once again, the Rothermeres rented Bailiffscourt on the Sussex coast. Although it was built between 1928 and 1935, Lord Moyne had replicated an original fifteenth-century manor house. He was so determined to recreate medieval life with his home that he furnished the house in fifteenth-century style, right down to the crockery and cutlery. That Christmas, the Rothermeres and their guests ate in the Great Hall on a medieval-style dining table, using authentic three-pronged forks.[14]

The previous Christmas, Laura and Ann had been together when Ann and her two children had spent Christmas at Himley Hall. When Ann had asked to stay for an extra day, Eric had exploded. As Laura recalled in her divorce papers, 'I asked my husband and he was most unpleasant … saying he would not have his house used as a hotel for my relations.'[15]

Ann was furious and made plans to leave Himley immediately, but not before going to Eric's room and accusing him of 'unreasonable and unforgivable' behaviour.[16] Despite being far from enamoured with her brother-in-law, Ann wanted to spend Christmas 1945 with her sister. In an effort at rapprochement, Ann and Esmond invited the Dudleys to Bailiffscourt for the festive period. Their fellow guests included Cecil

Beaton, Ed Stanley and Loelia, Duchess of Westminster. The party also included Laura's daughter, Sara, as well as Ann's children, Raymond and Fionn O'Neill – 'a whole hunk of children,' as Sara recalls.[17]

Post-war rationing was still in place but included in the Bailiffscourt estate was a farm, so the party had plenty of meat, cream and milk during the festive period. The party also had a huge amount to drink. Having boozed throughout Christmas Day, Ann suddenly declared that dinner that evening would be fancy dress, triggering a mad scramble as guests tried to assemble costumes. Some of the ladies borrowed items from the household staff, with Ann dressing as a medieval wench. Laura, for reasons known only to herself, decided to wear stockings, suspenders and a scarf and nothing else.[18] When Eric saw his scantily dressed wife, his mood darkened.

As the drink continued to flow, a game of pre-dinner bridge turned into a round of strip poker between Loelia Westminster, Esmond, Eric and Ed Stanley. When Eric lost and resolutely refused to take off any more clothes, the drunken party decided that the loser's penalty would be to find Cecil Beaton and kiss him. Eric had the good grace to find Beaton and give the perplexed photographer a kiss on the cheek.[19] But privately he was furious. Eric insisted that he and Laura left first thing the following day, barely bidding goodbye to Ann and Esmond.

9

LAURA AND ERIC

As their marriage entered its third year, Laura was not unfamiliar with her husband's temper. His flashes of anger would always be short, followed by extreme contrition. But during the last years of the war, and in the years following, Eric became increasingly short-tempered. As Laura stated in her statement to the High Court during her divorce from Eric in 1954, 'It would be untrue to say that I did not know his character before I married him, but ... he has steadily grown worse and deteriorated year by year.'[1]

Eric was getting older and he was worried about the future. Britain was nearly broke following the expenditure of the Second World War and, as a captain of industry, Eric knew that he would be forced to pay a high rate of tax. He also realised that a Labour Government would seek to nationalise Dudley coal and steel, which would mean a terrifying loss of income.[2]

Immediately following the end of the war, Eric looked to re-establish his business contacts in the United States in order to sell Dudley steel in America. Aged 51 and exhausted from his war work, Eric was at the point in his life when he should have been winding down. Instead, for the second time in his life, he was faced with the prospect of having to rebuild his family fortune.

Realising that the costs of running Himley after the war would be prohibitive, Eric decided to sell the family home and move to a smaller house, Larkshill Court, near Sunningdale, which he had bought before the war. Laura was devastated at the prospect of leaving Himley. As well as being the site of her very own hospital, she also genuinely loved the house. To her, Himley was the perfect example of a country house, with classical Palladian symmetry as well as the Capability Brown-designed parkland.[3] Himley also reminded Laura of the happiest times of her relationship with Eric as the background to their initial affair.

Built in 1911 in the Queen Anne style, Larkshill Court was large by the standards of today. But in comparison to the grandeur of Himley, the house seemed a small, poor alternative. Now renamed Ednam Lodge, Eric relished being in a more manageable house, but Laura hated their new home, nicknaming the house 'the suburban villa'.[4] 'It was a joke place to go to,' Sara Morrison remembers of her new home. 'The swimming pool was the one redeeming feature.'[5]

Himley Hall was emptied of furniture and remained on the market for two years before finally being sold to the National Coal Board in 1947.[6] But Ednam Lodge was not to be a forever home. In 1946, the house became notorious and made headlines around the world when Eric and Laura hosted the Duke and Duchess of Windsor. In a highly suspicious crime that remains unsolved to this day, someone stole the duchess' jewels.

Laura had met the Duke and Duchess of Windsor for the first time in August 1946.[7] The duke and Eric had been friends since childhood, and Eric's first wife, Rosemary, had been touted as a potential bride for the future king. After Rosemary had married Eric, the young Viscount and Viscountess Ednam had remained close friends with the prince, naming him as godfather to their eldest child.

Crucially, Eric had happily accepted Wallis Simpson as royal mistress, including her in a house party at Himley in April 1936. As the abdication crisis loomed, Eric continued to offer support to the king. On Friday, 4 December 1936, Edward travelled to Himley Hall, where he spent his final weekend as monarch, away from the prying eyes of the press and the general public. On the following Tuesday, Eric returned to Fort Belvedere with the king, staying until the instrument of abdication had been signed on Thursday, 10 December.[8]

Eric had not attended the wedding of the Duke and Duchess of Windsor in France in 1937. But the couple, who notoriously dropped friends and acquaintances for any perceived minor slight, remained on good terms with Eric. Wallis, in particular, was devoted to him because of his kindness to her, as well as his unwavering support for the duke. After a disastrous stint in the Bahamas during the war, where the duke had been governor, the Windsors returned to Paris and leased a house in Antibes.[9]

When Eric wrote to say that he and Laura would be in Cannes in August 1946, they were invited to dinner at Château de la Croë, the Windsors' home at the Cap d'Antibes peninsula, which the duchess ran on a grand scale suitable for an ex-king.[10]

Laura was initially in awe of the Windsors. The night of the dinner was a boiling hot evening, typical of the Riviera. While the Dudleys had chosen light evening dress, the duke was in full Scottish regalia, showing no sign of breaking a sweat. As well as the duke's apparent lack of normal bodily functions, the duchess' abilities as a hostess impressed Laura. She was staggered to realise that the duchess missed nothing, noting the likes and dislikes of her guests in a small gold notebook by her side, so that in future the guests would be served only food and wine that they had previously enjoyed.[11] Laura was inspired by the duchess' style and her clothes, as well as by her skills as a hostess. A Buckinghamshire neighbour of Laura's would later remark, 'She [Laura] looked like the Duchess of Windsor.'[12]

Laura and the duke established an instant rapport, while Wallis was kind and indulgent to the younger woman. In contrast to the accepted portrayal of the duchess as cold and sterile, Laura found Wallis to be good company, with a quick sense of humour and a keen sense of the ridiculous. Laura developed a friendship with the Windsors which was to last beyond her divorce from Eric. She would visit them in Paris and the duke and duchess were welcoming to Laura's daughter when she attended finishing school in Paris in the 1950s. Sara would take tea with the Windsors once a week, 'Every sentence would begin "When I was King",' she dryly remembers of the duke.[13]

Following the dinner in Antibes, Eric offered the use of Ednam Lodge to the Windsors should they ever come to England. The Windsors were expert freeloaders and instantly accepted the offer. Ednam Lodge was close to both Windsor Castle, where the duke's private papers were stored, and Fort Belvedere, which the duke was desperate to visit.

The visit was duly arranged and the Windsors arrived at Ednam Lodge on 11 October 1946, with three army lorries full of their luggage, all under the command of an officer of the Royal Army Service Corps. Despite the Windsors wanting to maintain a low profile during their visit and avoid the press, their visit caused a media furore. The duke and duchess reluctantly had to give a press conference and pose for pictures outside the lodge.[14] Laura and Eric had tactfully, and sensibly, vacated the house, staying at their suite at Claridge's but leaving their staff in situ.

The duchess was renowned for her jewellery collection, and whenever she travelled, much of her collection travelled with her. The jewellery would be contained in one of three identical suitcases, the other two serving as decoys to distract any eagle-eyed thieves. On arrival, the Dudleys' butler, Bullock, asked if the duchess would like to leave her jewellery in the strong room. The duchess refused, preferring to store the suitcase under her maid's bed, so she could change her jewellery more easily throughout the day.[15]

During their first few days in Sunningdale, the duke visited Windsor, and both the duke and duchess travelled to London and had dinner with the Dudleys at Claridge's. On Tuesday, 15 October, the Windsors again travelled to Windsor, while Eric and Laura remained at Claridge's. The duchess' maid, Joan Martin, and the duke's valet, Rowe, took the suitcase containing the jewels to the room of Miss Blaisdell, the duchess' secretary. Joan Martin was due to go on holiday the next day, so the jewels had been moved in preparation for her departure.

Martin went down to the servants' supper at 5.35 p.m., returning to the secretary's room at 6.45 p.m. She found the suitcase open and empty. The police were called and surmised that thieves had broken into the lodge by an open upstairs window while the staff were all dining in the basement.[16]

At 8 a.m. the next day, police found a jewellery case on a nearby golf course, which had been dug up by Sara Long's dog, Topsy.[17] Scattered around the jewellery case in the long grass were several priceless items, including a string of pearls which had once belonged to Queen Alexandra.

Press reports of the time wildly exaggerated the value of the stolen jewels, with values as high as £500,000. The duke claimed that the value of the jewels was closer to £20,000. In total, eleven pieces of jewellery were missing and never recovered. Inspector J.R. Capstick of Scotland Yard was put in charge of the case and questioned all of the visiting staff members as well as the resident staff.[18]

On hearing of the theft, Eric and Laura immediately returned to Ednam Lodge, where tensions were running high. The duchess wanted all of the Dudley staff to be questioned thoroughly, which Laura refused. The duke was close to tears for much of the day while the duchess' anger boiled to a hard rage. By the time the Windsors departed, the duchess had defrosted enough to write rather pithily to Laura:

> It really was a lovely stay in England and it would never have been as nice if you and Eric had not loaned us Ednam Lodge – I can only hope that every servant etc is not leaving as a result.[19]

None of the missing jewels were ever recovered and rumours persist to this day that the robbery may have been an inside job. One theory is that the duke, who was pathologically and irrationally worried about money, staged the theft in order to claim the insurance money. Another outlandish theory is that the British royal family wanted to retrieve family jewels given by the duke to the duchess and were actually responsible for the robbery. The police case was finally closed in 1961, with the police records made available to the public in 2003.[20]

After receiving the insurance money for the stolen jewels, the duchess continued to amass one of the largest and most expensive jewellery collections in the world. Following her death in Paris in 1986, her inimitable collection was sold at auction in 1987 for a record US$50 million, the proceeds of which went to fund AIDS and cancer research.[21]

Even before the robbery of the Duchess of Windsor's jewels from Ednam Lodge, the Dudley marriage was under strain. The war years had taken their toll, with both of them having to adjust to post-war life. Though only married since 1943, the Dudleys had been in a relationship since 1936 and living together since 1939. With Eric's temper and arguments about 'the suburban villa', the couple needed something drastic to repair the marriage.[22] They hit on a disastrous path of action. Laura and Eric decided to try for a baby.

Neither Eric nor Laura had excelled at parenting, seeming to prefer their stepchildren to their own biological children. By the end of the war, Sara was 11 and was rapidly blossoming into a pretty young woman. Laura was barely 30 and did not like any woman stealing her thunder, especially not her own daughter. 'She was threatened by me. It was an almost pathetic active dislike of her own daughter,' Sara remembers.[23] Eric, on the other hand, absolutely adored Sara and made plans to adopt the girl. While this never came to fruition, mainly due to Lady Glyn's intervention, Sara recalls Laura rather cruelly telling her, 'You've been bought. You're going to be adopted.'[24]

Eric had a low opinion of his own children, with his teasing bordering on spiteful. Sara remembers Eric laconically telling her to 'go and exercise Peter on the tennis court' when Peter returned from Eton for the holidays.[25]

The eldest of Eric's sons, William 'Billy' Dudley, was only five years younger than Laura and was nearing adulthood by the time Laura moved into Himley. Having attended Eton, Billy entered the Royal Hussars when war was declared. Between 1942 and 1943, Billy served as ADC to the Viceroy of India, so was not able to attend his father's wedding. Nor did he have the opportunity to get to know his new stepmother until the war ended, by which time the Dudley marriage was on the rocks.

When Billy became engaged to Stella 'Baby' Carcano Morra, the eldest daughter of the Argentinian Ambassador to Britain, in 1945, Laura attempted to play some sort of maternal role. She travelled to Paris with Stella and introduced her to Pierre Balmain, who designed Stella's wedding dress and much of her trousseau. Having spent the majority of the war in uniform, Laura was also desperate to buy some new clothes. A trousseau for her stepson's fiancée provided the perfect excuse for Laura to splurge in Paris.

Following their wedding, at which Sara Long was a bridesmaid, Billy and his wife led very separate lives from the Dudley seniors. Billy, a self-effacing, warm but reticent man, was horrified by the later gossip about Laura vacillating between various lovers and his father.[26]

Eric's youngest surviving son, Peter, was Laura's favourite. 'She clucked over Peter,' Sara remembers. 'She did try to be a good stepmother to him.'[27] Born in 1926, Peter was only 8 when his mother died and he regarded Laura as a mother substitute. She endeavoured to give Peter a more normal home life at Himley. Before he attended Eton, Peter was raised alongside Sara, with both children left to the care of Old Pinny, the Dudley family nanny, who ruled the top floor of Himley.[28]

But Laura's kindness to Peter rankled with her own daughter and there was no love lost between the step-siblings. 'He was dreary,' Sara recalls of him. 'But it must have been hard for him to come home and find me in situ.'[29] As the war progressed, Peter was eventually dispatched to a relation in Canada, returning in 1944 to join the Fleet Air Arm.[30]

Just as the Dudleys were about to try for a baby in 1945, Laura suffered a collapsed uterus. She was given emergency surgery at a clinic at 19 Bentinck Street, after which she and Eric were assured that there was a good chance of her conceiving and carrying a child to full term.[31] During Laura's recovery, the Dudleys attempted an alternative patch-up operation and travelled to America in January 1946. Eric was hoping to kick-start his businesses again by brokering a deal for Dudley Steel to supply the US firm, Bethlehem Steel.

The Dudleys travelled on the *Queen Elizabeth*, alongside fellow passengers Lord Kemsley and his wife, Marie. Bizarrely, Kemsley was travelling to New York to meet with the new foreign manager of his newspapers, Ian Fleming, who was staying in New York en route to Jamaica to oversee construction of his new house.[32]

Arriving in America for the first time, Laura was blown away by the myriad twinkling lights of the Manhattan skyline after years of blackouts in England.[33] She relished life in New York, which felt so vibrant after war-torn Britain. The Dudleys were staying at the Waldorf Astoria, where they entertained several business associates of Eric, with Laura oozing charm and allure.[34] But then disaster struck as Laura began to feel seriously unwell. The handsome society doctor, 'Piggy' Wees, was summoned, much to Laura's delight. Despite a diagnosis of pneumonia, Laura managed to flirt her way through her various consultations, further baiting her husband.[35]

Dosed up on antibiotics, Laura was well enough to fly with Eric to Palm Beach in early February 1946, where Laura and Eric were due to stay with Consuelo Balsan, the former Duchess of Marlborough, at her enormous home, Casa Alva, in Manalapan. Thrilled to be feeling better and heading to the Palm Beach sunshine, Laura and Eric arrived to find Winston and

Clementine Churchill also staying. The Churchills were on an extended recuperative visit following the crushing Conservative defeat in the 1945 general election. Winston spent his days painting in the boiling sunshine with a valet on hand to top up his brandy glass.[36] Sarah Russell (*née* Spencer-Churchill), the daughter of Bert Marlborough and the granddaughter of Consuelo, was also staying at Casa Alva and she and Laura formed a strong friendship which was to last for the rest of their lives.

In the luxurious surroundings of Casa Alva and surrounded by old friends, Eric was in a calmer, happier mood. Laura threw herself into the Palm Beach party circuit, despite still suffering the after-effects of pneumonia. However, one morning she woke up 'completely yellow', having contracted jaundice and hepatitis.[37]

Eric immediately arranged for Laura to be admitted to a clinic where she was kept busy entertaining a string of visitors from her hospital bed. A frequent visitor was Consuelo's lecherous husband, Jacques. Warned by Sarah Russell about Balsan, who had chased his pretty step-granddaughter around a swimming pool, Laura was on her guard. When the 76-year-old attempted to grope her, Laura handled the situation with her usual aplomb. She managed to jump out of bed and summon the nurses, insisting that a nurse be present for all future visits from Balsan.[38]

When news from Britain reached Eric that the government was in discussions to nationalise the coal industry, he immediately made plans to return home. Laura was still too unwell to travel, so the Dudleys agreed that she would stay in Palm Springs to convalesce and then follow her husband once she recovered.[39]

While convalescing in Palm Springs, Laura thought about the future of her marriage. Giving little consideration to the pressure her husband was under, Laura decided that she would leave Eric. She returned to New York, where she decided to prolong her stay, panicking Eric, who wrote and telephoned, begging his wife to return. But Laura flatly refused.

Eventually Laura did return, sailing on the *Queen Mary* in March of 1946.[40] A furious Eric was in London, waiting to meet her. The couple returned to Ednam Lodge, where days of rows ensued. Finally, the couple agreed to spend some time apart, with Laura returning to London and Eric remaining in Sunningdale.

This agreement was not a trial separation but more an opportunity for both Eric and Laura to think about the future of their marriage. However, Laura regarded 'time apart' as free rein to do what she pleased. On 10 May 1946 she had dinner with Randolph Churchill, fanning the flames of Randolph's crush, after which he wrote to her, 'Every minute last night was sheer enchantment […] I only wish I could do one tenth as much to make you happy as you did for me.'[41]

She also embarked on an affair with Philip Dunn, son of the millionaire Canadian industrialist Sir James Dunn. Laura had been friends with Philip's ex-wife, Mary (*née* St Clair-Erskine), since before the war. Philip and Mary had divorced in 1944 (but would later remarry in 1969) and Mary had married Captain Robin Campbell in 1946. On the rebound following his ex-wife's remarriage, Philip was the perfect target for Laura. On meeting him again after her trip to the United States, the couple began an affair and planned a romantic holiday abroad.

In a bid at subtlety, Laura set sail for Gothenburg in May 1946 with her friend, Didy Asquith.[42] On arrival, the women feigned surprise to find Philip and his friend, Toby Milbanke, already in situ. 'I remember receiving endless postcards from Mummy and Philip Dunn in Sweden,' Sara says.[43] But the holiday was not a success and Laura and Philip argued. She broke off the affair and Philip returned to England.

Remaining in Stockholm, Laura soon began a brief affair with Alfred Bloomingdale, the heir to the department store, who was staying in Sweden after a failed stint as a theatrical agent. But this affair was equally unsuccessful and Bloomingdale soon set sale for Los Angeles. When a dejected Laura received a plea from Eric to meet him and Sara in Cannes at the end of July, she happily agreed. In Cannes, Laura agreed to give her marriage another chance. She had to. She was pregnant.[44]

10

ANN AND ESMOND ... AND THE *DAILY MAIL*

As Laura's marriage went into extra time, Ann's new marriage provided her with a fulfilling new role. As Esmond's wife she had access to the *Daily Mail* and she was determined that the newspaper, and her position within it, would become ever more powerful and influential. Esmond, on the other hand, had different plans. He had come out of the war exhausted and hoped that his new marriage would allow him a quieter life away from his newspapers.

Esmond had worked hard during the late 1930s and during the war years to ensure that the *Daily Mail* moved away from the pro-Nazi stance that his father had imposed. In a deliberate and considered PR move, Esmond made the *Daily Mail* pro-Churchill, adopting a deliberately patriotic tone and keeping criticism of the government to a minimum. By the end of the war, the *Daily Mail* was still outsold by Beaverbrook's *Daily Express*, but the readers of Middle England were returning to the *Daily Mail* in their droves.[1]

While Ann had the obvious advantage of being the owner's wife, she was also bright and wanted to learn. She surrounded herself with academics and the intelligentsia from whom she could learn. 'Aunt Ann continued to educate herself throughout her life,' her great-niece Anabel Loyd explains.[2]

In the first year of their marriage, Ann became a formidable presence in her husband's newspapers. She was fervent when it came to whom Esmond should hire to work on the *Daily Mail*. By October 1946, the editor of the *Daily Mail*, the superbly named Stanley Horniblow, was complaining about being made to hire so many of Ann's 'precious boyfriends' for the newspaper.[3] These hires included Peter Quennell, who worked as book critic for a salary of £1,000 per year, and Frank Owen, a former editor of the *Evening Standard*, to whom Ann had taken a shine. She was also not above pressuring Esmond to employ members of her family either – her brother

Hugo was found roles within the *Daily Mail*, firstly as a sub-editor and later as Paris correspondent.[4]

Another of Ann's 'precious boyfriends' was working for a Rothermere competitor. Ian was now the foreign manager of Kemsley Newspapers. As part of his very generous contract, Ian received two months' holiday allowance, alongside his £4,500 salary and £500 annual expenses, allowing him to realise his dream of wintering in Jamaica.[5] He had absented himself from a post-war Christmas and travelled to Jamaica to oversee the initial building work of his house, 'Goldeneye'. But upon his return in 1946, the friendship between Ann and Ian intensified.

Ann was a naturally dominant and assertive woman who made the rules for the Rothermere marriage. She decided where they would live and how they would entertain. Meanwhile, Esmond was even disinclined to stop her interference in his newspapers. As her niece recalls of her aunt, 'Ann has been made to seem unkind, which she wasn't. But she could be extraordinarily ruthless.'[6] For Ann, there was nothing more attractive than a man who did not bend to her whim. The challenge was tantalising. Surrounded by men and a husband who were unable to say no to her, Ian's aloofness and his complete unobtainability made him irresistible.

By 1946, the sporadic sexual affair between Ann and Ian had resumed in earnest. Ian ran a huge risk by having a dalliance with the wife of a rival newspaper baron. But Ann proved equally as irresistible to him as he did to her. She was beautiful, intelligent and sexy. Unlike many of the other debutantes and the daughters of aristocrats whom Ian met in his social life, the slightly older Ann had a glamour, sophistication and polish that was missing from the other women he romanced. For a determined bachelor, who was still grieving for Muriel Wright, a relaxed and permissive relationship with a married woman suited Ian. Above all, the affair was deliciously *verboten*. For two people who relished dancing on a knife edge, the very illicitness of their relationship was a huge attraction.

Ann needed excitement in a life that was becoming increasingly official. As well as the parties and entertaining, Ann was expected to fulfil a public role as Lady Rothermere. Many committees or voluntary groups wanted the benefit of her name and fortune. Ann was not uncharitable and was generous with her time, as well as with her money, but she only gave up her time for organisations or initiatives that were of interest to her. From a young age, she had been fascinated by politics and always made herself available to help people seeking election. In the summer of 1931, aged just 17, Ann had volunteered to help Duff Gordon during his successful parliamentary run in the Westminster St George by-election.[7]

She would later campaign for Sara's husband, Charles Morrison,[8] and would frequently canvass for candidates and even drive elderly people to polling stations.[9]

Ann would also happily devote time to promoting fashion and the arts. Soon after the end of the Second World War, the *Daily Mail* agreed to sponsor the inaugural National Film Awards, which subsequently became known as the *Daily Mail* National Film Awards. The awards were the first to be given based on a public vote, with cinemagoers voting for their favourite actor, actress and film at their local cinemas.

On 21 June 1946, the first National Film Awards took place at the Dorchester Hotel in London. The ceremony was intended to be a glitzy, opulent bash during the post-war gloom. As the new Lady Rothermere and the wife of the sponsor, Ann was asked to present the awards. In a black taffeta ballgown, Ann looked slightly awkward but glamorous. With an impressive diamond necklace at her throat, she looked every inch the viscountess, her dark hair piled elegantly on her head. She presented the Most Outstanding British Actress award to Margaret Lockwood, and the Most Popular and Outstanding British Actor prize to a young James Mason.[10]

Ann would go on to present the prizes at every *Daily Mail* Film Awards ceremony until she divorced Esmond. While she always complained about the evening, the pictures show her growing in confidence every year, beaming and vibrant in a succession of elegant and expensive outfits.

During the opening of the annual *Daily Mail* Ideal Home Exhibition, Ann had to be on her very best behaviour. Devised by the *Daily Mail* in 1908 to boost advertising revenue, the exhibition showcased modern household items as well as new housing designs. In the late 1940s and 1950s, excited housewives crowded the exhibition for glimpses of the latest labour-saving devices like the microwave oven and the dishwasher.[11]

Suspended during the Second World War, the exhibition relaunched in 1947. Ann opened the first post-war exhibition accompanied by Esmond. The Rothermeres were treated like royalty and toured the exhibition, seeing examples of prefabricated housing as well as a kitchen made entirely from recycled aircraft propellers. For several hours the Rothermeres managed to feign interest in the latest household items, talking to stallholders and visitors. Ann would go on to attend every opening of the annual Ideal Home Exhibition while married to Esmond, despite having little interest in the practicalities of housekeeping.[12]

While Ann dutifully carried out the responsibilities expected of her as Viscountess Rothermere, her natural inclination to fun meant that her social life was her main focus. When the renovation work on Warwick House finished in early 1947 the Rothermeres were finally able to take up residence. The parties started immediately and did not stop for the next seven years. Guests poured into the grand house to enjoy both the flowing champagne and the company.

While Ann used the Rothermere money to provide the best catering for her parties, she cared little for food. Her lunch and dinner parties were generally comprised of simple, typically English dishes. For Ann, the food, wine or champagne were never the focus. The mix of guests, the conversations, discussions, and especially the arguments, were the motivations for her parties. She would oversee every party like a ringmaster or conductor.

Many of her acquaintances described Ann as being like an actress with the party being the show. Even Ann herself said that she would rev herself up for an 'evening performance'.[13] Whatever her mood, she had to be scintillating and dazzling.

Ann also had the eyes of a hawk. She watched her guests to ensure no one was standing alone. And no one arrived or left without a word from Ann. Like the director of a film or play, Ann would work to get the best out of her guests. Shy guests were put at their ease and drawn out on subjects with which they felt comfortable.

Arriving on the threshold of a roaring room, abuzz with conversation, a guest could feel apprehensive. But Ann would quickly glide across the room to welcome them, introducing them around, helping the conversation to flow. The consummate hostess.

Above all, Ann's parties were fun. She mixed together guests from across the political and social divides. As Noel Annan described her, 'She did not exist to please, to flatter and cajole. She possessed the art, as every great hostess does, of mixing incongruous people together.'[14] Ann wanted her guests to have a good time and enjoy themselves, which inevitably they did. As her niece recollects, 'We had such fun at Warwick House.'[15]

The one facet that made Ann a controversial hostess was her need for argument. Ann's love of mischief manifested in her desire for drama. 'She loved turmoil, she provoked, she led her friends on, she wanted movement, and hated the pale and the placid,' Noel Annan recalled.[16] Frequently, she would bring up a controversial subject in order to start a squabble between guests. Like a soldier lobbing a grenade, Ann would fire off a contentious comment and wait for an explosion. She was intelligent and well read, and fundamentally fair, but sometimes she would say something completely outrageous or untrue simply to spark a row. 'She definitely enjoyed conflict,' says Anabel Loyd. 'She enjoyed a maelstrom around her as long as she was at the centre of it.'[17]

Esmond did not thrive on socialising like his wife, but he realised the benefit of hosting powerbrokers and captains of industry within his home. Crucially, he could also find out insider gossip which he could funnel back to his journalists. But he could never match the social stamina of his wife. Esmond was not a natural host and relied on Ann to ensure that their guests felt comfortable. He tended to focus on conversations with people he liked or people that were useful for business. And when Esmond had had enough, he would quietly slip upstairs to bed.[18]

As time went on, Ann's interests developed and changed. And the guests invited to Warwick House reflected this shift. Immediately after their marriage, the Rothermeres' parties had been dominated by politicians and journalists. As Ann became increasingly interested in art and culture, more artists and writers tended to make the invite list. Lucian Freud, Frederick Ashton and Francis Bacon became regulars at Warwick House.

Esmond was not thrilled with the change. As a Conservative, he was not keen on the liberal, arty type of person who now so interested his wife. Nor could these new guests benefit him or his newspapers. Instead, many of them had to be found jobs on the family newspapers. But, as always, Esmond accepted this change with equanimity.[19]

Esmond also seemed to accept his wife's growing relationship with Ian with equal equanimity. 'I always presumed Esmond knew absolutely,' Sara Morrison recalls.[20]

Ann and Ian did endeavour to keep their relationship secret. When Ian was en route to see the completed Goldeneye in early 1946, he implored Ann to take pains to be discreet. In a letter from New York in January 1946, Ian begged Ann to hide any of his letters which made their affair obvious:

> I know how you leave things around like a jackdaw and I expect everyday [*sic*] that it will be the end. I do wish you'd take trouble and not leave my letters among your brassieres and your pants. Do please try. I know perfectly well that you are going to come along one day with a tragic face and say that all is discovered.[21]

His apprehension about discovery was not solely because of his fear that he would lose Ann. Discovery of his affair with a rival newspaper proprietor's wife would have resulted in his immediate dismissal from the Kemsley Press.

Ann also worried about discovery and took trouble to conceal her relationship. When the Rothermeres travelled to the United States in September 1946, Esmond travelled to Canada, where he had timber and paper concerns, leaving Ann alone in New York. Romantically, Ian flew from England to

New York to see Ann. Less romantically, Ian invented a work assignment which allowed the Kemsley Press to pick up the tab for the trip.[22] When he arrived at the Rothermere suite at the Plaza, Ann panicked, worried that her maid would report back to Esmond. Ian became angry, telling Ann to 'get rid of the bitch', which she immediately did.[23]

By the following year, when Ian again travelled to New York en route to Jamaica, the letters from Ian to Ann show that their relationship continued unabated. The couple had also discovered a mutual love of sadomasochism. Ann and Ian dominated the people around them – Ian with the women he romanced, Ann with both of her husbands and the majority of her male admirers – enjoying the sexual side of dominating a partner made sense. The fact that they both also enjoyed *being* dominated is more difficult to understand. A lifetime of subservience at the hands of his mother goes some way to explain Ian's sexual attraction to a strong, domineering woman like Ann. Ann is less easy to understand. Throughout her life she seems to have been the dominant figure – as the eldest child and the assertive partner in both of her marriages. As a woman who was always in charge, being under the total control of a sexual partner must have been both refreshing and titillating.

In a letter in December 1946, Ian compliments Ann, saying that she 'charmed New York to death' during her visit in September. Then, in an explicit allusion to their sadomasochistic relationship, he goes on to say, 'You have made bruises on my arms and shoulders. All this damage will have to be paid for some time.'[24] However, Ann's niece makes light of the sadomasochism within the relationship, explaining the acts as simply:

> Mawkish curiosity [...] I think that it's entirely possible that they were simply trying new things. A suck it and see approach. That curiosity and open-mindedness to all of life's experiences united Ann and Ian. They scratched at almost every experience in life.[25]

Outside of the bedroom, life continued for Ann as Lady Rothermere. In 1947, she was elected to the board of the *Continental Daily Mail*, which necessitated trips to Paris. She had also taken over as director of the British Fashion Council, so she used her time in Paris to visit the fashion houses and buy new clothes, as well as visiting Diana Cooper at the embassy. Esmond would frequently accompany his wife on her trips, after which the Rothermeres would travel down to Monaco where Esmond had inherited his father's home, Villa Rocque Fleury. Here, Esmond would relax by playing tennis – exactly the kind of energetic activity which Ann loathed.

In the spring of 1947, the Rothermeres rented South Wraxall Manor in Wiltshire for the summer. Esmond, despite a demanding job, managed to work remotely from his various homes, conducting business over the telephone and by telegram. He accompanied Ann and her children to Wiltshire and managed to stay there almost permanently, with occasional business trips to London.

Ann's thoughts during the summer were almost entirely consumed with Ian. Being in the countryside and away from her lover made her miserable. Whenever she attempted to ring Ian, she would be constantly interrupted by Esmond or her children and was unable to speak freely, her reticence demonstrating that she was still endeavouring to be discreet for the sake of her husband.[26]

When Esmond sailed for Montreal on Wednesday, 20 August 1947, Ann travelled to Shane's Castle in Ireland, ostensibly for Raymond to spend time at the estate that he had inherited. On arrival in Ireland, Ann dispatched the children to Shane's Castle while she stayed in Dublin, where she was joined by Ian for four days. The couple rented a simple fisherman's cottage on the coast and spent blissful days together, entirely alone. Ann relished her role as pseudo-wife to Ian, cooking for him, keeping the small house clean and sleeping beside him every night.

As Ian prepared to return to London and Ann made plans to meet her children at Shane's Castle, the dynamic of their affair fundamentally shifted. For the first time in their relationship, Ian told Ann that he loved her.[27]

11

LAURA AND ERIC, *DEUXIÈME PARTIE*

Laura's pregnancy seems to have temporarily halted hostilities between her and Eric. When the Dudleys returned from Cannes in early August 1946, Laura went to see her gynaecologist, Cedric Lane-Roberts, who confirmed that she was pregnant. Laura assumed that the baby had been fathered by her husband and stated as much in court papers during her divorce from Eric.[1]

Admittedly, Eric could well have been the father, but the Dudleys had only been reunited in Cannes in July. The baby would have to have been conceived almost immediately if Laura knew she was pregnant by August. As the Dudleys had been trying unsuccessfully to conceive since they married in 1943, the possibility that their reunion in Cannes resulted in a baby seems remarkably slim. Given her open affair with Philip Dunn in Sweden, as well as a fling with Alfred Bloomingdale, Laura's baby was presumably fathered by someone other than her husband.

By the time the pregnancy was confirmed, Laura was 31 and Eric was 52. The pregnancy was not easy for Laura. She was in constant pain and soon left Ednam Lodge for Claridge's in order to be looked after by a nurse. As her health continued to deteriorate, Lane-Roberts suggested that she be admitted to a nursing home at 18 Bentinck Street.[2]

Eric became frantic with worry as Laura became seriously unwell. Eventually, an ectopic pregnancy was discovered. The developing baby had ruptured one of Laura's fallopian tubes, causing excruciating pain. She was immediately rushed into surgery, the foetus removed, and Laura's fallopian tube was repaired. When she recovered, Laura was told that future pregnancies would be unlikely.[3]

As he had been pinning his hopes on a baby to repair the cracks in their marriage, Eric was devasted. Laura was less upset than her husband. She had been incredibly ill during the pregnancy and was relieved to feel better. She was also not a natural mother and, while she wanted to have Eric's child, she did not relish the idea of having another baby. She had not been pregnant since the age of 19 and she was worried about the effect that pregnancy would have on her body, as well as kiboshing her social and sex life. There may also have been a slight tinge of relief. If the baby was indeed fathered by someone other than Eric, the termination may well have been a blessing in disguise.

As Laura struggled with her pregnancy and convalescence, her daughter Sara went to boarding school for the first time. Having left the day-to-day responsibilities of raising her to a nanny and governess, Sara's departure to Mrs Fife's school near Cirencester made little impact on her mother's life.[4] After recovering from her surgery, no longer pregnant, with her daughter in boarding school and a marriage that was steadily disintegrating, Laura looked around for an activity that would fill her time and give her a purpose.

Following the theft of the Windsor jewels from Ednam Lodge, Eric agreed that he would buy another house and sell Ednam Lodge. Like Ann, Laura had impeccable taste when it came to property and interior design. She had a knack for finding unique and picturesque houses and making them beautiful. Both Charteris sisters were able to see the potential in property and would stop at nothing to make their vision a reality. Eric wanted to remain near London, so Laura began searching in the Home Counties.[5]

Laura had her pick of available country houses that had flooded the market after the war and she relished the process of house-hunting. For the first time in her life, she was looking for her very own home, having previously always moved into homes belonging to her husbands. Laura also had the advantage of Eric's wealth behind her and hoped that a new house might ease the tensions in her marriage.

Laura finally found a Queen Anne house near the village of Kings Langley, Hertfordshire, in the summer of 1947. Originally built for the Earl of Clarendon in the early eighteenth century, Westwood had passed through several owners before being placed on the market following the war. The red-brick house consisted of a large, three-storied, single block and a large basement which contained the kitchen. Neglected during the war, the house was in need of major refurbishment when Laura first visited.[6] While she loved the house, the main attraction of Westwood for the Dudleys were the stables where they could house their growing collection of horses.[7]

Not quite a manor house but by no means 'a suburban villa', Westwood was perfect for the Dudleys; in the middle of the countryside, but only 30 miles from Windsor and 20 from London. Today, Westwood and the village of Kings Langley is part of London's expanding suburbs and is just a few miles from the M25. But in 1947, Westwood seemed to meet the needs of both Dudleys.

Laura completely altered the interior of the house. Unrestricted by regulations, she knocked down interior walls to convert the smaller rooms into large, light, entertaining rooms and created five main bedroom suites. One of the suites became known as the Windsor Suite, intended for the Duke and Duchess of Windsor. Laura decorated the rooms in a pale blue known as 'Wallis blue' – the favourite colour of the duchess.[8]

During the autumn, Laura moved between Westwood and Ednam, supervising building work at her new home while packing up her old house. The renovation work on Westwood took its toll on the Dudleys' marriage, with Eric choosing to spend much of his time at their suite at Claridge's. Tactically, Eric left for an extended shooting trip to Scotland when Laura, Sara and the staff moved into Westwood. Tensions were not eased when Eric returned to find that his wife had purchased massive amounts of new furniture and antiques with which to furnish Westwood, despite the abundance of furnishings left over from Himley and Ednam Lodge.[9]

Expense aside, the move to Hertfordshire seems to have given the Dudley marriage a temporary boost. But once the move was complete, the marriage began to stall again. Eric started to complain that the house was not suitable for a peer of the realm. Having claimed that he wanted a small, manageable home, Eric made a complete volte-face and instructed an architect to design and construct two large rooms or 'wings' on either side of the house, with a dining room and a library. He also rechristened the house 'Great Westwood'.[10]

While Eric kept himself busy aggrandising the house, his wife began to look for something to keep her entertained. With the move to Westwood and the renovation of the stables, Laura and Eric began to take their riding more seriously. Laura had always been a keen horsewoman and she had begun to attend horse shows and compete in amateur showjumping classes. Sara was also a budding horsewoman and Laura's interest in showjumping was initially motivated more for her daughter's benefit. 'I remember lots of fictional dentists' appointments as an excuse to be taken out of school to attend events,' Sara recalls.[11]

Showjumping is not a sport for the poor and Eric happily indulged Laura and his stepdaughter. Laura was allowed to buy thoroughbred horses, including Come Closer, Princess and Doodlebug. Originally purchased for Sara, Doodlebug was later commandeered by Laura as her own career took off.[12] Laura was also able to afford the best training. Following a bad fall at the Frankfurt Horse Show in September 1949, Eric invited the renowned horseman Colonel Paul Rodzianko to come and train Laura and Sara.[13]

Born in Russia to an aristocratic family, Rodzianko escaped during the revolution and eventually joined the British Army, where he developed a talent with horses. A fierce and demanding instructor, Rodzianko moved into Great Westwood to train Laura full time in the winter of 1949.

One of his more bizarre practices was to do a Russian dance in his bathtub every morning. Initially amused by this odd ritual, Laura soon became irritated as she was woken morning after morning by water cascading across the floor of the Great Westwood bathroom.[14]

Following her six months with the colonel, Laura turned professional and competed throughout 1950 and 1951 in Paris, Nice, Windsor and the London International Horse Show at White City. Eric accompanied her, having given himself the honorary title of *chef d'equipe*. In Paris, he brought the Duke and Duchess of Windsor along to watch his wife compete. Laura was paralysed with fear at the thought of the Windsors watching her, especially as the duchess was no fan of the horse. Given a tranquiliser to calm her nerves by a fellow rider, Laura became so relaxed that she jumped the wrong course and was disqualified, much to Eric's embarrassment.[15]

As Sara Long became an ever more accomplished rider, surpassing the skill of her mother, Laura began to lose interest in showjumping: 'I rode better than her which stoked her jealousy.'[16] But for the late 1940s and early years of the 1950s, showjumping kept Laura busy.

Keeping Laura occupied had become Eric's top priority. And for good reason. Soon after moving into Westwood, Laura had left her husband and bolted.

During the winter of 1947, as the renovation and redecoration of Westwood neared completion, Laura and Eric began to realise that a new house had done little to repair their marriage. In a bid to distract themselves from their problems, the couple filled their individual diaries with social engagements. Eric was busier than ever with his work. He sat on many company boards as a director and continued to maintain the Dudley industrial interests in the Midlands, which involved an evening a week in Birmingham – which Laura tellingly began to refer to as 'my night off!'[17]

The Dudleys also began to spend the majority of the week in London. Eric owned a house on Brook Street in Mayfair which had been damaged during the Blitz. Following the war, believing that repairing the townhouse would be long and costly, Eric and Laura took a permanent suite at Claridge's. After two years at Claridge's – and the accompanying bills – Eric decided to repair the Brook Street house, just as work at Westwood began.[18]

During weekends at Great Westwood, Eric and Laura would entertain religiously, desperate for any company to stop them from being alone together. Frequent visitors were Freda and Bobby Casa Maury.[19] The former Freda Dudley Ward had divorced her first husband and married the Marques de Casa Maury in 1937 – a handsome, roguish, racing driver.

Freda had never approved of Laura. She had known and liked Eric for a long time, having been part of the social set of him and his first wife, Rosemary. While Freda was not exactly restrained in her extramarital affairs, she disapproved of Laura's dalliances. As a result, Laura flirted outrageously with Bobby whenever the Casa Maurys stayed at Westwood, mainly to annoy Freda.[20]

In December 1947, Laura and Eric travelled to Paris to attend a ball at the British Embassy.[21] During the Coopers' residency, the British Embassy on the rue du Faubourg Saint-Honoré had become a focal point of European social life. The ambassador, Duff Cooper, and his wife, Lady Diana, were throwing a party to mark their retirement. The Coopers were known for lavish entertaining and their retirement ball was to be no exception, with the crème of European society attending, including Ann and Esmond Rothermere.[22]

Travelling light, the Dudleys flew to Paris for the evening. At the ball, Laura was looking her most radiant. She wore a pale, off-the-shoulder tulle dress made in Paris, with a thin band of leopard skin across the bust.[23] Laura also wore the Dudley family tiara. Originally a vast and imposing crownlike diadem, topped with spokes of diamonds capped with large pearls, the tiara was cumbersome and heavy to wear. With little thought to history or preservation, Laura had instructed Cartier to refashion it. The tiara had been simplified to make a circlet consisting of three bands of small diamonds. The tiara also had five detachable diamond ovals positioned intermittently along the band, which could be added for grander occasions.[24]

In her simple dress splashed with leopard skin and her magnificent tiara, Laura felt herself the belle of the ball. She looked ravishing. Laura was a woman who was genuinely in her prime. She exuded self-confidence and radiated sex appeal. With her dark, liquid eyes and her chestnut hair coiffed to secure the glittering tiara, Laura was breathtaking.

Perhaps the only other woman at the party to emanate such glamour and sex appeal was her sister. Ann wore a beautiful white tulle dress and a simple Art Deco-style tiara with cross patterns of diamonds, which had been a gift from her husband.[25] That evening, the Charteris sisters were at their zenith, drawing admiring glances from their fellow guests. Both were beautiful and young. And both were accompanied by their rich, older husbands.

Laura dazzled one man, in particular. Gerry Koch de Gooreynd was a delicately good-looking man with a Roman nose, pencil moustache and slicked-back blonde hair. Born in Belgium, the eldest of three brothers, to William and Manuela, Gerry was educated in Belgium, Switzerland and England. His father, a stockbroker, moved the family permanently to London in 1912 and the family settled in a large house in Belgravia.

Gerry was a cultured man with considerable charm and savoir faire, which made him good company and attractive to women. He was also fundamentally kind, considerate and gentle. 'He was a nice man. A truly, truly nice man. I was so fond of him,' Laura's daughter recalls.[26]

Gerry was also delicate and suffered from frequent bouts of ill health, having been diagnosed in his twenties with Hodgkin's lymphoma. He had followed his father into stockbroking, joining Panmure Gordon, the merchant bank, and lived in a house near Buckingham Palace. He had divorced his wife, Elizabeth Lawson, in the late 1930s after she fell in love with Barbie Wallace's stepson, Gerard, whom she married in 1940.[27] Gerry was devasted, which further added to his vulnerable aura.

Despite his ill health, Gerry had joined the British Army during the Second World War and fought in France, where he was wounded and captured. After two years in a prisoner-of-war camp, Gerry was repatriated and worked in Intelligence for the remainder of the war, receiving an OBE in 1948 for his services to the British Empire.

Laura had known Gerry for some time as he sat on the board of the Brompton Hospital, of which Eric was the chairman. But that evening she flirted outrageously with Gerry during the ball, enraging her husband. Furious that Laura was ignoring him and seemingly seducing another man on the dance floor, Eric 'behaved like a lunatic', as Laura recalled in her divorce papers.[28] He insisted that he and his wife return to their suite at the Ritz where the couple argued until six o'clock in the morning. Eventually, Eric returned to England while Laura remained in Paris.

In her memoirs, Laura claims that the day after the ball she left the hotel to find something to eat. On the Place Vendôme, she just 'happened' to bump into Gerry Koch de Gooreynd.[29] The pair went to Maxims for lunch, where Laura poured out her problems and Gerry listened.

As well as having a whopping great crush on Laura, Gerry offered her practical and helpful advice. His considerate manner and gentleness could not have been a starker contrast to Eric's jealousy and flaring temper. As Laura recalled in her divorce application:

> Mr Koch de Gooreynd then told me for the first time his feelings about me, and begged me not to return to my husband; told me to try and get a divorce from my husband and marry him […] I saw a chance of escaping from my husband's cruelty and a chance of happiness and agreed.[30]

After lunch, Laura telephoned Eric and told him that she would not be returning to him and she intended to marry Gerry. Eric was understandably furious and threatened to travel across to Paris to bring his wife home. Gerry then telephoned Diana Cooper and arranged for Laura to stay at the embassy.

As well as being a relation of Laura and Ann, Diana Cooper was a great friend of Ann's. But she tolerated Laura rather than liked her. 'Laura would *tell* you that they were great friends,' Hugo Vickers, a friend of both Laura and Lady Diana, recalls of the relationship.[31] However, she was surprisingly nice to Laura that evening. Lady Diana welcomed her to the embassy before explaining that as she and Duff were due at a dinner, Laura would be given supper on a tray. The following morning, Laura discussed the situation with her hostess who seemed to regard the whole thing as a joke. Despite looking nothing like Gerry, Diana melodramatically begged her husband, Duff, not to leave the embassy in case Eric mistook him for Gerry and shot him.

Laura then rang Ann, who had returned to London the previous day. She told her sister about leaving Eric. Ann, who had witnessed Laura flirting with Gerry, was outwardly calm and sympathetic. She offered her sister the use of rooms at Warwick House while Laura decided what to do. In reality, Ann was irritated and embarrassed by her sister's behaviour, describing Laura's 'latest caprice in preferring Mr Koch de Gooreynd to Lord Dudley' in a letter to Evelyn Waugh.[32]

Laura returned to London and moved into the top floor of Warwick House.[33] Eric was furious and refused to send his wife's clothes, dogs and maid, Biddlecombe, to London. He even dispatched his solicitor, Mr Humbert, to retrieve the Dudley jewellery from Warwick House. Laura made it clear that she wanted a permanent separation from Eric, later admitting in court papers, 'I sent a letter with hotel evidence to my husband at his Solicitors [*sic*] address, begging him to divorce me.'[34] But Eric refused and began to plead with his wife to return.

Laura refused and remained at Warwick House for the rest of the winter, rushing headlong into a new relationship with the doting Gerry Koch de Gooreynd. His home at 2 Buckingham Place was only a stone's throw from the Rothermere home, and when Laura was not on the top floor of Warwick House, she was at Gerry's house.

Warwick House was certainly big enough to accommodate Laura's semi-permanent residency. And, for the early part of 1948, there were only Laura and Esmond in residency. Ann had travelled to Jamaica and to Ian.

12

PREGNANCIES

Alongside her great friend Loelia, Duchess of Westminster, Ann had sailed for Jamaica on New Year's Day. Ostensibly, Ann and Loelia were in search of some winter sun. The rumour that Loelia was having an affair with Ian gave credence to the journey and provided cover for the real liaison. Ann happily peddled this story to ensure that she and Ian were protected from gossip, with Loelia playing the lonely role of chaperone.[1]

While Ann and Ian relished being together, spending their days fishing and exploring the reefs around Goldeneye, Loelia became resentful and bored. Realisation slowly dawned that her only purpose was to provide respectability for the lovers.[2]

On her first visit to Goldeneye, Ann was not overwhelmed by Ian's house. Stark and bare, with no glass at the windows and only basic furnishings, she was appalled by the lack of comfort. The house had no hot water and the plain concrete floor of the house was routinely covered in black boot polish. Bare feet tended to become blackened – a condition which earned the nickname 'Goldeneye foot'.[3] The house was so uncomfortable that when Ian's mother, Eve, and his sister, Amaryllis, had stayed in December 1947, mother and daughter moved to a hotel after just one night.[4]

But Ann adored her time with Ian, despite the surroundings. The pair had a mutual love and appreciation of nature, as well as a shared a love of birdwatching. Much time was spent at Goldeneye identifying birds using a recently purchased Macmillan edition of the *Field Guide to Birds of the West Indies* by a little-known ornithologist, James Bond. For the first time, Ann and Ian were able to spend a long period of uninterrupted time together.

But being with each other for days on end highlighted how different Ann and Ian were. Ian preferred the company of men and more serious conversation, while Ann thrived on being social and discussing gossip. She struggled with the stilted social life on the island and when the trio had dinner with a near neighbour, Ian implored Ann and Loelia to refrain from 'Mayfair talk'.[5]

Luckily for Ann, a roster of guests passed through Goldeneye. Ian's great friend, Ivar Bryce, whom Ann never approved of, arrived with his wife Sheila.[6] Patrick Leigh Fermor, whom she had met once at the Dorchester when they were both guests of Emerald Cunard, was a more welcome guest. Erudite, oozing charm and side-splittingly witty, Paddy was very like Hugo Charteris. He and Ann formed a close, platonic friendship which was to last for the rest of Ann's life, with the pair endlessly teasing each other. Ian was also fond of Paddy, despite his notorious clumsiness. True to form, Paddy managed to break an underwater speargun during his short stay at Goldeneye.[7]

In early February, Ann and Loelia departed for Miami, where they were due to meet Esmond. Ann had peddled the rumour that Loelia, rather than she, was having an affair with Ian, but gossip was rife. Earlier that year, on 24 January 1947, when Ian had attended the opening of the Sunset Lodge Club at Montego Bay, Lily Ernst, a former ballerina and mistress to Lord Beaverbrook, had drunkenly said to Ian:

> I was trying to remember which paper you were mixed up with. I was certain your boss was a woman, but the only woman possible was Lady Rothermere which was impossible of course.[8]

Ian believed that Lady Pamela Berry, the wife of Michael Berry, the chairman and editor-in-chief of the *Daily* and *Sunday Telegraph*, was fanning the flames of gossip. As the wife of a newspaper proprietor and a noted political hostess, Pamela Berry and Ann were great rivals. But this drunken quip was not just a strike in the ongoing rivalry between the two women. This was an admission that one of Esmond's fellow newspaper proprietors knew about Ann's relationship with Ian. The affair was public knowledge.

Having reunited in Miami, the Rothermeres spent a few days in New York en route to Britain. Here, Ann had a prickly meeting with Eric Dudley who was in New York on business. He implored Ann to convince Laura to leave Warwick House and return to him. Never a fan of her brother-in-law, Ann was coolly polite but refused his entreaties. Her thoughts were consumed with Ian, writing to him constantly from Miami, the Plaza in New York and from the *Queen Mary*. Clearly worried about competition, in one letter Ann is uncharacteristically vulnerable when she writes, 'It would be an interesting feat to be faithful to someone for three weeks, you have never done it before and it might make you feel very happy.'[9]

She also made a rather clunky attempt at making Ian jealous. She claimed that she had 'got off' with a governor in New York,[10] and described a stranger's attempt to pick her up at the Pierre Hotel.[11] Responding laconically, Ian promised Ann a lashing when he got back to London, '10 on each buttock', and detailed 'all the things I shall do to you one by one when you come through the door of Hays Mews'.[12]

Leaving New York on the *Queen Mary* on 19 February 1948, Ann wrote to Ian imploring him to 'please take me back next year'.[13] But the pattern of their affair was about to change. While enjoying the social rounds of New York, Ann had begun to feel unwell and nauseous. Suspecting the reason, she waited until she returned to London to confirm what was wrong. Ann was pregnant. And Ian was the father.[14]

In the oddest parallel, Laura also found out that she was pregnant in early 1948 with Gerry's child.[15] The natural course of events would have been for Laura to gain a quick divorce from Eric and marry Gerry, but she was reluctant to do this. While Gerry was engaging, warm and kind, he was not entirely what Laura wanted. 'He was real. He did not puff up her self-esteem,' Sara recalls.[16] While Gerry could not be described as a pushover, her daughter concludes, 'He was not tough enough for her. He was not assertive. Just too straightforward. Literally too nice.'[17]

When Eric returned from his business trip to America in the spring of 1948, he asked his wife to return to him. Laura agreed to move from Warwick House back to Brook Street but first she went to Buckingham Place to tell Gerry that the relationship was over. Typical of his kind, compassionate nature, Gerry was more concerned for Laura. But the break was devastating for him. On 27 May 1948 he wrote plaintively to Laura, 'This is the ultimate of pain and suffering. I thought I was strong but this is beyond any strength. Take pity on me, my darling, I beg of you.'[18] He would remain in love with Laura for the remainder of his life. After she had returned to Eric, he wrote again, saying, 'My love for you is complete, unchanged and unchanging [...] no matter what happens, as long as I live I am there for you to talk to.'[19]

Later, when Gerry became ill with leukaemia as a result of his Hodgkin's lymphoma in 1954, he wanted Laura by his side. When he died, on the evening of 19 October 1954, Laura was there. And at his funeral mass at Farm Street Church in Mayfair, she was treated like a widow by his family. This was further compounded when Gerry made Laura the main beneficiary of his will. He left her the remainder of the lease on his house in Buckingham Place as well as the majority of his stocks and shares. As Sara concludes, 'Gerry was genuinely in love with her. I really held that against her – choosing not to marry Gerry.'[20]

But back in May 1948, Laura returned to Eric, leaving Gerry alone. Laura and Eric discussed the issue of her pregnancy. Eric professed to be happy at the thought of raising another man's baby, but Laura, mindful of her previous ectopic pregnancy, decided to have a 'procedure'. Abortion was illegal in 1948 but she found a nursing home where a miscarriage would be 'promoted'.[21]

Eric and Laura then left for the South of France for a recuperative holiday at the luxurious Hotel du Cap-Eden-Roc in Cannes. As Laura brutally detailed in later court papers, the holiday was far from a romantic reunion:

> We went over to France and my husband was by then completely impotent. He was in a shocking state, crying and screaming [...] I was unhappy but I could not help being sorry for him. My husband nauseated me by his conduct. He insisted on pawing my body in the bedroom, in the bathroom and, in fact, almost everywhere.[22]

★ ★ ★

Ann was in a better frame of mind than her sister when she delightedly told Ian that she was pregnant on his return from Jamaica in March 1948. Ian was less than enthusiastic, worried that a baby would upset the established dynamic between himself, Ann and Esmond.

Nevertheless, Esmond, who publicly, rather than privately, acknowledged the baby as his, arranged a golfing holiday to Gleneagles in Scotland for himself, Ann, Ian and Loelia Westminster in August 1948. Here, they were joined by Laura for a few days following her return from Cannes. When rain prevented golf, the group were playing bridge in the hotel when Ann suddenly started contractions, a month prematurely. She was rushed to Edinburgh and admitted to a clinic at 11 Randolph Crescent, where the baby was born by caesarean section. The baby, named Mary Ann, survived for just eight hours.[23]

Ann was understandably devasted and remained in hospital, with Esmond staying loyally at her bedside. She was still too unwell to attend the christening and burial of her baby daughter in Aberlady. Here, Mary Ann was buried next to Ann and Laura's mother, with Esmond, Laura and Anne Tennant in attendance.

The death of his baby brought out an incredibly tender and caring side to Ian. He poured out his grief and sadness in heart-wrenching letters to Ann. While she remained in the clinic, he wrote:

> I have nothing to say to comfort you [...] I can only send you my arms and my love and all my prayers. I can't be there to wipe your eyes and kiss you.[24]

Ann was later to admit that Ian's letters during her convalescence really made her love him.[25]

The death of the baby also marked a shift in Esmond's acquiescence in his wife's relationship with Ian. Choosing not to act while Ann remained in hospital, Esmond returned to London ahead of Ann and hatched a plan. He solicitously sent his chauffeur to collect her when she returned from Scotland by sleeper train so that Ann could not stop en route to visit Ian at his house in Hay's Mews. Back in Warwick House, Esmond laid out his plans for Ann's further convalescence. He would take her to Paris for the *haute couture* shows, and then on to Portofino in Italy.[26] Despite her protestations that the trip was unnecessary, Esmond was determined to impose distance between his wife and her lover.

In Portofino, Esmond finally challenged Ann about the nature of her relationship with Ian and she admitted to the extent of the affair.[27] Publicly Esmond's attitude towards Ian remained friendly and genial, but behind the scenes he swung into action to force an end to the relationship. He asked the newspaper proprietor Lord Kemsley to speak to his foreign manager. In a hideously awkward meeting, Kemsley duly gave Ian a dressing down, warning him to stay away from Lady Rothermere.[28]

By Christmas 1948, Esmond had relented enough to include Ian on the guest list for Christmas at South Wraxall, which the Rothermeres had rented for the latter part of the year. Then on 6 January, Ann once again set sail for Jamaica.[29] She claimed to be staying with Noël Coward, but the excuse was flimsy, to say the least. Ann was accompanied by Ian, as well as Ian's great friend Robert Harling and his wife, Phoebe. The only person to make a stab at discretion was Coward himself. When a photographer from *Life* magazine arrived at his house, Ann was hustled back from Goldeneye.[30]

When Ann left Jamaica in February 1949, she asked Ian to think about a more permanent future together. 'I cannot contemplate life without you,' she wrote.[31] In response, Ian agreed with Ann. But he subtly applied the brakes on their relationship, claiming that he did not want to take Ann out of a 'basically happy life into one that would be more difficult in a thousand ways'.[32]

However, any decision was soon taken out of their hands. Esmond chose that moment to play his trump card. When Ann arrived back at Southampton Docks, she was greeted by a staff member of the *Daily Mail*, who delivered a letter from her husband. The letter was an ultimatum. Either Ann give up Ian or Esmond would divorce her.[33]

Instead of ending Ann and Ian's relationship, the ultimatum forced another meagre attempt at discretion. In the latter part of 1948, Ann and

Ian had been lent Noël Coward's house, White Cliffs in St Margaret's Bay, Kent, for illicit weekends. When Coward's neighbour, Eric Ambler, decided to sell the remaining lease on the neighbouring cottage, Summer's Lease, in the spring of 1949, Ian took over the tenancy.[34]

Ann enjoyed 'playing' at domesticity in the relative simplicity of a smaller house. Because of Esmond's ultimatum, the couple only socialised with Noël Coward and his guests, rarely venturing further than the bay. Their enforced solitude in the relaxed environs of Summer's Lease gave Ann and Ian a false sense of confidence in their relationship. Neither appreciated that life away from St Margaret's Bay would bring other pressures. Domestic bliss seemed to be within reach, with Ian writing to Ann, imagining married life, 'I could commute and you could put out my slippers in front of the fire and ask me about my day at the office.'[35]

But before Ann could make any decisions about her own marriage, another Charteris sister was walking up the aisle. On 15 December 1949, the Rothermeres and Dudleys attended the second wedding of their sister, Mary Rose. Having made a wartime marriage to Roddy Thesiger, Mary Rose spent precious little time with her husband while he served abroad. The couple eventually separated shortly after the end of the war and divorced in 1946. The end of her marriage had led to a further descent into alcoholism for Mary Rose, but she valiantly tried to stop drinking, undergoing several attempts at rudimentary rehabilitation. In 1948, aged 30, she met the 54-year-old Nigel Grey. In what seems like a pattern for the Charteris sisters, Mary's second husband was older than herself. Like Esmond and Eric, Mary Rose was Nigel's second wife. And, just like her brothers-in-law, Mary Rose's new husband had a child who was only a few years older than she was.

While Ann hoped that Mary Rose would make a success of her second marriage with a confident, older man providing the support she needed, other members of the family were less enthusiastic. Guy Charteris was heard to say, 'I always struggle to remember my sons-in-law. But Grey I find easy: Grey by name. Grey by nature.'[36] Despite having a son, Francis, in 1951, the marriage was not a success and Mary Rose continued to drink.

Ann and Esmond spent Christmas 1949 at South Wraxall without Ian. Mindful of Esmond's ultimatum, Ann decided against her annual trip to the Caribbean and Ian departed for Goldeneye alone. While there, he seriously began to ponder how marriage to Ann might work. When he returned to London in February 1950, he wrote to Ann listing all the obstacles to a possible marriage. Top among his concerns were her love of socialising, her children and her surrendering of all the 'flim flam' of her life as

Lady Rothermere.[37] For his part, marriage would mean a complete change of lifestyle, surrendering the freedom and independence of bachelordom.

Ann and Ian were separated in June when Ann went to Bailiffscourt, which the Rothermeres had taken for the summer. Ian travelled to Scotland, where he was due to undertake naval training in order to retain his rank of commander with the Royal Naval Volunteer Reserve. Then he travelled to America to stay with Ivar Bryce and his new wife, Jo Hartford, at their farm, Black Hole Hollow, on the border of Vermont and New York.[38]

Before leaving for America, Ian had taken a decisive step towards a shared future with Ann. He decided to move out of his bachelor digs in 21 Hays Mews, which he had leased after leaving Ebury Street, and rent a larger apartment in Chelsea. He found an apartment in an imposing block of Victorian mansion flats on Cheyne Walk. The flat had uninterrupted views of the Thames as well as Chelsea Old Church, which had just been rebuilt following a direct hit by a Luftwaffe bomb in the war. Ian took a five-year lease on 24 Carlyle Mansions for £480 per year.[39] His mother, who had moved to Cannes for tax reasons, helped Ian with the expenses of the move. Crucially, the flat was big enough for him and Ann, as well as her children, should she ever decide to leave Esmond.

When Ian returned from America and Esmond departed for a business trip to North America in late September, Ann and Ian were reunited and able to spend time together at Carlyle Mansions. The couple also travelled to France, spending a weekend at Chantilly, where Diana and Duff Cooper had retired after leaving the British Embassy in Paris.

Ann was able to conceal illicit trips to Paris under the auspices of business. As well as being a member of the British Fashion Council, she was a director of the *Continental Daily Mail*, which involved regular business meetings in Paris.[40] Ann's brother Hugo was also living in Paris with his wife and working as Paris correspondent for the *Daily Mail*. Ann would stay with Hugo and Virginia Charteris at their apartment on the Boulevard Suchet, while Ian would stay at the Hotel Continental. Ann's sister-in-law, Virginia, claimed that 'Ann enjoyed the clandestine aspect of the thing'.[41]

While Ann and Ian may have thought they were being clandestine, their affair was an open secret among the *Daily Mail* staff. When visiting Paris, Ann would ask to use the firm's car and driver, causing the chauffeur to remark, 'Madame la Comtesse is here with her lover.'[42]

When Esmond returned to London at the end of October 1950, he told Ann that the marriage was over. He had started an affair with an American woman he had met earlier in the year and seen during his recent trip to America. Ann had become aware of the affair in the summer but seemed unperturbed, writing to Hugo, 'He has deserted – for an American blonde – but I don't think it is serious.'[43]

Ann was far from devastated. She had loved Esmond and she had relished the role of being Lady Rothermere. But after six years, she had tired of the man and the role. While she adored the wealth and status that came from being the Viscountess Rothermere, she was no longer enamoured of all the accoutrements that came with her lavish life. She explained to Hugo that she was tired of 'the paraphernalia of people who gnaw away one's vitality and whom one has not sufficient character to resist'.[44]

Formal separation was discussed but abandoned until the new year as arrangements were made for a last family Christmas in Gstaad. Following the festivities, the Rothermeres would, temporarily at least, go their separate ways. The children would go to Ireland, Esmond to the house in Monte Carlo, and Ann would travel to Jamaica. Joining Ian at Goldeneye in January 1951, Ann was delighted to find that Cecil Beaton and stage designer Oliver Messel were also staying on the island, as was the dress designer Edward Molyneux.[45]

Ann was less delighted when the Bryces arrived in Jamaica as part of their extended honeymoon on board their yacht *Vagrant*. The Bryces were accompanied by Tommy and Marion 'Oatsie' Leiter, as well as Jo Bryce's daughter, Nuala, and her husband, Claiborne Pell.[46] Always threatened by Ian's friendship with Ivar Bryce, Ann was less than thrilled when Oatsie, a vivacious, sporty brunette whom Ian knew from previous visits to America, flirted with Ian.

The drama reached a crescendo one night when the Bryces came ashore to dine with Ann and Ian at Goldeneye. A tropical storm broke and the crew of the *Vagrant*, who had taken advantage of the Bryces' absence to raid the ship's liquor store and become paralytically drunk, were unable to prevent the boat slipping anchor and smashing into a reef. The Pells and the Leiters, who had remained on board, eventually made the decision to abandon ship, grabbing as many valuable items as they could before climbing aboard a dinghy to make for the safety of the shore.

The Bryces collected the bedraggled and sodden Pells and Leiters and took them straight to Goldeneye. In a letter to Diana Cooper, Ann recalls the four guests crashing into Goldeneye with 'black marks of lifejackets round their necks and purple bruises from diamonds crushed between skin and jacket'.[47] She then goes on to say how Ian went to attend to the crew while she 'poured disinfectant into the diamond wounds and handed out rum to dull the pain'.[48]

However, the other people at Goldeneye remember Ann's behaviour differently. Nuala Pell said Ian did little to help the rescue operation and was 'conspicuous by his absence'.[49] Similarly, Ivar Bryce recalls Ann being far from sympathetic after he gashed his head dragging the dingy to shore. 'Don't bleed on the floor!' she reportedly barked at him.[50]

Ann was further irked when the staggeringly beautiful writer Rosamond Lehmann arrived in Jamaica determined to have an affair with Ian, who was equally enthusiastic. However, Ian had thought Lehmann would arrive after Ann had departed for England. With Ann still in situ, Ian begged Noël Coward to take Rosamond off his hands. Coward reluctantly agreed but only after he mercenarily asked for both Ian's brand-new camera and tripod.[51]

Understandably, Ann returned to England in a sour mood, no longer sure about her future with Ian. Esmond had also had a change of heart while in Monte Carlo. Loath to get a second divorce, and still having some semblance of love for Ann, he suggested that they give their marriage another go. Ann agreed to the reconciliation before Esmond delivered the blow of another ultimatum. He said that their marriage would only stand a chance if Ann agreed not to see Ian for six months.[52]

While Ann was still irritated by Ian's attempted philandering in Jamaica, her long, solitary journey back to England had cooled her anger. Missing Ian, who had remained at Goldeneye, Ann asked Esmond for time to think over the ultimatum, to which he reluctantly agreed. After a long discussion, Ann said that she would give Esmond her decision after an upcoming trip to Paris to attend a board meeting of the *Continental Daily Mail*.

While in Paris, Ann wrote a wrenching, emotional letter to Ian, debating whether the couple could manage a six-month absence from each other. 'If it is real love it should easily survive that length of time,' Ann deliberated.[53] But her decision seemed to have already been made up when she wrote, 'I want you so much; you have been so wonderful in the last month [...] so deeply loving and affectionate that I don't see how I can really leave you.'[54] In response to her letter, Ian joined Ann in Paris, where the couple spent Easter 1951 together.

As a result, the Rothermeres called time on their marriage, agreeing a legal separation in September 1951. There were social obligations for which the couple agreed to retain a united front, after which they would publicly announce their separation. First, there was a dinner hosted by her sister Laura and her brother-in-law Eric, at the Dudley's Brook Street house on 27 September for the Duke of Windsor, who was visiting London. There was an awkward moment after dinner when the duke turned to Esmond and asked, 'You know Jamaica well ...' The tension could have been cut with a knife before the 'painful silence' was broken by Ann, who explained that it was she, and not Esmond, who had been to Jamaica.[55]

The Rothermeres' final social engagement was an election party on Friday, 26 October 1951, which they held at the Dorchester. Laura joined her sister, as did Eric.[56] The other guests included Greta Garbo, Ed Stanley, Patrick Leigh Fermor and Harold Nicolson. The loud and raucous party was full of tension as the predominantly wealthy aristocratic guests were hoping for a Conservative win after the post-war Labour Government. Although a friend of many Labour politicians, Ann loudly whooped and cheered every time a Conservative seat was retained or gained, 'as though at a boat race,' Leigh Fermor recalled.[57] On the afternoon of 26 October, Clement Attlee tendered his resignation and King George asked Winston Churchill to form a Conservative Government.

In early November 1951, Ann left Warwick House to spend December at Shane's Castle. From Ireland, she would travel to Grindelwald in Switzerland for the new year, after which she planned to sail for Jamaica, Goldeneye and Ian.[58]

Before leaving for Ireland and as part of her official separation from Esmond, Ann had negotiated a substantial financial settlement of £100,000. While this settlement would allow Ann to live comfortably, she was concerned that, having lived so opulently as Lady Rothermere, her standard of living would be significantly changed by her divorce. Esmond later remarked to his friend Alastair Forbes that the settlement was the 'going rate' for divorce,[59] while Ann wrote to her brother and sister-in-law from Grindelwald, saying, 'I am not an unjust woman and I know that Esmond owes me a great deal.'[60]

This comment may seem obtuse, given Ann's behaviour, but she had already begun a concerted campaign to change the narrative around the divorce. She attempted to portray the breakdown of her marriage as inevitable, despite Esmond's repeated attempts to save the marriage and her blatant infidelity with Ian. She also described the separation as without rancour, claiming that 'there are no hearts to break'.[61]

In reality, Esmond was devastated by the end of his marriage. A fundamentally reticent man, the publicity and gossip surrounding his wife and the separation was painful. Immediately following the divorce, he moved in with his daughter Esme and her husband at their farm in Kent and came out in a nervous rash. He did not marry again for fourteen years. Much later, the *Daily Mail* did not review nor even make any mention of the James Bond books.

13

ANN AND IAN ...
AND JAMES BOND

While Ann hammered out the financial details of her separation from Esmond in late December 1951, there was still no guarantee that she and Ian would marry. While she was determined to become Mrs Fleming, the perennially single Ian still had his reservations, not least whether he would be able to support a wife, which may explain why Ann gunned so hard for a vast settlement. However, just before Christmas 1951, Ian purchased the lease of White Cliffs in St Margaret's Bay from Noël Coward. Larger than the adjoining Summer's Lease, White Cliffs would act as a temporary home for Ann and Ian after the divorce, should they choose to marry.

The separation of Ann and Esmond did not come as a shock. As Sara Morrison recalls, 'We got a lot of information about the household from the staff, with comings and goings dealt with more discreetly and elegantly than today.'[1] But the actual split was fast. Raymond and Fionn were told by their mother that the family would be leaving Warwick House for Carlyle Mansions. 'They had to move in twenty-four hours,' Sara remembers. 'Raymond rang me up and told me, "Mummy is going to marry Ian".'[2] Sara helped her cousin to pack up his beloved miniature trains at Warwick House and does not remember Raymond or Fionn being unduly upset by the breakdown of the Rothermere marriage. 'We all felt that the aunt on the whole seemed to be doing the right thing,' she concludes.[3]

By the end of December, Ann and Ian had decided to marry – their decision motivated by the fact that Ann was pregnant again. Working backwards from the birth of Caspar on 12 August 1952, Ann and Esmond would have already agreed to separate before Ann became pregnant. But an impending baby may well have forced a proposal from Ian. As Sara confirms, 'Ann was determined to a) have a baby and b) have Ian's baby.'[4]

Ann may not have known she was pregnant when she told her children that they were leaving Warwick House. But she did tell them of her intention to marry Ian, which suggests that she had determined on a proposal by whatever means. As Ian's friend Robert Harling muses, 'I wondered whether the situation had been manipulated by Ann [...] by again becoming pregnant.'[5]

By the time she and Ian left for Goldeneye in mid-January 1952, the pregnancy had been confirmed and they had decided to marry. In preparation, Ann was taken to meet Ian's mother. The previous year, Eve Fleming had decided to leave her tax exile in Cannes and buy a house on Cable Beach in Nassau. En route to Goldeneye, Ann and Ian were to spend a few days in the Bahamas and tell her of their plans to marry.

Staying in a nearby hotel, the visit did not go as planned. Before leaving London, Ann had developed haemorrhoids due to her pregnancy. These had worsened while she was in New York and completely floored her in Nassau.[6] She received treatment from a local doctor and stayed in bed, giving her the neat excuse to spend minimal time with her future mother-in-law. By 16 February, she felt well enough to travel and the couple departed for Jamaica.

Noël Coward came to Goldeneye on the evening of their arrival for dinner to celebrate the engagement of his two friends. The trio had a fun, boozy dinner, playing several rounds of the card game Canasta. Despite her impending marriage, Coward noted in his diary that he 'sensed that Annie was not entirely happy'.[7] However, this may have been more to do with her pregnancy and piles, rather than worry about her engagement and her future.

With a baby on the way, Ann and Ian were determined to marry quickly and with relatively little fuss. They decided that they would marry in Jamaica as a way to avoid the press. Ian was not inclined to make his wedding a big event, while Ann was just delighted to be finally marrying the man she loved. The Rothermeres' decree nisi was granted on 10 February 1952, with the decree absolute coming into effect forty-three days later, as per British law. This meant that Ann and Ian would be free to marry at the end of March. As Esmond's highly paid lawyers were pushing the divorce through as speedily as possible, no delays were expected, and Ann and Ian tentatively set their wedding date for 25 March 1952.[6]

At Goldeneye, wary of losing another baby, Ann slowed down her pace of life completely – not an easy task for a woman with such a low boredom threshold. She spent her time contentedly lying on the terrace of Goldeneye, painting pictures of Caribbean fish and flowers.

Ian, on the other hand, was nervous. After forty-three years of bachelordom, he was going to marry and become a father – all in the space of six short months. For the rest of his life, Ian would claim that he started writing *Casino Royale* to take his mind off his upcoming nuptials – an oft-repeated legend which rankled Ann with the implicit suggestion of Ian's dread at marrying her.

Ian may have started writing his first James Bond novel as a distraction, but the many motivations for the start of his writing career were all bound up with Ann. He had been talking about writing a book for many years. As early as 1942, when Ian first visited Jamaica during the war, he had said to Ivar Bryce, 'When we have won this blasted war, I am going to live in Jamaica ... and write books.'[9] But his impending marriage to Ann provided the catalyst. 'She baited him to start writing,' Sara confirms. 'She said he couldn't be anything but a journalist.'[10]

His marriage would give him financial stability. Ian had never been poor and his earnings from Kemsley Newspapers were good, but the £100,000 that Ann achieved through her settlement from Esmond gave the future Flemings financial security. He would no longer be dependent on his salary and could have the financial freedom to write full time.

And for the first time in his life, Ian would also have emotional stability. Having been a perennial bachelor, moving from one love affair to another, he would use the energy to write which had previously been spent on romances as well as managing his affair with Ann.

Despite the money that would come with his marriage to Ann, Ian was well aware that his future wife had become used to a certain standard of living. Ian wanted to do his best to provide the money to allow Ann to live well and continue the lifestyle which she so enjoyed. In addition, with a child on the way, Ian wanted to find an additional source of income.

Finally, as Ann was pregnant and in a delicate condition, sex was off the cards at Goldeneye. Sex had been a pivotal part of their relationship and with no other available outlet for his sexual energy, Ian turned to writing to relieve his frustration.

There is much debate among Bond fanatics about when Ian actually started writing. Ian's official biographer, John Pearson, dates the start of *Casino Royale* and the invention of Bond to the morning of 15 January 1952.[11] Ann's diary dates the creation of James Bond as later. While awaiting their marriage at Goldeneye – after their arrival on 16 February – Ann writes, 'This morning Ian started to type a book.'[12]

But this is not the story of James Bond, nor even the story of his writer. These details are included solely to demonstrate that whenever James Bond was born, Ann was there, providing the stimulus for the creation of one of the most famous literary characters of all time.

The wedding of Ann and Ian took place on Monday, 24 March 1952, a day earlier than originally planned. The location was the town hall in Port Maria, a few miles from Goldeneye. Noël Coward and his secretary, Cole Lesley, were the only witnesses. Ann and Ian arrived together by car. Ian looked casual, dressed in a belted, blue, short-sleeved shirt and blue trousers. Ann looked pretty in an eau-de-Nil silk dress – an imitation of a Christian Dior dress made by a local seamstress.[13]

The ceremony was quick and informal. The registrar had nuclear halitosis, causing Ian to warn his bride to 'keep upwind of him'.[14] The registrar also managed to confuse both Ann and Ian's names. Ann was alternately referred to as Mary and Geraldine (her middle names), while Ian was referred to by his second name, Lancaster.

Greeted by the cheers of the small crowd waiting outside the town hall, the new Mr and Mrs Ian Fleming made for Noël Coward's house, Blue Harbour, for celebratory drinks. The group toasted the recent marriage with strong martinis, before boozily making their way back to Goldeneye, where Violet, the Goldeneye cook, had prepared a wedding breakfast.

Ian had chosen the menu carefully. The starter was turtle soup, made from turtles caught fresh by Ian, followed by black crab still in the shell, and a cake with green icing.[15] Whether the party actually tasted any of the food is debatable, given the amount of alcohol consumed following the wedding. After pre-lunch martinis and copious amounts of wine with the meal, Coward insisted that the party finish with a creation of his, called 'Old Man's Thing' – a lethal mixture of peeled fruit slices and a whole bottle of rum. Several rounds of Old Man's Thing were consumed as the group made endless toasts.

Showing remarkable stamina, given the industrial amounts of alcohol they had consumed the day before, the Flemings left Jamaica on 25 March 1952.[16] Flying via Nassau, on arrival in New York Ian found a telegram from his boss, Lord Kemsley. The cable generously announced that Ian was to be given an extra two weeks of leave, so the newly-weds decided to have a brief honeymoon in New York.

Anxious that she would be shunned by New York society, Ann was stunned to find that New York welcomed her with open arms. For four days, Ann and Ian were the toast of the town as they attended endless parties thrown to celebrate their marriage. Regretfully, on 30 March 1952, the Flemings left New York for London and the start of their new life together.

LAURA AND THE 1950S

With the dawn of the 1950s, the Dudley marriage limped on, with Eric's anger and jealousy intensifying. In early 1952, Eric and Laura had dinner with Ann and Ian at Dropmore Park in Buckinghamshire, the home of Lord and Lady Kemsley. After a game of Canasta, Eric accused Ian of being a 'filthy cheat', after which the Dudleys left.[1] In the car, Laura said to Eric, 'Can't you ever behave?', to which Eric became furious, saying, 'If you do not like the way I behave go with your filthy tart of a sister. If the Rothermere marriage is washed up, ours is just as much or worse.'[2]

But it was to be Laura's affair with Bobby Casa Maury which would sound the death knell for the Dudley marriage. Eric and Laura had continued to see much of the Casa Maurys, who would often stay at Great Westwood. Their marriage was also in trouble. Bobby would complain to Laura that his wife was bored of him. He also made the outlandish claim that Freda wanted to marry Eric.

Casa Maury was tremendously good-looking, charming and confident. Having previously only flirted with him to irritate Freda, Laura now embarked on a full-scale affair. As she herself admitted in her divorce petition, 'In February 1952 I was associating with the Marquis [sic] de Casa Maury and in order that we could meet, a friend said I could use her flat at Park West.'[3]

On Thursday, 21 February 1952, Laura and Casa Maury were interrupted at Park West by a private detective, Mr Wyatt, who had been hired by Eric to search the flat.[4] That evening, the Dudleys agreed to separate.[5] Laura would take up residence at Brook Street for the start of Sara's season and Eric would remain at Westwood.

After the separation was officially agreed in April, Eric departed with the words, 'I will always love you', before archly telling Laura that she had 'three months to find a rich husband'.[6]

But Laura's affair with Casa Maury was more than simple lust. Her daughter Sara was now 17 and about to come out in society with a London season. All eyes would be on this beautiful and eligible young woman as she took her place in society and inevitably attracted the eyes of young men. A gossip-garnering affair with Casa Maury ensured that public attention would be focused back on Laura. 'That was the aunt's [Ann's] reading of the situation,' Sara Morrison confirms. 'The aunt felt that the affair was more coincidental than anything else.'[7] Ann wrote to her sister, blasting Laura for her behaviour. She told her that Sara should come first and entreated Laura to end the affair. Laura was furious and in retaliation she refused to send a note of congratulation when Ann married Ian.

When Laura officially left Eric, announcing her plans to her daughter as the pair took up residency in Brook Street for the summer, Sara was devastated, 'I felt like my childhood had been obliterated. She ought never to have left Eric. He was the only serious person that she was married to.'[8]

With Laura permanently in London and publicly separated from Eric, she could openly pursue her relationship with Bobby. The affair precipitated the end of his marriage to Freda, who booted her husband out of their home in Albert Mansions, Kensington, with him taking up residency in the Berkeley Hotel. The relationship between Laura and Bobby instantly cooled when he confided that he had no money, admitting that his lifestyle had been funded by Freda. In her autobiography, Laura is honest enough to say that after her separation from Eric, she was bored by her affair with Bobby, 'The forbidden fruit, once permitted, was not one bit to my taste, as so often happens.'[9] Sara is more forthright, 'Bobby Casa Maury was a real creep. A shit actually. I really disliked him.'[10]

Following Sara's season, Laura left the Dudley home on Brook Street and took a flat in Bryanston Court, on George Street in Marylebone – the same building where Wallis and Ernest Simpson had lived during her affair with the Prince of Wales. Laura also managed to talk herself into a job with Christian Dior on Maddox Street.

She was employed as an early public relations representative within the company, which explains how she managed to obtain a job so easily with few qualifications. She was well connected and was frequently featured in the press herself. As well as placing Christian Dior products in newspapers and magazines as a form of free advertising, Laura was given free rein to wear Christian Dior clothes, her employers rightly believing that her frequent appearances in the press would provide free advertising for the brand.[11]

She relished the job and brought the same verve and determination to the work that she had previously brought to her relationships with men. Laura had style and had always enjoyed clothes, so a career in fashion was a good fit for her. She worked hard and was obviously good at her job, remaining with Christian Dior for three years. Even Ann was impressed by Laura's industriousness, bitchily describing her sister's success in the fashion world as 'the only objective that she has achieved that isn't a man'.[12]

Working hard but playing harder, inevitably Laura was not alone for long. The next man to wander into her life had a bizarre connection to her former lover, Bobby Casa Maury. In May of 1953, Bobby introduced Laura to Anthony Pelissier, the former husband of Freda's daughter, Penelope. Even in the tight establishment circles of that age, the links between Laura and Pelissier were uncomfortably close. 'The incestuousness of it all,' Sara ruefully recollects.[13]

Born in 1912 to the theatrical producer H.G. Pelissier and actress Fay Compton, Pelissier had grown up in the theatrical world. After a brief career as an actor in the 1930s, he turned to writing in 1937, before making his directorial debut in 1949. In the four years preceding his meeting with Laura, he had written and directed four smash-hit films – *The History of Mr Polly* in 1949, *The Rocking Horse Winner* in 1950, *Night Without Stars* in 1951 and *A Personal Affair*, released in 1953.

With three well-received films under his belt and the daring drama, *A Personal Affair*, finished and due to be released later in the year, Anthony was at the top of his game.[14] Like a moth to a flame, Laura found herself irresistibly attracted to this quietly forceful man. With his short, stocky body, receding hairline, high cheekbones and a thin, pencil moustache, Pelissier could not be described as physically attractive. But there was something about his penetrating gaze and his almost hypnotic manner that drew people in. 'He was very glamorous,' Sara recalls. 'He had this intensity. A presence.'[15]

Opinions were mixed about Anthony. While Sara found the match 'very odd', she liked him.[16] He was bright and intellectual. And he was one of the first men to really challenge Laura, berating her for wasting time in 'society' and not using her brain. Even Laura's maid, Rosemary, approved of this new man, asking her mistress hopefully, 'Is this one a keeper?'[17]

But many of Laura's friends disliked Pelissier. He made little effort with her more frivolous friends and she later blamed him for distancing her from her social circle. But Laura's own behaviour, rather than her choice of man, may be the more likely explanation for a dwindling number of invitations. 'She always said that women were worried that she would run off with their husbands,' Hugo Vickers remembers of Laura's perceived rackety reputation.[18]

Unusually for Laura, during their five-year relationship she was not in control. Like Eric, Pelissier was a strong, determined and intelligent man, and the relationship with Laura was volatile. He would frequently leave

Laura. In one letter, he wrote to her explaining his absence, 'I just had to get away – or else I would have split.'[19] As Sara notes, Pelissier would leave because he 'no longer wanted to be a play thing'.[20] In retaliation, when he inevitably asked to return to Laura, she would taunt him, leading to more explosive rows. In one letter after a separation, Pelissier wrote to Laura, 'I thought you wanted us to be back together permanently […] marriage was talked of […] But no: I misunderstood.'[21] He also admits, 'I can understand you wanting to punish me.'[22]

But the pair seemed unable to either separate or stay away from each other. As Pelissier later wrote to Laura, 'I am an "obsessional" type of human being […] For some years you were my obsession.'[23]

An exhausting relationship with Anthony coincided with the final illness and death of Gerry Koch de Gooreynd. Laura was by his bedside on the evening of 19 October 1953 when Gerry died. A requiem mass was held for him at Farm Street in Mayfair before his body was taken back to Belgium and buried in the family plot at Gooreynd. Laura inherited the remainder of the lease of the house on Buckingham Place. Worrying about money and the spiralling costs of her divorce proceedings from Eric, Laura almost immediately gave up her flat in Bryanston Court and moved into the house at 2 Buckingham Place.[24]

In March 1954, after the two years of official separation, the Earl of Dudley applied to the court for a divorce from Laura on the grounds of her adultery with Bobby Casa Maury. Eric had quite a list of men to choose from and initially also cited Gerry and Philip Dunn, but his solicitors persuaded him to remove any additional names. The Casa Maurys were also getting divorced, with Freda citing Laura. With an affair between Laura and Bobby Casa Maury providing a catalyst for two divorces, the court was unlikely to refuse either application. Laura was represented by the solicitors Gordon, Dadds & Company.[25]

The decree nisi for the Earl and Countess of Dudley was granted on 2 February 1954. The Casa Maurys were also granted a decree nisi a few minutes after the Dudleys. Unlike Freda Casa Maury, who attended court and then was photographed climbing aboard a bus to travel home, Laura did not attend the court proceedings and had travelled to Paris.

As soon as the decree nisi was granted, Eric tracked Laura down. Bizarrely, he asked her to return and have dinner with him. In a typically contrary romantic act so typical of Laura, she immediately flew back and had dinner with her now ex-husband that evening at Mirabelle.[26]

Laura's daughter, Sara, was 19 when her mother and stepfather divorced. Pretty, outgoing and enormous fun, she had been a hit during her season.

With her delicate features and elfin appearance, Sara bore more than a passing resemblance to her Aunt Ann.

At the age of 19 she became engaged to Charles Morrison, a handsome, stolid scion of the wealthy Morrison family. Charles' great-great-grandfather, James Morrison, cleverly stockpiled black crêpe in preparation for the mourning of King William IV in 1837, earning a fortune when the monarch died.[27] James then bought land in Wiltshire, which consolidated the family wealth. Charles' father, John Morrison, served as MP for Salisbury from 1942 to 1965 before entering the House of Lords as Baron Margadale of Islay in the county of Argyll. Charles had attended Eton before National Service with the Life Guards. He then went up to Cambridge before leaving to attend the Royal Agricultural College in Cirencester.[28]

Sara and Charles married on 28 October 1954 at St Margaret's Westminster in a grand high-society wedding. As many brides will empathise, Sara remembers little of the day. She was escorted down the aisle by her beloved grandfather, Guy, who had egg on his tie.[29] While her ex-stepfather Eric was included in the celebrations, Anthony Pelissier was not.

Despite her own divorce and her bombastic relationship with Anthony, Laura threw herself into helping her daughter with wedding plans. 'She handed me over to Christian Dior,' Sara recalls. 'Mummy had a lovely time at my wedding. She really enjoyed the whole thing.'[30]

Free of her mother for the first time in her life, Sara and Charles moved into South Wraxall Manor, which she had inherited after the death of her father. Ann's son, Raymond O'Neill, joined them as a permanent house guest. Both Charles and Sara became actively involved in politics, with Charles later becoming MP for Devizes.[31] The Morrisons would have two children, giving Laura a granddaughter, Anabel, in 1955, and a grandson, David, in 1959.

Whether driven by Anthony Pelissier's criticism of her not using her brain, or by her own ambition, Laura left Christian Dior in 1956 to establish a fashion boutique of her own. With financial support from her ex-mother-in-law, Lady Glyn, as well as the money she received from Gerry, Laura opened a shop which sold clothes, fabric and objets d'art.[32] Shrewdly, Laura named the shop 'Contessa', knowing that people would be intrigued by a store that was run by a countess. She even went so far as to decorate the Contessa wrapping paper with the Dudley coronet.[33]

The first Contessa store opened in mid-1956 on Rayners Lane in Harrow.[34] As a woman used to getting what she wanted and refusing to take no for an answer, Laura was a phenomenal saleswoman. She also never let the truth hold her back. When women came to Contessa to buy fabrics,

Laura pretended that she had made her own clothes by copying a pattern. In fact, most of Laura's clothes were made for her by Christian Dior, which set an impossibly high sartorial expectation for the housewives of Harrow.[35]

By early 1957, Laura was able to establish another Contessa store in Borehamwood, closely followed by an outlet in Radlett. Laura would eventually lease seven sites for the Contessa chain and showed remarkably canny business sense by establishing the shops in new 'commuter towns', where residents had disposable income, rather than the more fashionable areas of London. And, baldly, Laura knew that a shop run by a countess had more prestige in suburban towns.

Like her nursing career, Laura was genuinely fulfilled by her work in the Contessa shops. Having been supported by men for all of her adult life, she found that she was able to support herself. 'She nearly found out that she could be a grown-up with her Contessa shops,' her daughter remembers. 'Arguably the only time she ever had been.'[36]

Laura continued to see Anthony Pelissier but the dynamic between the pair was antagonistic and unpredictable. As Pelissier noted in a letter to Laura during one of their frequent separations, 'attempting to handle you was way too tough and twice I broke out'.[37] The combative relationship continued until Laura bought Hertfordshire House, in the village of Coleshill in Buckinghamshire. Laura later recalled that Pelissier demanded a country house, while she, worried about money, preferred to stay in London. Pelissier had a love of the country and felt that taking Laura out of London might remove her from her frivolous social life.[38] For her part, Laura wanted to stabilise her relationship with Pelissier. By buying a country home she hoped to gain some semblance of control.

Bearing more than a passing resemblance to her former home, Great Westwood, Hertfordshire House was built around 1780. A beautiful three-storied, red-brick house with a low, angled roof, bow windows and imposing entrance porch, Laura described Hertfordshire House as a small 'grand' house.[39] In the heart of the Chilterns, the house had sweeping views across rolling fields to the village of Winchmore Hill. The house had originally been a farmhouse but had been largely neglected since the war, as had the surrounding 14 acres of land and the two staff cottages. When Laura first viewed the house in 1957, she fell instantly fell in love. She was unworried by the extensive refurbishment needed and, using the money from her divorce settlement to obtain a mortgage from Coutts, Laura managed to purchase Hertfordshire House in June 1957 and moved in the following August.

Laura loved her new home with a passion and poured her heart into the renovation and redecoration. Having found that her existing furniture would only fill her bedroom and drawing room, Laura happily began to scour antiques shops across the country for suitable items. She decided to realise the shares left to her by Gerry, making her a wealthy woman. Selling her shares in a copper firm which was going public netted Laura £80,000.[40] As a result, she was able to decorate Hertfordshire House to exactly the style and standard that she wanted.

Laura's happiness with her new home was short-lived. In the late summer of 1958, Pelissier permanently called time on his relationship with Laura. She was devastated and tried in vain to get him back. But Pelissier was adamant and wrote to Laura rather dramatically, 'Darling – You were always a gambler and like all gamblers you knew the right moment to play. This, I assure you, was the wrong [...] There's a billion things to say – yet there's nothing.'[41]

Laura even went so far as to enlist her daughter's help in winning Pelissier back. She instructed Sara to bicycle over to White City, where Pelissier was working on a programme for the BBC. Over lunch, he brutally explained his reasons for terminating the relationship, saying to her, 'Your mother is a mixture of cannibal and vulture. I am fed up with having bits picked out of me.'[42]

Laura was distressed by the loss of Pelissier. 'She was depressed after Anthony left,' Sara remembers. 'She had lost another prop.'[43]

Having got through Christmas 1958 and still licking her wounds, Laura was at a loose end on 31 December when she received a call from Frankie More O'Ferrall. He and his wife Angela were having an impromptu party in London and asked Laura to join them. Initially reluctant to attend, Laura was told that there would be an eligible man for her at the party. Galvanised, Laura changed and drove to the More O'Ferralls' home on Curzon Street in Mayfair.[44] Entering the party, Laura realised that she knew everybody, except for one man. This was the eligible man that Frankie had mentioned – Michael Canfield.

Ann and Laura
as children.

Ann, Laura and Sara
Long at a Warwick
House party, 1949.

Ann and Shane O'Neill on their wedding day, 6 October 1932.

Laura (front row, second from right) and the staff of the Himley Hall Hospital, 1943.

Laura and David Long depart
for their honeymoon in Paris,
14 November 1933.

Laura and Eric Dudley
playing tennis at Himley
Hall around 1950.

Laura in Red Cross commandant uniform, in a picture taken for the Red Cross fete at Himley Hall, 1943.

Ann and Diana Cooper, Warwick House, 1949.

Laura's wedding to Michael Canfield, 13 June 1960.

Laura playing croquet with Bert Marlborough and Nancy Lancaster at Hertfordshire House in the 1960s.

Laura dancing in Venice, summer 1986.

Ann and Caspar at Hertfordshire House

Ann, Caspar and Francis Grey,
Sevenhampton.

Laura striking a pose in the South
of France, the early 1960s.

A picture taken by Laura of
John F. Kennedy when he
stayed at Himley Hall in 1939.

Laura and Roy Jenkins leaving
Sevenhampton, Christmas 1968.

Diana Cooper in the loggia
of Hertfordshire House,
the 1960s.

Laura at work at her Contessa
shop, around 1958.

Laura, Randolph Churchill and 'Grock' the donkey, Hertfordshire House, Christmas 1964.

Ann with Randolph Churchill (centre), and his son, Winston Spencer-Churchill (left), at Warwick House in 1949. Laura is in the background talking to Anthony Eden. (Reproduced wit the kind permission of Hugo Vickers)

15

ANN AND IAN ...
AND FAMILY LIFE

When the Flemings arrived back in the UK at the end of March 1952, Ann moved into Ian's flat on Cheyne Walk. She was accompanied by her children, 18-year-old Raymond and 16-year-old Fionn, as well as a parrot who welcomed visitors with the words 'Hello darling'.[1] Used to the spacious surroundings of Warwick House, Carlyle Mansions felt small to Ann. But selflessly, her worry was all for how Ian would cope. Just before her marriage Ann had expressed her concerns to Hugo and Virginia, writing from Goldeneye, 'I fear Ian's martyrdom *is* imminent with intrusion of talking parrot, saxophone, R, F and self to his perfectly run bachelor establishment [...] the immediate future looks rather chaotic'.[2]

But Ian seemed to thrive in this new domestic arrangement, spending weekdays in Chelsea and weekends at White Cliffs. After a weekend with the Flemings, Laura recalled the house as 'full of laughter'[3] and friends noticed that both Ann and Ian seemed to shine with happiness, each clearly adoring the other.

As Ann's pregnancy progressed, she chose to spend more time at St Margaret's Bay. Happy as she was, her pregnancy was difficult. Her birthday on 13 June 1952 coincided with a heatwave in Britain, which Ann found arduous and uncomfortable. At the age of 39, Ann was an older mother and she found her pregnancy increasingly tiring. Having had an emergency caesarean in 1948 with the birth of baby Mary Ann, Ann hoped that she would be able to have a natural birth with this baby. But her doctors advised against carrying the baby to full term and a caesarean was recommended for 12 August.[4]

The caesarean section, which took place in the private Lindo Wing of St Mary's Hospital in Paddington, was long and complicated, with Ann becoming extremely ill. As a first-time father, Ian was naturally nervous.

But as the hours ticked by and Ann became increasingly unwell, Ian was reduced to tears. On the evening of 12 August 1952, the baby was finally delivered, weighing 9lbs 4oz,[5] but Ann was in a bad way.[6]

In 1952, caesarean section incisions were made vertically down the abdomen, rather than the modern transverse incision. The invasive surgery, following the earlier caesarean, left Ann with a severe lesion from her rib cage to her lower stomach and permanent scars.[7]

Ann was kept in hospital for three weeks after the birth of her son, whom the Flemings initially called Kaspar, before deciding on the more traditional spelling of Caspar. For five days, Ann was fed intravenously and had to endure the use of catheters while she recovered. While in hospital she received flowers from Esmond with the simple note, 'Dearest Ann, best wishes to you and your son.'[8] Already low and understandably emotional from the effects of the surgery and the birth of her son, Ann was 'awash with tears of what might have been'.[9] An odd sentiment, given that she had just married the man she loved and given birth to his son.

Leaving hospital on 1 September, Ann travelled to St Margaret's Bay with the baby for further recuperation. She was incredibly low after the birth of her son, which suggests that she may have suffered from postnatal depression. In a letter to her brother, she wrote, 'I am pursued by demons […] and can't stop crying.'[10]

But Ann's unhappiness may also have stemmed from a shift in Ian's behaviour towards her. Ian had a repugnance of any physical abnormality and he had been horrified by the drips and catheters that his wife had used following the birth of their son. On her return home, he appeared to be sickened by the deep scars that two caesareans had left on his wife's body. For a couple who had thrived on such a strong sexual connection, Ian's reluctance to make love to his wife shattered an already weakened Ann. As she later wrote of this time in a letter to Ian, 'You mention "bad old bachelor days" – the only person you stopped sleeping with when they ceased was me.'[11]

Ian was also worried about his work. He had shown a first draft of *Casino Royale* to his friend William Plomer, a reader for the publisher Jonathan Cape. The publisher was initially unenthusiastic and only capitulated after Peter Fleming, Ian's brother, applied pressure. With two successful travel books under his belt, Cape was worried about losing Peter and agreed to publish *Casino Royale*, but drove a hard bargain. Conducting his own negotiations, Ian initially agreed to Cape's terms in September before retracting his agreement. He pushed for an initial first print run of 10,000 copies, which Cape refused. On 10 October, Ian was forced to climb down and accepted the publisher's terms.[12]

While Ian conducted negotiations on *Casino Royale*, as well as continuing his role as foreign manager for the Kemsley Press, he was also made managing director of the Queen Anne Press, a small publishing house acquired by Lord Kemsley in 1951.[13] His various activities kept Ian busy while Ann made a slow recovery. Apart from a sojourn to Paris, Ann remained at St Margaret's Bay with Caspar for the autumn of 1952. Joan Sillick, the nanny who had taken care of Raymond and Fionn, returned to take charge of Caspar.[14]

Ann returned to London in October for the christening of Caspar at Chelsea Old Church. Her choice of godparents for her son were Clarissa Eden, who had married Foreign Secretary Anthony Eden the previous year, Noël Coward and Cecil Beaton. Ian's choices as godparents were his brother Peter and an old golfing friend, Sir George Duff-Sutherland-Dunbar.[15]

With a new baby, the flat in Carlyle Mansions was becoming increasingly claustrophobic and Ann chose to spend the majority of her time at White Cliffs. She wanted to resume her role as hostess and Carlyle Mansions had neither the space nor the setting for her to entertain. As her health recovered, she began to lobby her new husband for a suitable London townhouse. Ian, who was preoccupied with the upcoming publication of his book, was reluctant to move, despite being aware that the flat in Carlyle Mansions was ill suited to a family. And, to a lesser extent, he recognised that the flat was incompatible with Ann's ambitions as a hostess.

His friend Robert Harling was responsible for finding the Flemings their next home when he heard of a house for sale in Victoria Square.[16] The small, residential square between Buckingham Palace and Victoria Station is remarkably quiet, given the proximity to two major London throughfares. The house was also just a stone's throw from Ian's original bachelor digs on Ebury Street.

No. 16 Victoria Square is a beautiful, white, stucco-fronted, early Victorian town house designed by Matthew Wyatt. The house is differentiated from the other buildings in the square by a circular corner tower on the left-hand side of the building. The tower, which runs the full height of the house, is dominated by large windows, providing an unusual round-corner room on every floor. Ann was completely enamoured of the house, envisioning hosting small, but glamorous salons. Ian was less enthusiastic but capitulated to his wife.

Using the money from her divorce settlement, the Flemings purchased 16 Victoria Square in the autumn of 1952. Bringing her exquisite eye to the interior design of the house, Ann employed a fleet of painters and decorators to renovate the house, while she and Ian spent early 1953 in Jamaica, leaving Caspar with Nanny Sillick.[17]

For the first time, Ann travelled by air, having previously always pre-ferred to travel by boat, which took two weeks. By the early 1950s, air travel, with the introduction of the jet plane, had become safer and was a much speedier way to travel around the globe. For Ann and Ian, who were founding members of the 'jet set', their international journeys between the United States, Jamaica and the UK became much quicker and easier.

Leaving London on a cold January evening, the Flemings travelled over-night to New York, where they stayed for one night.[18] Breaking their normal routine of travelling on to Jamaica, the Flemings journeyed to Florida on the *Silver Phantom* train, where Ian planned to do research for his next novel, *Live and Let Die*. The couple then flew onto Jamaica for their first full stay on the island as husband and wife.[19]

Despite only being married for less than a year, the marriage began to fray as the Flemings had different attitudes towards a holiday at Goldeneye. Ian established a rigid routine of writing in the morning and spending the afternoon swimming and looking at the fish in the bay below Goldeneye. In the early evening, he would proofread what he had written earlier, before settling into evening drinks and a boozy dinner. For Ann, there was little to occupy her. With her notoriously low boredom threshold, her ideal holiday was a constant stream of visitors and regular socialising.

Both Ann and Ian initially worked valiantly to find a compromise. When Lord Beaverbrook invited the Flemings to stay at Cromarty, his lavishly luxurious house in Montego Bay, Ann was thrilled at the prospect of two days and nights of solid socialising. Ian agreed to accompany his wife but only in return for a two-night camping trip in the Blue Mountains.[20]

The Flemings also established a routine of inviting guests to join them at Goldeneye. Their resident guests that winter were Ann's father, Guy, and her stepmother, Violet, who had married in 1945. The Charteris seniors arrived just as a storm broke. Ann remembered the arrival archly, 'My hair was blowing perpendicular and we could not hear each other speak.'[21]

The Charterises were easy guests, who settled well into Goldeneye life. Guy relished exploring the Caribbean island in search of flora and fauna, and sharing his discoveries with a delighted Ian. He also joined Ian on his regular afternoon diving trips in the private cove at Goldeneye to search out exotic fish. But these calm, sun-soaked days were accompanied by a hectic social schedule devised by Ann. There were parties up and down the north coast, including dinner with Noël Coward at Port Marina, where a fellow guest was Katherine Hepburn, much to Ian's delight.

But his good humour began to fray and he soon began to decline invi-tations, citing work. Ann navigated this by arranging to host several gatherings at Goldeneye, forcing Ian to play host. Ian retaliated by pressing so much alcohol on a particularly boring guest that he passed out on one of the Goldeneye beds.[22]

★ ★ ★

Leaving Goldeneye on 14 March, the Flemings returned to England via a visit to Eve Fleming in Nassau and a stopover in New York. While the Flemings had been in Jamaica, the lease on the Carlyle Mansions flat had come to an end, so Caspar and Nanny Sillick had moved into Victoria Square, despite the ongoing building work.[23] Expecting the refurbishment to be finished, Ian was furious to discover that the renovation was on a much larger scale than he had expected, with a fleet of builders needed to complete the work.

The conflict between the Flemings had been caused by Ann not being entirely truthful about the extent of the refurbishment, but the finished house demonstrated her enormous talent and flair for interior design. She created one of the most exquisite townhouses in London, crafting a flawlessly decorated entertaining space in which she could perform as hostess. The house was small, with no garden or garage, but Ann's designs made the most of the space. Ann had had the kitchen moved to the ground floor of the house. Here, she installed a modern kitchen with the latest gadgetry, allowing the basement to be converted into self-contained staff accommodation. Opposite the kitchen on the ground floor was an intimate dining room, created from the bow-window area of the base of tower. Ann had purchased the previous owner's oval dining table, which fitted neatly and allowed Ann to host the maximum number of dinner guests that the small room would allow.[24]

Upstairs on the first floor was a large L-shaped drawing room, which contained the Flemings' best furniture, as well as their art collection – including a portrait of Ann by Lucian Freud and Ian's beloved inlaid-brass drawings. Despite spanning four floors and a basement, the house suffered from a dearth of bedrooms. Ann took up most of the second floor with a suite of bedroom, bathroom and dressing room. Ann and Ian had decided that Nanny Sillick and Caspar would spend the majority of their time at White Cliffs, but there was just enough room on the second floor to accommodate baby and nanny during their occasional visits.[25]

On the top floor were two small bedrooms divided by a bathroom. One was for Fionn, while the other, smaller one was for Ian. Rigid orderliness reigned in this small attic room. Designed to be like a ship's cabin, the room contained a small, single bed, covered with an extraordinary quilt depicting Queen Victoria. Two of the walls were decorated with oppressive striped wallpaper, while the other two walls were devoted to bookshelves which housed Ian's impressive book collection and assortment of busts. The whole effect was small, cosy and individual – an eclectic room reflective of a diverse inhabitant.[26]

The Flemings' contrasting tastes in interior decoration was reflective of the disparity in their marriage. Ann preferred delicate, regency furniture displayed in light rooms, mixing modern watercolours and oils with more traditional portraits and pictures. Ian preferred more masculine, dark furniture, favouring heavy family portraits and oils. In the main rooms and most of the house, Ann's taste was largely on display, with much of Ian's individual taste relegated to his small bedroom.[27]

The household was completed by a new cook, Mary Crickmere, and her husband Edgar, who worked as Ian's valet and served at table in the evenings. Ann had no real enthusiasm about catering for her parties and would leave the menus to Mrs Crickmere, while she focused on the guest list and the ambiance. Later, when Ann complained about the money spent on food, Mrs Cricklade furiously listed the number of people who had been entertained at the house in the previous month. Ann had hosted at least one dinner and two lunches every week. As Ann spent every Friday to Monday in Kent, Mrs Crickmere pointed out that over half of all the meals cooked at Victoria Square had been for guests.[28]

Escaping the ongoing building work at Victoria Square, Ian undertook an assignment to the South of France to profile the underwater diver Jacques Cousteau for *The Sunday Times*.[29] Ann decided to accompany her husband. She planned to stay with Somerset Maugham at the Villa Mauresque, in Antibes, while Ian spent time with Cousteau in the bay of Marseilles. The trip also meant that Ian would be away from London when his first novel was published on 13 April 1953.[30]

Ann and Ian were reunited at the Villa Mauresque in mid-April before heading back to London via Chantilly, where they spent a night with the Duff Coopers. When Ian's car refused to start, Ian was introduced to Diana Cooper's infamously terrifying driving. Famed for mounting pavements to avoid traffic jams, scattering terrified pedestrians, Lady Diana roared the Flemings from Chantilly to Dieppe in record time.[31]

Returning to London, Ian was gratified to find that *Casino Royale* had received generally good reviews, although there had been some shock at the torture scenes. Ann was reticent about the publication. When Ian had offered to dedicate the book to her, she had refused, as she was not keen to be associated with the themes of gambling and torture. However, she did complete a small but concerted PR campaign on her husband's behalf. She wrote to important, powerful friends like Lord Beaverbrook to ask for the book to be reviewed.[32]

As the Victoria Square renovations neared completion, Ann revved up for a round of ambitious entertaining. In early October 1953, she hosted a party to celebrate Cyril Connolly's fiftieth birthday. Ian valiantly tried to engage with his wife's social plans, sitting next to the former Lady Mary Dunn and making animated conversation.[33] The evening was loud, drunken and very successful.

Determined to re-establish herself as one of the great hostesses, Ann went into overdrive, precipitating further conflict within the Fleming marriage. As Ann became more social, Ian retreated into himself. This, in turn, drove his wife even further into the arms of her social circle.

On 1 January 1954, the Flemings were preparing for their departure to Goldeneye when they received news that Duff Cooper had died on board the French liner *Colombie*. En route to the Caribbean, between France and Spain, he had suffered a gastro-intestinal haemorrhage and died in the early hours of New Year's Day, 1954.[34] Lady Diana Cooper, who had been with her husband when he died, was grief-stricken. Ann met her old friend on her return to London and did her best to comfort her as Diana rehashed every detail of the death. Worrying that Diana was drinking heavily and to excess, Ann was reluctant to leave for Jamaica until other friends rallied around the widow.[35] Ian was suffering from a bad case of flu, so the Flemings decided to miss Duff Cooper's small funeral at Belvoir Castle and headed straight to Goldeneye and a warmer climate.

Having left the UK feeling morose, things did not improve as Ian's health continued to suffer. Following their annual tradition of inviting a couple of guests to Goldeneye, Ann had invited her friend Tanis Philips and her husband, Teddy. Born Tanis Guinness, the sister of Loel Guinness, she had first married the son of the Earl of Sandwich, then the American songwriter Howard Dietz, before divorcing him and marrying Charles 'Teddy' Philips. Ann had known Tanis before the war, and Laura had stayed with Tanis during one of her separations from Eric.

But the visit was not a success. Ann and Ian were nauseated by the Philips' habit of using endless endearments and pet names which included Lion, Bear and the vomitous 'Bearingtons'.[36] Ian, who was busy writing his third James Bond novel, *Moonraker*, was particularly irritated and demanded that Ann ask their guests to refrain from using pet names. Understandably, Ann was too embarrassed to comply. When the Philips decided to leave

Goldeneye early, a row erupted when Ian angrily accused his wife of being a traitor for attempting to mollify their guests, rather than back him up.[37]

Ann and Ian returned to the UK in March 1954 in time for the UK publication of Ian's second novel, *Live and Let Die* on 5 April. While Ian enjoyed a jaunt to the South of France to enlist Somerset Maugham as a contributor for the Kemsley Press, Ann returned to her duties as a hostess with a vengeance. Initially, Loelia Westminster and Ann were to host a joint fancy dress ball at Send Grove, the regency house that Loelia had bought in 1947 after divorcing the 2nd Duke of Westminster. But Ann rapidly took control and the event became known as 'Ann's ball'.[38] The evening clearly took a toll on the normally calm and composed Ann: when Evelyn Waugh and Diana Cooper arrived over an hour late for the pre-ball dinner, she was furious and seemed barely able to spit a welcome.[39] But she perked up as the alcohol flowed and the dancing began, with guests partying until the sun came up.

This was also the year that the Flemings started another tradition which would continue for the whole of their marriage: separate holidays. For the next few years, Ann and Ian would spend the early part of the year at Goldeneye together, while Ian wrote another book. Then, in the summer, Ian would travel to the United States to stay with the Ivar Bryces, generally using the time to tinker with his manuscript. The Fleming marriage thrived when Ann and Ian were apart. Increasingly cantankerous in each other's company, when separated, husband and wife would pine for each other and write romantic letters to each other full of longing. As Sara Morrison concludes of the Fleming marriage, 'They were always better at courtship than marriage […] it was the excitement that put them on their mettle.'[40]

Initially Ann was invited to join Ian in America but she always refused. Her initial low opinion of Bryce never improved and she would use Ian's absence to visit her own friends abroad. When Ian left for the United States in August 1954, Ann made for Greece, where she had been invited to Hydra by Paddy Leigh Fermor and his partner, Joan Rayner.[41] The only other guest was the academic Maurice Bowra, the warden of Wadham College. He and Ann had previously met through Cyril Connolly, but their time together on Hydra brought them closer. Paddy accompanied Ann and Maurice on the boat back to Athens, from where they would fly to London via Rome. After a dinner accompanied by lashings of ouzo and retsina, Maurice went to bed in their small hotel, while Ann and Paddy drunkenly climbed up to the acropolis and explored.[42]

Arriving back in London, Ann had to rush down to White Cliffs to relieve Caspar's nanny. Nanny Sillick had requested some time off, which Ann had happily agreed to and then forgotten all about. When the date for Nanny's holiday arrived and Ann was still in Greece, she furiously delayed her much-needed holiday.[43] Having bolted to St Margaret's Bay and appeased Nanny, Ann then charged back to London Airport to collect Ian.

A romantic reunion was ruined when Ian arrived covered in unattractive sores. Melodramatically assuming that the sores were caused by syphilis caught from a woman, Ann was furious until Ian explained that his affliction was caused by an allergic reaction to a cold relief pill.[44] A contrite Ann and a subdued Ian returned to White Cliffs for the remainder of the summer.

At the end of August, Ann and Ian travelled to Shane's Castle in Ireland to celebrate Raymond's twenty-first birthday on 1 September. As he had come of age, Raymond would now inherit the family land of 120,000 acres and what remained of the property. The previous house had been burned down in 1922 by the IRA and the family now used a house attached to the stables.[45] Ann was appalled by the state of the building, which was damp and had dry rot in the walls. Nevertheless, she helped Raymond arrange the party, decorating the house and digging out the ancient family silver and linen.[46]

In October, Ian went on another extended trip to the United States to research his next book accompanied by Ivar Bryce. As Ian was spending time with the friend that Ann liked least, she took advantage of her husband's absence and invited Ian's least favourite of *her* friends to stay at White Cliffs – Peter Quennell, James Pope-Hennessy and Lucian Freud.[47] The group were all part of the coterie that Ian described as Ann's 'boobies' – a derogatory nickname coined by Evelyn Waugh for the men he viewed as fawning over Ann.[48] He returned in time to accompany Ann to St Margaret's Westminster for the wedding of her niece, Sara Long, to Charles Morrison on 28 October 1954.

With the return of Ian came the return of conflict in Ann's life. Planning their usual post-Christmas trip to Goldeneye, the couple disagreed about whether Caspar was old enough to go with them. Their son was now 2 and Ian worried that Caspar and the attendant Nanny Sillick would hamper activities at Goldeneye, while Ann wanted her son with her.[49] Caspar was the intense focus of parental love and increasingly becoming the only harmonising aspect of Ann and Ian's relationship. The Flemings were unequivocally united in their love for Caspar and determined to do the very best that they could as parents. As Sara confirms, 'They did their damndest to be the best parents that they could be.'[50]

This time Ann gave in and agreed that Caspar should remain at White Cliffs. But as a compromise, Ann was allowed to invite Peter Quennell to

Goldeneye. To Ann's further delight, she discovered that Evelyn Waugh was planning to be in Jamaica after Christmas. Ian was less than thrilled that his island idyll was to be invaded by two of Ann's 'boobies'.

Before leaving for Jamaica, the Flemings celebrated Christmas 1954 in St Margaret's Bay. The festive period proved particularly exhausting for Ann. As well as hosting Peter Quennell and her father and stepmother, Ann had various domestic crises. Normally, White Cliffs was looked after by a general housekeeper-cum-cook, Mrs Davies. In order to deal with the extra guests, Ann had asked the redoubtable Mary Crickmere and her husband to come to White Cliffs for the Christmas period. This caused friction with Mrs Davies, who openly resented having Mrs Crickmere in the kitchen. The simmering resentment eventually exploded into a monumental row when Mrs Crickmere criticised Mrs Davies' cooking, resulting in Mrs Davies melodramatically threatening to drown herself in the sea.[51]

Ann calmed both domestics before another crisis loomed. As there was insufficient space for the guests as well as the staff at White Cliffs, the Flemings had rented the next-door cottage. When Ann had arrived ahead of the Crickmeres, she found the rental house in a squalid state. She was forced to do a frantic clean-up – throwing dirty items of clothing and bedding into a laundry cupboard. During dinner on Christmas Eve, smoke began emanating from the cupboard and soon the whole cottage was ablaze. The cause of the fire was initially blamed on Ann inadvertently throwing a cigarette into the laundry cupboard with the dirty bedding. She vociferously protested until faulty wiring was found to be the true cause of the fire.[52]

Exhausted and ready for a holiday, Ann then refused to leave for Goldeneye on 1 January. She had been horrified when a flight from Heathrow to New York had landed short of the runway at Prestwick and burst into flames in the early hours of Christmas Day, killing twenty-eight passengers. Worried that Caspar would be left an orphan if both she and Ian were wiped out in a plane crash, Ann refused to fly. Ian was furious and left for Jamaica anyway, leaving his wife to travel across the Atlantic by boat.[53]

Added to her reluctance to fly was Ann's overall reluctance to go to Goldeneye. She had enjoyed the Jamaica holidays at the beginning of her relationship with Ian, but the house remained the domain of her husband. Goldeneye was where he could be solitary and quiet with writing being his main focus. Ann lamented the lack of social life, finding the holidays increasingly dull. A social life also provided a diversion from her marriage. At Goldeneye, the atmosphere was becoming increasingly fractious as the Flemings only had each other.

Ann finally left for Jamaica on 19 January 1955, suffering from laryngitis. Glumly, she arrived in New York before flying to Nassau and then on to Goldeneye, arriving voiceless and exhausted in early February. Peter Quennell arrived shortly afterwards.[54] He immediately invoked the ire of Ian by marching across the garden to swim every morning. Ian was sensitive to any disturbances in his writing routine and claimed that the morning appearance of Peter interrupted his flow. When Ann was asked to speak to Quennell, she became furious, accusing Ian of finding any excuse to make her friends feel unwelcome. When a hugely embarrassed Ann eventually had to ask Quennell to use another route to the beach, he was amused rather than upset, antagonising Ian even more.[55]

Leaving Jamaica on 2 March 1955, Ann flew to New York and sailed back to London while Ian remained at Goldeneye. Refreshed and recovered from her health woes after a sunny holiday, Ann was looking forward to hosting several parties back in London. But Ian was surprisingly bereft without his wife. The day after Ann left the island, Ian wrote poetically to his wife, 'When I saw that the big bird got you up in its claws I went back to sunset [...] and loved you for an hour [...] I woke up earlier than usual and cursed you for not being there.'[56]

Ann was becoming increasingly fed up with the restrictions of the White Cliffs 'cottage'. Always fearing boredom, she wanted to be able to have people to stay for the weekend. During a July weekend house party, the shortcomings of the house were apparent when Ann had Peter Quennell and his girlfriend, Sonia 'Spider' Leon, to stay. Decorously, the pair were given separate bedrooms while fellow guest Evelyn Waugh had to be farmed out to a hotel in nearby Folkestone.[57]

Reluctant to move and understandably anxious about money after the Victoria Square renovation, Ian was not keen on Ann's idea for a new country house, causing more friction within the Fleming marriage. Ian was happy with the status quo, as St Margaret's was convenient for London and, more importantly, was close to several golf courses. But by the time he left for his annual trip to stay with the Bryces in America, he had tentatively agreed to the purchase of a house in the country.

After a restful three weeks away at Black Hole Hollow Farm, the Bryces' home in upstate New York, Ian returned to Victoria Square to find that Ann had started house-hunting in earnest. While Ian preferred to look for a manageable home in the Home Counties, near a golf course, Ann had bigger ideas. She wanted a grand country home in the smart countryside of Gloucestershire or Wiltshire, where there was a complete dearth of golf courses. Through a sequence of compromises, mostly made on Ian's part, the Flemings began to look in Oxfordshire, Gloucestershire and Wiltshire.

Ann yielded enough to see several properties in Buckinghamshire, after which the Flemings visited Pamela and Michael Berry at their home, Oving House, near Aylesbury.[58] The Berrys had purchased the Georgian property from Randolph Churchill the previous year and had ample resources to renovate and remodel the house, installing a pavilion and swimming pool. Seeing the results of the extensive and expensive building work, Ian began to quake, fearing Ann would take inspiration for their own country home.

When Ian travelled to Turkey in early October on another research trip, Hugo Charteris arrived to stay for a week at Victoria Square.[59] Like many sibling relationships, the bond between Ann and Hugo could veer from loving to volcanic within seconds. Although Ann was maternal towards her siblings, and particularly indulgent of her brother, she reacted badly when Hugo intimated that he wanted money. Hugo's writing career was not providing enough income for his growing family and he asked his sister to give him some of her divorce settlement. Ann was furious and refused. This triggered a row, which quickly turned ugly when Hugo accused his sister of marrying Esmond purely for his money.[60]

Hugo had unwittingly hit a sore point with his sister. While she appeared to lead a comfortable life, cushioned by the settlement from Esmond, Ann's lavish spending on entertaining and decorating, as well as her plans for a large country home, had dented her capital. Used to a life free from financial restraints as Lady Rothermere, Ann had become pathological over her money worries – a fear which was to last for the rest of her life. Both siblings were furious after the row and Hugo departed for Scotland without having made peace with his sister. In a petty last move, he even left money in an ashtray to pay for a phone call he had made.[61]

After Christmas at Shane's Castle, in early 1956 Ian departed for Jamaica. For the first time since their marriage, Ann chose not to go to Goldeneye. While publicly she claimed that she felt she could not leave Caspar and Nanny Sillick at White Cliffs, maternal instinct had never stopped her from travelling in the past. When Ian travelled to New York en route to Jamaica, the Bryces suspected a separation and implored Ian to make it up with Ann.[62]

The letters between the Flemings during this period are loving and affectionate, with Ian beseeching Ann to join him at Goldeneye. Ian describes leaving Victoria Square and mournfully saying goodbye to Ann's bedroom, before pilfering a picture of her and Caspar, which he keeps beside him in Jamaica. Ann replies in kind, recalling their 'wonderful lives at Goldeneye' and rather archly saying, 'I hope you won't learn to be happy there without me.'[63] As always with the Flemings, their marriage seemed to grow stronger by spending time apart.

But it was not just reluctance to go to Jamaica which stopped Ann from joining her husband. In mid-January she entered a health farm near Godalming in Surrey called Enton Hall. Ostensibly, she was going for treatment for fibrositis – a condition which causes tiredness and muscle pain and is frequently linked to stress.[64] The reality was that Ann was seeking help for her increasing dependency on barbiturates.

Barbiturates at that time were seen as a wonder drug, with amobarbital and phenobarbital used to treat everything from insomnia to anxiety. Barbiturates are, in essence, sedatives that have a calming effect on the body. The benefits of barbiturates are almost instantaneous, making the drugs popular the world over and widely prescribed during the 1950s. Patients suffering from insomnia were able to fall asleep quickly and sleep for longer, while patients with anxiety often reported feelings of euphoria after treatment. The dangers of barbiturates and their highly addictive nature only came to public attention in the 1960s following a number of high-profile deaths, including the overdoses of Marilyn Monroe and Margaret Sullavan.

Ann had been prescribed phenobarbital to help her sleep. Common side effects of the drug are a lack of co-ordination and slurred speech, with users appearing muddled and confused. She was also prescribed dextroamphetamine – known by the brand name of Dexedrine – to soothe the anxiety she was beginning to suffer from. This drug-taking, combined with the high level of alcohol consumed by Ann, could easily have been fatal. While by no means addicted to alcohol or drugs, Ann was worried about her barbiturate intake. As a disciplined, together character, she hated any loss of self-control. As her niece recollects, 'control mattered a lot. Losing control would have frightened her to bits.'[65]

Before the advent of rehabilitative centres, health farms were the only option for tackling drug dependency. Enton Hall had been opened as a hydropathic centre in 1949, with a focus on a naturopathic medicine. Known as the 'nature cure', life at Enton was dominated by regular exercise, massage, saunas and a natural diet of fruit and vegetables. Enton Hall had rapidly become the fashionable place to dry out from alcohol or drugs, with many society figures staying. During her treatment, Ann retained her sharp sense of humour, writing to Evelyn Waugh that Enton was 'less fashionable than Tring [Champneys] but I was encouraged by the brochure for although the dining room looked melancholy the plates were heaped with food'.[66]

Ann chose to stay at Enton for only two weeks, leaving on 24 January 1956.[67] She had temporarily weaned herself off using phenobarbital to help her sleep, but as her marriage to Ian began to break down, Ann would routinely resort to barbiturates to help her sleep and tackle her anxiety.

Feeling healthy after her stay at Enton, Ann began to look forward to Ian's return from the Caribbean in late February. In Jamaica, Ian was less than enthusiastic about returning to London. Unbeknownst to Ann, he had started an affair with Blanche Blackwell, the woman that Ann would later archly refer to as Ian's 'Jamaican wife'.[68]

16

IAN AND BLANCHE –
ANN AND GAITSKELL

Ian and Blanche met at a dinner hosted by Charles and Mildred D'Costa at the tail end of Ian's solitary stay at Goldeneye. Ian was instantly attracted to Blanche, who was petite with dark features and lovely legs. But he was far from his usual charming self. When the dinner conversation turned to the growing homosexual community on the north coast of Jamaica, and Blanche talked of her family-owned property in the area, Ian crassly asked if she was a lesbian.[1]

Despite his clumsiness, Blanche later asked Ian for drinks at her temporary home in Kingston. Ian managed to parlay this into an overnight stay – which he naturally played down in letters to Ann. In return, Blanche was invited for a swim at the beach at Goldeneye, where they discovered their mutual love of swimming and snorkelling, as well as a shared interest in exotic fish.[2] Their burgeoning friendship was greatly encouraged by their mutual friend, Noël Coward. Blanche was open, warm and friendly, whereas many islanders, including Coward, felt Ann was distant and cold. As Sara Morrison confirms, 'Because of the aunt's ever decreasing visits to Goldeneye […] she was made to seem unkind.'[3]

Born in 1912 in Costa Rica, Blanche belonged to an old Jamaican family, the Lindos, who had come to the island in the seventeenth century. Returning to Kingston as a child, she was later sent to England at the age of 16 to attend Garrett Hall, a pseudo-finishing school near Manchester. In 1936, she married Joseph Blackwell, a captain in the Irish Guards and heir to the Crosse & Blackwell food fortune. The couple had a son, Christopher, in 1937, before returning to Jamaica to run the Blackwell family estate. The Blackwells separated in 1945, divorcing in 1949, and Blanche returned to England to oversee her son's education at Harrow. In 1955, she moved permanently back to Jamaica and in early 1956 she started construction on a house at Bolt, only 4 miles from Goldeneye.[4]

Leaving Blanche behind, Ian returned to Victoria Square on 21 March 1956 to find Ann both ill with flu and embroiled in another Charteris family row. Guy had been admitted to hospital in Birmingham and Ann, despite her own illness, found herself in the invidious position of having to relay news of their father to all of her siblings separately – Hugo, in Scotland, Laura, who was in Paris, and Mary Rose, who was staying in Braintree.[5] For Ian, the contrast could not have been starker. He had left behind the warmth and sunshine of Goldeneye, as well as an exciting new romance, for a cold, rainy London and an ill-tempered and embittered wife.

But Ian was not the only Fleming to be straying from his marriage. Ann and Ian were part of a generation and social circle which accepted infidelity with equanimity, despite the occasional flash of jealousy. An affair alone would never have threatened the Fleming marriage, but it is curious that, by some bizarre synchronicity, in 1956 both Flemings embarked on affairs which were to become pivotal in both of their lives.

Towards the end of 1955, Ann had met the Labour leader Hugh Gaitskell. Always attracted to power, Ann found herself fascinated by the politician, despite being vastly different in outlooks. 'Politically they were poles apart,' Sara recalls.[6] With her upbringing, wealth and aristocratic friends, Ann was staunchly Conservative, while Gaitskell was firmly on the side of social equality. But Gaitskell was an absorbing paradox.

His background and upbringing should have placed him squarely on the Conservative right. After spending his early years in Burma, Gaitskell attended the Dragon Prep School in Oxford before Winchester College. After his father's death in 1915, his mother married Charles Wodehouse and returned to Burma, while Hugh remained at school in England. From 1924 to 1927 Gaitskell read PPE at New College, Oxford, where his left-leaning sympathies began to form.[7]

During the General Strike of 1926, Gaitskell supported the workers and fundraised for the miners who remained on strike until November 1926. After graduating, he lectured in economics for the Workers' Educational Association – a charity founded to supply free education to adults. The experience changed Gaitskell. For the first time, he could see the huge imparity between the upper and working classes and he vowed to bring about change.

Having gained experience of government during the war as an adviser to the Ministry of Economic Warfare, in 1945 he was elected as Labour MP for Leeds South. Gaitskell rose quickly through the ranks of the Labour Party. As a protégé of the Labour Chancellor of the Exchequer Hugh Dalton, Gaitskell was regarded as one of the rising stars of the post-war Labour Party. In May 1946, he was made Parliamentary Undersecretary for

Fuel and Power, before being promoted to Minister of Fuel and Power on 7 October 1947.

After the Labour Party scraped a re-election victory in February 1950, Gaitskell was appointed Minister for Economic Affairs. When Stafford Cripps privately announced his intention to resign as Chancellor of the Exchequer in the spring of 1950, he was persuaded to stay but take a long holiday to recover from ill health. Gaitskell took on the role of Chancellor *in loco*. When Cripps resigned in October 1950, Gaitskell was selected as Chancellor, despite his relative inexperience.

Labour survived the 1950 general election and Gaitskell remained as Chancellor, but when the Conservatives won the snap election of 1951, Gaitskell moved to the opposition benches as Shadow Chancellor of the Exchequer. When the Conservatives again won the 1955 election, the Labour leader Clement Attlee announced his intention to resign, prompting a leadership contest.

At that time, leaders of the Labour Party were chosen solely by incumbent Labour MPs. Ministers had to choose between Gaitskell, Herbert Morrison and Aneurin Bevan. Gaitskell was popular with many of his colleagues and seemed assured of victory, but his great rival Aneurin Bevan made a last-ditch attempt to stop Gaitskell from becoming leader. He suggested that both men stand aside for Herbert Morrison, who was a popular public figure, having been instrumental in the national morale boosting Festival of Britain in 1951. Gaitskell refused Bevan's suggestion. On 14 December 1955, Gaitskell was elected opposition leader with 58 per cent of the Labour MPs' votes and a whopping eighty-seven-person majority.[8]

Gaitskell's political and public persona were at odds with the private man. In public, Gaitskell seemed austere and patrician. Opinions about him were mixed. 'He seemed pretty humourless. A bit arrogant. Sonorous. Just no lightness to him,' recalls the political historian David Edington.[9]

He was also not universally popular with the general public and was viewed as a killjoy because of his association with austerity measures. As Chancellor of the Exchequer in 1951, he had introduced prescription charges on spectacles and dentures in a desperate bid to bring down the already escalating costs of the NHS. The introduction was viewed as a direct contradiction of the Labour Party aims for the NHS as set out in 1948.[10] He introduced further austerity measures after the 1951 spring budget, when he increased purchase tax on luxury items such as cars and television sets, and even levelled an entertainment tax on cinema tickets.[11]

In private, Gaitskell was very different from his rather dour public image. He enjoyed dancing and could be charming and funny, with a sharp wit.

On 9 April 1937 – his thirty-first birthday – Gaitskell married Dora Frost. A keen Labour supporter since the age of 16, Dora was an admirable and much-admired political spouse. Serious, down to earth and rather dumpy and unglamorous in appearance, Dora was everything that Ann was not.[12]

On the face of it, the relationship between Gaitskell and Ann made no sense. Ann herself would later admit to her niece that during her regular Tuesday afternoon trysts with Gaitskell she would picture the much more handsome Labour MP, Anthony Crosland.[13] When questioned further by her niece about the reasons for her attraction to Gaitskell, Ann responded, 'I honestly can't tell you, darling.'[14]

The attraction can be explained by Ann's character. 'She had a fascination with power,' her niece remembers. 'Aunt Ann's love for the powerful was the ultimate aphrodisiac.'[15] And Gaitskell was certainly powerful. His premature death and the passage of time have resulted in his legacy largely becoming forgotten, but in the 1950s he was a dynamo on the political scene.

He had been the youngest Chancellor since Peel and now he was leading a political party that seemed assured of victory in the next election. Like the appeal of Tony Blair in the 1990s, Gaitskell seemed like a palatable leader to those who would not have traditionally voted Labour. For someone like Ann, who did not seek power for herself but loved to be surrounded by it, Gaitskell was a rising political star and she was determined to be in his orbit.

The relationship did not influence Ann politically. She remained right-leaning and would campaign for the Tories throughout her life. But the relationship affected Gaitskell. While he remained publicly socialist, Gaitskell privately began to loosen up and shed his dour image.

Dora was remarkably unperturbed by her husband's affair with such a noted political hostess. 'Dora did the grown-up thing of rising above it, which annoyed the aunt,' Sara remembers.[16] Initially included in social events at Victoria Square, Dora quickly extricated herself, choosing to completely ignore the affair, despite Gaitskell's increasingly ludicrous reasons for seeing Ann.

Later that summer, while Ian made his annual pilgrimage to the United States to stay with the Bryces, Ann made for Antibes and Somerset Maugham at the Villa Mauresque. The atmosphere was particularly charged during her stay as Maugham was in the process of writing his will. Always a lover of intrigue, Ann enjoyed oscillating between secret chats with the potential beneficiaries – Maugham's daughter, Liza, as well as Maugham's companion, Alan Searle.[17]

The end of her stay coincided with the arrival of Lady Diana Cooper. Keen to gain the approval for her new relationship from her oldest friend,

Ann confided in Diana about her relationship with Gaitskell. Having heard gossip, Diana was unsurprised, but questioned her friend's taste, as she had a low opinion of both the Labour Party and their leader. But she signalled her approval by extending an invitation to both Ann and Gaitskell to Chantilly in November – the lovers' first trip abroad.[18]

Returning from her jaunt to Chantilly, Ann received a call from the Conservative MP Alan Lennox-Boyd, who discreetly asked if he might borrow Goldeneye. Knowing of Ann's inability to keep a secret, the MP urged her to stay quiet about his request. Feeling that the gossip was worthless, Ann promptly forgot about the conversation.[19] But then Lennox-Boyd came to see Ian and admitted that the loan of the house was for Prime Minister Anthony Eden and his wife, Clarissa. The prime minister was shattered by the debacle of the Suez Crisis and needed a break away from prying eyes.

Ian could be relied upon to be discreet but Ann was a different matter. Ian eventually confided in his wife, who managed to keep quiet until the official announcement of the prime minister's departure for Jamaica on 24 November. Then Ann went into overdrive, giving indiscreet interviews to the press and almost immediately regretted her rash comments. In a letter to Evelyn Waugh on the day of the Edens' departure for Jamaica, Ann says, 'Ian was cross that I said anything detrimental about his beloved house [...] and would I keep my trap shut: alas, I did not take his advice.'[20]

The holiday was recuperative for the Edens but it was a bad political move. In the prime minister's absence there were rumbles about potential successors. When the Edens returned to Downing Street, Ann was invited to Number 10 in December 1956 as a thank you for the loan of Goldeneye. The atmosphere was tense as pressure mounted on the prime minister to resign due to his mishandling of the Suez Crisis, as well as his ongoing health problems.

Ann innocuously asked Clarissa Eden whether the couple had met anyone interesting during their stay at Goldeneye. The prime minister's wife explained that the couple had been very antisocial while on holiday, before adding that Blanche Blackwell had been a frequent visitor.[21] As a result, Ann immediately decided to resume her annual trip to Jamaica after Christmas, convincing Ian to allow 4-year-old Caspar to accompany his parents to Goldeneye for the first time.

The Flemings travelled separately to Jamaica. Ian flew to the island via New York while Ann travelled aboard the *Coronia* with Caspar, Nanny Sillick and Raymond O'Neill. Leaving Liverpool on 2 January 1957, the crossing was very stormy, with Nanny becoming seasick and Ann resorting to Dramamine and gin. After a brief stopover in Bermuda, the *Coronia* arrived in Kingston on 14 January.[22]

Arriving at Goldeneye, Ann was irritated to find that Blanche had made some interior design improvements to the spartan house, which included whitewashing the walls and installing new furniture. Ostensibly, this was in preparation for the Edens' visit the previous year, but Ann suspected that the redecoration was the sign of a rival marking her territory, causing more rows between Ann and Ian.

While she was peeved at the changes, Ann did not view Blanche as a threat to her marriage. She suspected an affair between Ian and Blanche but she was not possessive of her husband. She took an 'academic and objective approach' to her husband's infidelities.[23] 'There was a sort of "that's what little boys do" approach,' her niece recalls.[24] But her dispassion did not mean that Ann was happy to condone Ian's behaviour. 'She went to Goldeneye for an ever-shorter time after the advent of Blanche,' notes Sara.[25] Nor was she friendly to Blanche, treating her in an offhand, cold manner.

Blanche was so irritated by Ann's dismissive behaviour that she felt justified in continuing an affair with Ian. When Ann left Jamaica, leaving Ian alone at Goldeneye to finish *Dr No*, the affair between Ian and Blanche resumed in earnest.[26]

Ian travelled back to London in time for his stepdaughter's twenty-first birthday party on the evening of 9 March. Known traditionally as 'coming out', the party was a meshing of Fionn's young social circle and her mother's older friends. While the young danced, Ann surrounded herself with a coterie of friends including Maurice Bowra, David Cecil and Livia Deakin. Ann enjoyed seeing her daughter and her young friends dancing, despite Bowra complaining about the noise. Mindful of her ever-dwindling capital and in sharp contrast to her days of outré entertaining at Warwick House, Ann later grumbled about the cost of the party. She resented the £83 cost of the warm champagne and bemoaned the lack of food.[27]

Money continued to worry Ann and became another cause of conflict with Ian. In June, the Flemings hosted Hugo Charteris at Victoria Square. He came to stay for a week and Ann found herself caught between loyalty to her husband and her adored younger brother. Having capitulated to her brother's repeated entreaties for money, she had tentatively agreed to buy Hugo and his wife Virginia a house, using some of her settlement from Esmond. When Ian heard of the plan, he flew into a rage and forbad his wife to do anything of the sort.[28] The animosity between the two men blew into a full-scale row that continued for the majority of the week. Ann did not help matters by asking her brother to join her and Ian for a weekend at St Margaret's Bay. Ian was furious and refused to drive either sibling to Kent, forcing Ann and Hugo to take the train while he drove down alone.[29]

Despite their anxieties about money, after months of unsuccessful house-hunting, the Flemings purchased the Old Palace in Bekesbourne, Kent, in September 1957.[30] Originally built for the sixteenth-century Archbishop of Canterbury, Thomas Cranmer, the manor had been largely demolished during the English Civil War. The remains had been incorporated into the eighteenth-century building that replaced the original palace, creating a smorgasbord of styles. With tall chimneys and castellated parapet surrounding the roof, the house gives a grand impression but on a small scale. There were six bedrooms, so Ann finally had space to entertain her friends for country weekends.

From the beginning, the Old Palace was a disaster for the Flemings and placed huge strain on the marriage. Shortly after moving into the house in late November, Ann claimed that the house was haunted after she heard ghostly footsteps and doors banging. A more tangible disturbance was the nearby railway line.[31] Ann began to complain vociferously about her new home – laying the blame for the purchase squarely at her husband's feet.[32]

Ann was shaken out of her grump over the Old Palace by a rather embarrassing lawsuit brought against Ian's mother in November 1957. After moving to the Bahamas, Eve Fleming had become engaged to the penniless Marquess of Winchester. Despite the temptation of becoming a marchioness, Eve eventually called off the engagement, after which the 90-year-old marquess married the 50-year-old Bapsybanoo 'Bapsy' Pavry.

The marriage had not been a success and the marquess had quickly resumed his relationship with Eve Fleming. The furious marchioness sued Eve in a Bahamian court for enticement of her husband, winning a settlement from Mrs Fleming. But when Eve left the Bahamas to live in Monte Carlo, accompanied by the marquess, Lady Winchester brought a new action against Eve in the British High Court.[33]

The action was mortifying for Ian and his brothers but Eve seemed to relish the attention. She dressed in progressively more outlandish, eye-catching outfits every day for court. Like her mother-in-law, Ann enjoyed being in the eye of the storm. She revelled in the hilarity of the situation and delighted in her mother-in-law's ludicrous wardrobe choices. Eventually, the Fleming brothers were forced to take their mother in hand.

The brothers coerced Mrs Fleming into a more conservative wardrobe, which Ann described as 'hospital matron clothes. On Friday the poor old thing wished to wear a yellow satin picture hat with grey pearl hatpins the size of tennis balls – they had her out of that in a trice.'[34]

The presiding judge, Mr Justice Devlin, ruled that Eve had financed the marquess' attempted annulment of his marriage to Lady Winchester. On appeal the following year, the finding was overturned and Lady Winchester was ordered to pay costs. Eve returned to Monte Carlo and lived with the marquess until his death at the age of 99 in 1962.

Back at Bekesbourne, the Fleming marriage had reached crisis point. The purchase of the house had been a mistake and Ian resented being blamed for buying a property he never wanted. The rows escalated, affecting the health of both Ann and Ian. Ann became increasingly anxious and, unable to sleep, resorted to Dexedrine. Ian was already in poor health and resorted to drink and cigarettes.

In December 1957, over dinner at Scott's restaurant, both Flemings agreed to air their grievances about each other and their marriage. Ian went first, detailing his concerns over his wife's excessive spending and her recurrent barbiturate usage. Ann was so upset by her husband's litany of criticism that she was unable to offer her own feedback and the dinner came to a premature end.[35]

In the short term, Ann and Ian agreed that they both needed space from one another. After Christmas 1957 at Bekesbourne, Ian travelled alone to Goldeneye while Ann remained in Kent. The parting had been so acrimonious that Ian later admitted that he had seriously thought about spending the night before his departure at his club.[36]

Responding to one of Ian's criticisms, and worried that her use of barbiturates could be contributing to her increasing ill health, Ann again chose to enter the health farm at Enton Hall in January 1958. In a letter from Goldeneye, Ian pleaded with his wife, 'I pray that Enton's prison walls have mended your darling heart and somehow got you off this tragic switchback of pills which I implore you to stop.'[37] In a pitiful, searing exchange, Ian brutally describes Ann's behaviour, 'You've no idea how they change you – first the febrile, almost hysterical gaiety and then those terrible snores that seem to come from the tomb!'[38]

Ann came away from Enton feeling a little better, but her marriage still weighed heavily on her mind. Previously, periods of separation had made the Flemings' marriage stronger. But in early 1958, the letters between Ann and Ian were less loving and the couple continued to row about the Old Palace. Ian was furious that Ann did not recognise how hard he had worked to install the family in their new home in time for Christmas. Ann responded with more complaints about the house, claiming that she genuinely believed another move would help their marriage.

In what was fast becoming a pattern in the Fleming marriage, Ian eventually capitulated again and agreed that Ann could look for another country house. But his agreement came with a stark warning: 'Your pot is down to about 70,000 and two more years at 10,000 a year will reduce it to your iron ration of 50 after which we shall just have to live on income.'[39] The insinuation of the message was clear. Any further house purchases would be Ann's financial responsibility.

When Ian returned to London in March 1958, he and Ann were both determined to make their marriage work. Ann's intention was hampered slightly when she discovered that Blanche Blackwell would be staying at Goldeneye, free of charge, while the building of her own house was completed.[40]

Despite this, Ann and Ian decided to embark on a second honeymoon. Following a trip to the Seychelles on assignment for the Kemsley Press, Ian intended to meet Ann in Rome before the couple would travel on to Venice for Ian's fiftieth birthday on 28 May. However, the gods seemed to conspire against the Flemings as Ian cut his shin on some underwater coral during his stay in the Seychelles. When the wound became infected, Ian was transported to the capital city of Victoria, where he was pumped full of penicillin and forced to stay in hospital for a week.[41]

When the Flemings were reunited in Rome, Ian was in a foul mood following his exhausting journey. Making the best of it, the couple spent a few days in Rome before boarding the Laguna Express for Venice – Ann's first trip to the city – where Ian had booked the hugely luxurious Princess Margaret Suite at the Gritti Palace Hotel. The world's most romantic city seemed to successfully cast its spell on the Flemings. Spending their days walking and talking, with Ann exploring the churches while Ian necked Campari, the Fleming marriage finally received a vital transfusion.[42]

But their halcyon holiday soon came to an end as Ian was due to fly to Monte Carlo to meet with Aristotle Onassis to talk about a film script.[43] Ann complained vociferously when it was time for the couple to fly to Monte Carlo – a city she had never liked. By the time Ann and Ian boarded their flight from Venice to Nice, the rows had started again.

By the summer of 1958, the couple were once again pursuing very separate lives. Ian flew off on his traditional holiday to New York in June, leaving his wife behind. The crisis talks at Scott's the previous year had served little purpose beyond a grudging acceptance that neither Ann nor Ian wanted a formal separation or divorce. And both Ann and Ian were demonstrably resigned to each other's extramarital affairs. When Ian was in New York he asked Blanche Blackwell to join him but she refused.[44]

In his turn, Ian accepted the presence of Gaitskell in his wife's life. While Ian was in America, Ann attended the Encaenia celebrations at Wadham

College in Oxford, where the guests of honour were Gaitskell and Prime Minister Harold Macmillan.[45]

Gaitskell even turned up during a Fleming family holiday. When Ian returned from America in early July, the Flemings travelled to Kitzbühel with Caspar. Unwisely, the Fleming family decided to make the long journey from England to Austria by car.[46] By the time the family arrived at Villa Pengg in Kitzbühel, Ann and Ian were barely on speaking terms. Even given the *laissez-faire* attitude of the Flemings towards their marriage, Gaitskell's less than subtle arrival in Kitzbühel is staggering. The fact that he came with his wife and children in tow seems even more astonishing.

Ann feigned surprise when the politician arrived, but the constant presence of Dora and the children put the kibosh on any romantic moments on the mountainside. Ian accepted Gaitskell's appearance with equanimity and even seemed to enjoy the Labour leader's company. Dora Gaitskell continued to ignore the affair but obstinately refused to leave Ann and her husband alone.

Returning to London in September, Ann resumed her relentless social life – having dinner parties several nights a week in the oval dining room of Victoria Square. By now, their social circle accepted that the Flemings were operating as individuals rather than a couple. 'Ian was never there,' Sara remembers.[47] Ann entertained alone while Ian would dine at his club, frequently returning home to find Gaitskell et al. in the dining or drawing room. Ian would bid a hasty greeting before beetling up to his little room on the top floor.[48]

Ann's friends, and particularly her literary friends, were disparaging about Ian's writing. Allegedly, Ian once returned home to Victoria Square to find a collection of Ann's 'boobies' reading a James Bond novel aloud, guffawing at the writing. Ann was always publicly dismissive of the James Bond novels. She referred to the novels as 'pornography for the masses and the ill-educated' and claimed never to have read one.[49]

While these comments may seem harsh, Ann's attitude is typical of the classic British upper-class habit of mocking any sort of professional success. Ian was not unduly perturbed by his wife's vocal lack of support. Whenever she described the Bond novels as pornography, Ian would clap back, 'Well, we'll retire on the proceeds.'[50]

In November, Ann was forced to take a break from her manic social schedule. Having had a cyst removed from her womb, she recuperated at Bekesbourne.[51] With little to entertain or amuse her, Ann resumed her criticisms of the house. She lobbied hard for a move as she and Ian departed for Christmas in Ireland. Having only just recovered from her surgery, Ann was appalled to find that Raymond had done little to prepare for his Christmas guests. The house had insufficient bedding or food, so Ann went into frenetic maternal mode. She travelled into Belfast to buy supplies on Christmas Eve, as well as organise the castle staff – an experience she found so shattering that she was too exhausted to go to church on Christmas Day.[52] She and her son had ongoing battles over the central heating, which she would turn on and then he would turn off as an economy. First Fionn became ill, then Caspar got a fever. Guy and Vi Charteris were also staying and Ann worried constantly that her elderly father would fall ill, plying him with brandy to fortify him against the cold.[53]

Exhausted by Christmas in Ireland, the Flemings returned to Victoria Square. For the second year running, Ann and Ian found a convenient reason not to holiday together. In January 1959, when Ian flew off to Goldeneye, the Flemings claimed that Ann was too exhausted from Christmas to travel. This excuse was made laughable when Ann made a post-Christmas jolly to Chantilly to stay with Diana Cooper, where Gaitskell would soon join her. Ann made half-hearted attempts to play down the relationship, referring to Gaitskell in a letter as 'my unrewarded but ever devoted admirer', but by now the relationship was common knowledge.[54] While Ann was always cool about Gaitskell in her correspondence, he clearly wanted to spend as much time as possible with her, and she happily assented.

On her return to England, Ann did a complete volte-face and flew to Jamaica via New York. Diana Cooper had warned her friend that her affair had become too blatant. Ann's impromptu holiday served to protect Gaitskell, who was worried for his political reputation after the press had reported his visit to Chantilly.[55]

On their return from Goldeneye in March 1959, Ann renewed her house-hunting efforts. Once again, the Flemings could not agree on a location. Ann continued to push for Wiltshire or Gloucestershire, an area that felt familiar, given her childhood at Stanway. Ian wanted an area with a propensity of golf courses, favouring Petworth in Sussex.[56] Eventually, he gave in and agreed to Oxfordshire. His main concern about buying in the Cotswolds was that a home would become a focal point for gatherings of Ann's 'boobies', from which he would have no escape. Nor could the Flemings agree on the size or style of a potential country home. Ann wanted something grand. Ian preferred a smaller, more practical home. Unsurprisingly, the house-hunt quickly descended into a series of rows.

On 23 March, *Goldfinger*, Ian's seventh James Bond novel, was published. While reviewers were less than enthusiastic, the book quickly climbed to the top of the bestseller lists. When *The Sunday Times* was sold by Lord

Kemsley to Roy Thomson, Ian felt that the time had come to resign in order to focus solely on his books. As well as the phenomenal success of the James Bond books, Ian was shrewd enough to realise that as a Kemsley stalwart, he would always be associated with the 'old guard'. He did not want to have to contend with a new proprietor and new editorial staff. When a requested pay rise was refused, Ian resigned on good terms and was retained on a freelance basis by the paper for £1,000 per year.[57]

Ian was not the only person considering a resignation. After years of loyal service, the Crickmeres attempted to resign from Victoria Square. Ann was genuinely horrified at the prospect of losing Mary and Edgar Crickmere, who were used to Ann's excessive entertaining. With the dawn of the 1960s just around the corner, Ann was well aware that good domestic staff were a rarity. As Ann wailed in a letter to Evelyn Waugh on 1 May 1959, 'They are a unique and dying species.'[58] The Crickmeres' demand for a wage increase was more successful than Ian's had been. After weeks of wrangling, the Crickmeres agreed to stay. Ann was happy, but Ian became increasingly nervous of their household expenses, exacerbated by his wife's increasingly grandiose plans for a country house.

But domestic problems were not the only thing troubling Ann. Fionn had fallen in love and wanted to marry.[59] The man Fionn had chosen was earnest, serious and intelligent. John Morgan seemed like a solid, reliable and appealing son-in-law, with a budding career at the Foreign Office. But Ann did not approve. Her remarkably progressive views when it came to her friends, and her lovers, did not extend to that of her family. 'Ann was a snob,' her niece confirms. 'She would much rather Fionn had married Jacob Rothschild.'[60]

Educated at a state school in Chingford and then the London School of Economics, Morgan had the intellect that Ann respected in others.[61] But he did not have the breeding. When she had been looking to marry, at a similar age to her daughter, money and status had been forefront in her mind. She had gone on to marry her second husband in no small part because of his vast fortune and his power. Ann was of the generation and breed that believed that relying solely on income from a job equated to having no money.

Expressing her views about Morgan in a series of letters to friends, Ann shows a rare glimpse of the hypocrisy she could sometimes be capable of. She was conveniently forgetting that she had married Ian for love when his only source of income had been his wage from the Kemsley Press. After meeting her future in-laws, Ann acidly describes the Morgan family to Evelyn Waugh, 'His parents are chapel-going folk and do not drink or smoke, his mother has only once been to London.'[62]

Morgan was equally cool towards Ann when he came for a weekend at Bekesbourne.[63] As one of a new generation of men determined to change the world and hasten the death of the British Empire, Morgan viewed Ann as a relic. He also suspected, quite rightly, that she was a snob. During the weekend, he refused to talk of his background or parents, guessing that Ann would be charming to his face, then disparage him in private to her daughter and her wide circle of friends. In letters, Ann would refer to her son-in-law by the withering nickname of 'Foreign Office Morgan'.[64]

In the summer of 1959, the Flemings continued their search for a new home, as well as looking for a prep school for Caspar. The deep love that both Ann and Ian had for their son, and their determination to be good parents, was rapidly becoming the only thing that the Flemings could agree on. As a result, they went to extensive lengths to find just the right school for their adored child.

Raymond had gone to Ludgrove, but this was dismissed by Ann, while Ian vetoed his own prep school, Durnford.[65] Ann and Ian also visited Wellesley House in Broadstairs, which was run by one of Ian's golfing friends. Ian liked the school but Ann, unaccustomed to British boarding schools, was horrified by the spartan dormitories that each contained thirty beds. Ann was also put off by the school ethos, which placed emphasis on character rather than bookish achievement. She much preferred Summer Fields School in Oxfordshire, which placed sufficient weight on academic achievement and had marginally more attractive dormitories.[66] The main attraction of Summer Fields for Ann was the school's proximity to the country house she hoped to buy.

In the late summer of 1959, Ann had found the country house she'd been dreaming of. Her friend, Robert Heber-Percy, who lived in the exquisite Farringdon House, had found out that Lord Banbury was selling Warneford Place in nearby Sevenhampton. Ann immediately travelled to Wiltshire to have a look.

The original Warneford Place was a vast sixteenth-century house with forty bedrooms and a ballroom. Having been bought by the first Lord Banbury in 1902, alterations had been made to reduce the overall size of the house. Situated in a small park with a large ornamental lake, the house had been largely neglected since the death of the 1st Lord Banbury in 1936. When Ann viewed the house, the whole property was in a sorry state. But she relished the challenge of a full-scale renovation, envisioning a home in which she could live and entertain on a grand scale.[67]

Ian was less keen. Having cautioned Ann earlier in the year against 'some huge palace that we cannot afford to heat or staff and where we have to dress for dinner every weekend',[68] Warneford Place seemed to fly in the face of his concerns. A few miles from the small town of Highworth, on the edge of the Cotswolds, the location of Warneford Place was exactly the sort of area that Ian had hoped to avoid. Adding insult to injury, the house was miles from the nearest golf course.

Ian had his first view of the house with his friend Robert Harling, who had found the Flemings their Victoria Square home. In his memoirs, Harling describes Ian as being in a dour mood as the men drove to Sevenhampton. Ann had been deliberately vague about the house, leading Ian to speculate to his friend, 'Ann's keeping pretty quiet about the size of the damn place, but I've heard whisper it's got over thirty bedrooms, three bathrooms and only one ballroom.'[69]

Ann did substantially reduce the size of Warneford Place. She tore down much of the old house and commissioned a new building which incorporated parts of the original house, creating a beautiful home that Ian eventually came to love. But on that first visit, neither Ian nor Harling liked what they saw. Knowing the scale of the renovations that would be required, Harling reflected that Warneford Place would 'demand far more attention and cash than Fleming would wish to provide for such a gloom-ridden scheme. Above all, I judged, he was physically incapable of managing such a project.'[70]

As the men finished their tour of the near-derelict house, Ian's thoughts on Warneford Place were written across his face. As Harling archly recalled, 'Quite clearly, Fleming wished the house to be razed to the ground. Preferably that afternoon.'[71]

To avoid further argument, Ian agreed to the purchase and Ann immediately commissioned an Oxfordshire architect to oversee the massive renovation and refurbishment.

Ann paid a fleeting visit to Shane's Castle in the late summer before returning to England, intending to pack up the Old Palace, which was to be sold in preparation for the move to Sevenhampton. But the impending general election began to take up a lot of her time. Having become ever more fascinated in politics – in no small part due to her affair with Gaitskell – Ann eagerly embraced the pre-election tension. She even went so far as to volunteer to drive voters to polling stations on 8 October.[72] Despite Gaitskell's popularity, the Conservatives increased their majority and were returned to power with Harold Macmillan remaining as prime minister.

The winter of 1959 was mired by further ill health for Ann. Firstly, she was laid low by a bout of the flu. Then she contracted a chest infection and was advised by the Fleming family GP, Dr Beal, to give up smoking, which made her feel fractious and irritable.[73]

Ian made himself scarce. He embarked on an extended research trip to Hong Kong and the Far East, before looping around to California, with stays in Los Angeles and Las Vegas.[74] He returned to find Ann still out of sorts. Thinking that a warmer climate might be beneficial for her health, Ian floated the idea of Christmas in Monte Carlo, triggering another row between the couple. As usual, Ian capitulated to avoid further argument and the family made for their traditional Christmas in Ireland in mid-December.

The Flemings flew to Goldeneye in early January, with Ann plugging herself full of tranquillisers to combat her nerves. Caspar also travelled with his parents, accompanied by a new governess, Mona Potterton. Unfortunately, Potterton immediately irritated Ian with her Victorian-style bonnet. He insisted that his wife take her shopping for a less-offensive sunhat, much to Ann's embarrassment.[75]

Having spent much of the previous year apart, the Flemings found themselves chafing in the small confines of Goldeneye, exacerbated by the presence of Caspar and Ms Potterton. Ian was struggling to get down to work on his next book. Then, incredibly, Gaitskell arrived on the island.[76]

The risks that the leader of the opposition took to spend time with Ann were hair-raising. Even in an age when newspapers were more respectful of the private lives of politicians, the affair between Gaitskell and Ann was breathtakingly blatant. He claimed to be in Jamaica on a 'fact-finding mission' – a laughable excuse which few believed.[77] For the first time, several London newspapers printed the gossip, hinting at an affair between a politician and a leading society hostess.[78]

Unfortunately for Ann and Gaitskell, a stringer for the *Daily Express* was determined to try and prove evidence of the affair. Fed up with being constantly pursued, Ann cabled Lord Beaverbrook and begged him to call off his stringer. While she sent the cable from Oracabessa, Gaitskell waited in the car, where he was spotted by the very same stringer. Terrified, Gaitskell ungallantly sped off to Port Maria, leaving a bewildered Ann to make her way back to Goldeneye on foot.

A dishevelled Ann returned to Goldeneye to find her husband hosting a lunch party from which she had previously absented herself. Ann babbled an excuse and hurriedly joined the table. Lunch was then interrupted by Morris Cargill, the deputy leader of the local Labour Party and Gaitskell's host in Jamaica. Cargill asked if he could see Ann privately.[79] She left the lunch and travelled with Cargill to Gaitskell's hotel for a final tryst before the MP left for the UK the following day.

Ian professed to find the whole situation hilarious. But the situation demonstrates how hostile the Fleming marriage had become. On arrival at

Goldeneye, Ann had been annoyed to find that Blanche had planted trees and shrubbery in the gardens. Her retaliatory move was to flaunt her own lover in front of her husband. In his turn, Ian attempted to bribe Cargill to report the story of Gaitskell's flight from a *Daily Express* journalist to the London press. Cargill refused, despite Ian offering him more money.[80] This tit-for-tat exchange between husband and wife seems extraordinary and suggests that neither Fleming was as relaxed about the other's extramarital affairs as they claimed to be. Ian was publicly willing to be portrayed as a cuckold, purely to embarrass his wife and her lover – hardly a good look for the man who created James Bond.

17

LAURA AND
'THE ADORABLE CANFIELD'

The man whom Laura felt immediately drawn to on New Year's Eve 1958 was tall and attractive. At 6ft 3in and slim, with sleek, light-brown hair, Michael Canfield was diffident but exuded glamour. 'He was very attractive,' a friend of the time, David Edington, remembers, 'and he was charming, in a quiet way.'[1]

An American citizen, Michael had come to London in 1955 with his glamorous first wife, Caroline. Always known as Lee, she was the sister of Jacqueline Kennedy, the wife of then Senator John F. Kennedy. The adopted son of Cass Canfield, Michael had come to London to work in the British office of Harper & Row, the publishing house owned by his father. Shortly after arriving, Michael had been pressured by his socially ambitious wife to take on the role of special assistant to US Ambassador Winthrop Aldrich. This role immediately catapulted the young, attractive couple into the epicentre of London society. 'Lee was always in the headlines,' David remembers.[2]

But Michael had an even more intriguing back story, which was the subject of whispered gossip around London. Born in Bern, Switzerland, on 20 August 1926, Michael was given the name of Anthony Karslake, with his parents named as Violet and Ian Karslake.[3] But rumours abounded that Michael was, in fact, the illegitimate son of Prince George, the fourth son of King George and Queen Mary.

Michael did bear a striking resemblance to the duke and Laura wholeheartedly believed these rumours. She claimed that when she later introduced Michael to the Duke of Windsor in Paris, the duke was unusually silent and watchful. When Laura asked him if anything was wrong, the duke replied, 'I am certain your husband is my brother's son. Of course, it must have been when brother George was but a boy.'[4]

Laura's family always believed the rumours. 'I never doubted that he was the son of the Duke of Kent,' admits Laura's daughter. 'Katsie [Michael's mother] always said as much. She used to say that her son was "the nicest member of the Windsor clan".'[5]

Laura and Michael also discussed his potential royal heritage. When staying in Barbados in the mid-1960s, Laura wrote to Michael in England about a party where she had met another alleged illegitimate son, '____ particularly wants to get to know you as he says he's supposed to be the Duke of Kents [sic] son also'.[6]

There are myriad unsubstantiated rumours about Michael's parentage. Included in the more outlandish stories are that he was the result of an affair between Prince George and Alice 'Kiki' Preston – a leading member of the Kenyan 'Happy Valley' set – during a royal tour of Africa. There was another a rumour that Prince George was gay. As was standard practice for that era, the royal family arranged for 'treatment' – essentially, this was a form of conditioning in which gay men would be forced to sleep with prostitutes. The woman who was supposedly 'dealing' with Prince George ended up pregnant and she was sent to Switzerland to have the baby.[7]

Irrespective of the rumours that surround Michael's biological parentage, he was adopted by the American publisher Cass Canfield and his wife, the former Katherine 'Katsie' Temple Emmet, in 1926 and renamed Michael Temple Canfield. Cass was then working in London as the manager of Harper & Brothers Publishing, with the family living in a townhouse in Knightsbridge. The Canfields already had one biological son, Cass Canfield Junior, but Katsie had been unable to have more children and the Canfields had decided to adopt. 'She picked him out of a cradle in Switzerland,' Laura's daughter recalls.[8]

When Cass was made the president of Harper & Brothers in 1931, the family returned to New York. In 1937, the Canfields divorced and Cass Senior married Jane White, a noted sculptor, while Katsie married John D.W. Churchill and moved to Martha's Vineyard. After attending St Bernard's Prep School, Michael attended Brooks School in North Andover, Massachusetts. Graduating just as America entered the Second World War, Michael lied about his age – one of the few benefits of a hazy birth certificate – and entered the US Marine Corps. After receiving a minor shrapnel injury in the Iwo Jima landing, Michael left the marines as the war ended and entered Harvard, where he studied English literature.[9]

Michael was an elegant man, always impeccably dressed, with perfect manners and charm. A committed anglophile, he favoured tweeds and often spoke with a pseudo-British accent. But his adoption left a psychological mark. Despite growing up in the luxurious environs of the Canfield family, Michael always felt like an outsider. As well as his adoption, his childhood had been marred by his adoptive parents' divorce and the accumulated stress on the young Michael resulted in a facial tic and stammer, which would persist into adulthood. While Michael was a warm personality, he remained detached, almost apathetic. 'I was intrigued by him. But he ought to have been more interesting than he was,' his former stepdaughter recalls. 'He didn't seem to have engaged in his life with any interest.'[10]

As a teenager, Michael had met Lee Bouvier, the beautiful stepdaughter of leading financier Hugh Auchincloss. She was attending Sarah Lawrence College in Bronxville, New York, when Michael began to pursue her in earnest. But Lee had her own insecurities. She and her sister, Jackie, bore the stigma of divorce after their mother, Janet, had left their alcoholic father, Jack. Janet had remarried the wealthy Hugh Auchincloss, who was kind to his stepchildren, but deadly dull. Growing up close to the Auchincloss wealth, but not legitimately being part of it, the Bouvier sisters developed a complex about money. Both saw marriage as the ultimate goal for their lives but any potential husband would have to be rich.[11]

Lee and Jackie also had an intense rivalry. Lee was generally judged to be the prettier sister and had a certain sex appeal which Jackie seemed to lack. Lee, rather than the older Jackie, married first. And Lee, rather than Jackie, was thought of a trendsetter.[12]

After graduating from Harvard in 1951, Michael moved permanently to New York where he began work in his father's publishing firm. He and Lee began to see more of each other, attending parties and shows and even spending the odd weekend at the Canfield country home, Crowfields, in Bedford, New York.

In the spring of 1952 Michael travelled to England to undertake a temporary job in the British office of Harper & Row. Lee travelled to Italy with her mother during the summer and returned to the United States via London, where she was reunited with Michael. Despite being an anglophile, Michael was lonely in London and had started to drink heavily. He found himself impotent and unable to make love to Lee, curtailing their budding romance.

By the autumn of 1952, Michael was back in New York, while Lee had dropped out of college and was working as an assistant to the legendary editor of *Harper's Bazaar*, Diana Vreeland. Despite their abortive reunion in London, Lee determined that she would marry Michael. But no proposal was forthcoming so, anxious to beat her sister down the aisle, Lee proposed to Michael.[13] He accepted and the couple married on 18 April 1953, at the

Holy Trinity Catholic Church in Washington D.C. Michael was 27 while Lee was just 20.

Both Lee and Michael were under the mistaken impression that the other had money. Lee, as part of the extended Auchincloss family, had access to all the tokens of wealth: the home in New York, the vast Hammersmith Farm on Rhode Island for weekends and holidays, as well as the Merrywood Estate in McLean, Virginia. But in reality, she would not benefit from the Auchincloss wealth, receiving no allowance nor being named in her stepfather's will. Similarly, while Michael came from the wealthy Canfield family, he only received the income from a small trust fund, as well as his publishing salary.[14] Both Lee and Michael liked to live well and own lovely things, but neither had the solid financial resources needed to live the lives that they envisaged.

The young couple settled first in New York in a small apartment in Sutton Place South, decorated with money given to them by Janet Auchincloss. But the marriage quickly turned sour. Lee's obsessional need for wealth began to chafe Michael, especially when she began to suggest that he give up publishing and work in a more lucrative business, such as oil. As Michael became increasingly unhappy, he began to drink heavily, which again affected the physical side of their marriage.

In a bid to make their marriage work, in January 1955 the couple moved to London, where Michael had obtained work as a Harper & Row representative. The couple settled into a house in Chesham Place in Belgravia and immediately hit the London social scene.[15] The Canfields were hugely popular, being young, good-looking and very glamorous. The ever-passive Michael even gave up his job in publishing when Lee, wanting access to diplomatic circles, lobbied the American Ambassador to hire her husband.

But the marriage still foundered. When Lee failed to become pregnant, the Canfields discovered that Michael would never be able to father children, due to a low sperm count. This was the death knell for the marriage. When Jackie Kennedy, recovering from the stillbirth of a child, came to stay with the Canfields in November 1956, Michael asked his sister-in-law what he could do to keep Lee. 'Get more money Michael,' Jackie is reported to have replied. Michael was by no means poor and said as much. 'No, Michael. I mean real money,' Jackie responded.[16]

During Jackie's visit, Lee met a man who could give her real money. Prince Stanisław 'Stash' Radziwiłł was a Polish aristocrat who had escaped Poland during the Nazi invasion of 1939. Arriving in England in 1946, Stash quickly fell in with property tycoon Felix Fenston, and made a fortune in the post-war London property boom. Lee immediately began an affair with the older, sophisticated Radziwiłł.

When Lee's father died in August 1957, she and Michael returned to New York, taking a holiday to Martha's Vineyard in a last-ditch attempt to save the marriage. Returning to London, Michael moved back into publishing after Ambassador Aldrich retired. Without the social round of diplomatic parties to hold them together, Lee left Michael in February 1958 after Radziwiłł asked her to marry him.

Michael was devastated by the loss of Lee. His unstable upbringing had installed in him a pathological need for order and routine which was blown apart by Lee's departure. The divorce was finalised in the last months of 1958, hastened by the news that Lee was pregnant.[17] Radziwiłł's wife, Grace, was equally devasted. (In a bizarre twist, she would later marry Eric Dudley and become the Countess of Dudley.)

In her rose-tinted recollections, Laura remembers that she and Michael fell instantly in love on first meeting.[18] But the beginning of their relationship was not as fairy tale as she liked to recall. Michael was reeling from the breakdown of his marriage when he met Laura. He was also very drunk.[19] Laura was nursing her own broken heart, having been rejected by Anthony Pelissier, and was on the rebound. At 32, Michael was eleven years younger than Laura, and young and good-looking – the perfect antidote to her depression.

He was certainly very different from the men that Laura had had relationships with before. Like Gerry Koch de Gooreynd, Michael was a kind, gentle man. 'He was absolutely lovely. Just so nice,' Laura's granddaughter, Anabel, recalls. 'Michael must have been very easy to love.'[20] The playwright, William Douglas-Home referred to Michael as 'the adorable Canfield'.[21] He was also incredibly glamorous, with his connections to both the Canfield family and the Kennedys. But to Laura, this man was not marriage material. Stinging from her rejection by Pelissier, Michael was only ever meant to be a fling.

Laura and Michael left the party on Curzon Street and sloped off for dinner by themselves. According to Laura, Michael sobered up over dinner and the couple talked long into the night, exchanging life stories.[22] But he did not sober up enough to sleep with Laura that first night. She drove him home to Belgravia while she returned to Hertfordshire House. When Michael rang and asked her for dinner in early January, she happily agreed. And she and Michael were together again for a weekend in January when they were both guests of the More O'Ferralls at their Irish home, Balyna House, in County Kildare.[23]

Intending to join Peggy and Paul Munster in Kitzbühel at the end of January, Laura found a drunken Michael on the platform as she boarded the

Golden Arrow to Paris for the first leg of her journey. Seeing the benefit of having a young, handsome man in tow, Laura suggested he accompany her, to which Michael boozily agreed.

The Munsters were less than pleased at the arrival of Laura with an uninvited guest and quickly arranged for Michael to stay in a nearby hotel. In his hotel bedroom, Michael and Laura had sex for the first time. In her memoirs, Laura channels the very worst romance novelist as she describes Michael as 'shy but a wonderful lover'.[24]

After Kitzbühel, the couple flew to Paris, where further romance was blighted by Michael's admission that he had pubic lice. Clearly not as absorbed by his love for Laura as she liked to believe, Michael had gone to bed with a woman he had met at a party before joining Laura in Austria. 'Some strange Balkan tart type,' Laura acidly claimed.[25] Despite scouring the French pharmacies for a cure, by the time Laura and Michael returned to London, she was also suffering from an infestation.[26]

This was hardly the most auspicious start to a relationship, but rather than running a mile, Laura continued to see Michael on their return to England. She also successfully bated her former flame, Anthony Pelissier, with her new relationship. After dinner with Laura on her return from Kitzbühel, Pelissier wrote her a melodramatic letter, 'Seeing you again and that look on your face as I walked through the door [...] I at last had my heartbroken [sic].'[27]

But the eleven-year age difference between Michael and Laura continued to worry her. Writing to Michael from Hertfordshire House in 1959, she confessed her fears:

> Each day my love for you grows more deep. I can't take the prospect of the inevitable 'heart breaks' this must mean for me, for eleven years is too many years as well we both know: You must find happiness with someone of your age, you will, I know, but not with me around, and nor do I want to be around to watch it happen.[28]

Michael's mother was also disapproving of the age gap between her son and Laura when she visited London in 1959, and made her displeasure clear when invited to Hertfordshire House for a weekend. Seeing a picture of the young Anabel, Katsie asked who the girl was. 'My granddaughter,' Laura replied.[29] Katsie was unable to mask her horror at the thought of her son being with a woman who had a grandchild. Eventually, Laura and Michael decided to marry. 'She slightly married on the rebound,' Sara recollects.[30]

Never good on her own, Laura was happier being married. As she wrote to Michael in 1959, shortly before the couple became engaged, 'I have been in a sense on my own for eight years and I don't like it much, I want the complete togetherness that I now realize only marriage can bring.'[31] As a woman who gained her self-worth from the adoration of men, the younger, attractive Michael was good for her morale. As her daughter archly summarises, 'My mother acquired ego-boosters rather than husbands or lovers.'[32] Laura also loved the glamour that came with being Michael Canfield's wife. 'The American side, she loved,' Anabel Loyd acknowledges.[33] And Laura's family admit that she was at her best when married to Michael. 'She enjoyed life with Michael,' Anabel continues.[34] 'I think he was probably the love of her life,' Sara admits.[35]

For Michael, an older wife represented order and stability. As a man who had always felt like an outsider, a wife at the very epicentre of the British establishment gave him security that he had always lacked. Feeling rudderless in London following his divorce from Lee, Laura offered an anchor.

He also loved glamorous women. Lee Bouvier had been feted as one of the most stylish young women of her generation. Michael always noticed what women were wearing and appreciated women's fashion. He also had a good eye and excellent taste. Like Laura, he had a love of beautiful things and a skill for creating exquisite homes. In Laura, he found someone who shared his love of style. Always well dressed and glamorous, even as she approached middle age, Laura retained her appeal.

On 13 June 1960, Laura and Michael married at Amersham Registry Office. Laura looked radiant on her wedding day in a blue dress with a full skirt, decorated with polka dots and a three-tiered pearl necklace at her throat. Her only concession to being a traditional bride was a large white hat, complete with a blue ribbon. Michael looked glowingly handsome and happy in a light suit and tie.[36]

On the guest list was Michael's mother, Katsie, who travelled over from her home on Martha's Vineyard, although his father and stepmother did not come. Hugo Charteris also travelled down from Scotland. Anabel Morrison attended with her nanny, but neither Sara nor Charles Morrison were there. Nor was Ann.

The small troupe of guests travelled from Amersham Registry Office back to Hertfordshire House, where a wedding lunch was served in the garden.[37] That evening, the Canfields flew to Paris, where they stayed for two nights, before heading off to Majorca for three weeks, where Philip Dunn had leant the newly-weds his holiday home on a deserted coastline.

Before their marriage, Laura had been aware of Michael's drinking. He was naturally quiet and shy, so he drank to mask his insecurities and bolster his confidence. But alone on their honeymoon, realisation dawned that her new husband had a problem. 'Michael was an alcoholic,' Laura's friend, Hugo Vickers confirms.[38]

Returning to England in July 1960, the Canfields settled into their new life at Hertfordshire House. As part of their shared love of creating beautiful surroundings, the newly-weds decided to landscape the garden and grounds of Hertfordshire House.

Laura and Michael were introduced to Lanning Roper – one of the most revered garden designers of the twentieth century. Like Michael, Roper had grown up in America, in the wealthy enclave of West Orange, New Jersey. After studying at Harvard, he served in the US Navy during the Second World War, before settling in London in Little Venice. Always gently persuasive and with an incredible eye, Lanning would eventually design gardens for Prince Charles at Highgrove as well as Scotney Castle.[39]

A warm, engaging and talented man, Roper quickly became a firm friend of the Canfields, staying for extended weekends at Hertfordshire House as he planted and bedded. He would also go on to design the gardens for Ann and Ian at Sevenhampton, who became equally fond of him. Roper liked both Ann and Laura, but was a little in awe of the Charteris sisters. He would later recall their 'magnetic sexuality'.[40]

The Canfields' life in Hertfordshire began to revolve around an increasing menagerie of animals. Laura had a Pekinese called Beany, while Michael had a beautiful golden Labrador called Crumb. Over the years the couple acquired a goat, a donkey, a stallion donkey called Grock and several Shetland ponies. Despite her lack of maternal flair with her own daughter, Laura lavished love on her animals. Like her success as a nurse, Laura could show incredible kindness in certain situations. As a friend from Buckinghamshire recalls, 'Animals offered complete adoration [to Laura]. Much as she wanted from men, really.'[41] Laura poured her love into these animals. Like many childless couples, the animals became the substitute children of the Canfields.

During their first year of marriage, Michael and Laura were based mostly at Hertfordshire House, where they were soon joined by Pat and Jenny Duncan, who ran the house and looked after the Canfields. Michael had abandoned any idea of returning to America and remained working within the London office of Harper & Row. Hertfordshire House was on the outskirts of the village of Coleshill – an easily accessibly commuter village near Beaconsfield. Michael had retained a flat at 15 Eaton Square in Belgravia, and chose to spend a few nights a week there where he would be joined by

Laura, despite Hertfordshire House being more convenient for her work at the Contessa shops.[42] Laura was well aware that Michael had an eye for the ladies and she was resolute in not leaving him alone in London. 'She was possessive. She needed the self-affirmation,' her daughter remembers.[43] But Laura was not being unduly paranoid. 'When he died, Laura found that his diaries were full of lunch dates with ladies,' Hugo Vickers confirms.[44]

Laura would later portray her marriage as idyllically happy. There was certainly passion, with many letters between the pair referencing their sex life at the beginning of their marriage. As Laura says in one undated letter from Hertfordshire House, 'I am very "snoozly" as indeed you must be, we loved a lot last night and didn't have much sleep.'[45] But she and Michael were fundamentally different, and their individual characters did not complement each other. Michael was reticent and found himself unable to challenge his wife when she became too overbearing. Essentially, Laura needed boundaries, which Michael was unable to give her. Near neighbours of the Canfields remember a dinner party at which Laura repeatedly chastised Michael for minor misdemeanours. Michael began to drink heavily and retreated into himself. 'I remember my mother saying that if only Michael had stood up to his wife, the relationship might have been more successful,' the daughter of one of the dinner party guests declares.[46]

Occupied by her marriage to Michael and the ongoing renovation of Hertfordshire House, Laura decided to sell her chain of Contessa shops. In 1961, she received an offer but a price could not be agreed and no deal was signed.[47] Unfortunately for Laura, after she had declined the offer the 1960–61 American recession began to impact Britain. As the economy contracted, people began to sacrifice non-essential items and sales fell rapidly in the Contessa shops. Tax rates went up, as did commercial rents and Laura began to seriously struggle. Writing to Michael in 1962, she revealed the stress of the failing Contessa shops:

> Things go from bad to worse. I have seldom been more exhausted and generally hopeless about everything. Endless hours at St Alban's yesterday, piles of undisclosed accounts and threatening letters awaited me [...] I'm simply not tough or experienced enough to compete.[48]

In late 1962, Laura decided to close the chain and sell the remaining leases on the shops. She managed to cover her business debts but was left regretting her earlier decision not to sell in 1961.

When Mary Rose died on 21 December 1962 at the age of 43, Laura seemed outwardly unaffected. Mary Rose's marriage to her second husband,

Nigel, had been successful for a time and the couple had had a son, Francis. Early in 1960, Mary Rose had endeavoured to give up alcohol, causing hideous delirium tremens, known as 'the shakes', as the alcohol left her body. The withdrawal from alcohol had been so horrific that Mary Rose had started to drink again and she had caught pneumonia.

The drinking had continued and during the last years of Mary Rose's life, Ann had valiantly attempted to intercede. In March 1960, shortly before she married Michael, Ann had entreated Laura to speak to Mary Rose about her drinking.[49] Laura had refused. The younger sisters had never had an easy relationship, even as children, and, while Laura and Mary Rose had continued to see each other in adulthood, the relationship had been tense. When Mary Rose stayed with Laura and Eric at Himley, Laura had enraged her sister by clumsily trying to stop her from drinking. 'I remember being told to take her glass away,' Sara says.[50]

After Mary Rose's death, Ann and Laura essentially took on responsibility for her son, who was aged 11 when his mother died. 'Grandma and Aunt Ann took it in turns to have Francis,' remembers Anabel Loyd.[51] Ann would regularly take Francis on holiday alongside Caspar, while Laura would have the boy to stay at Hertfordshire House, alongside her granddaughter. 'He was the most beautiful boy,' Anabel says. 'Like a hero of Violet Needham.'[52]

As 1963 dawned, Michael remained unhappy with his work and talked loosely about changing careers. Even though he was a passionate anglophile and loved living in England, the Canfields discussed moving to New York where Michael could search out a more satisfying career. Laura had loved America since her first post-war visit and liked the idea of a temporary stint in New York.

While a permanent move was eventually discounted, the Canfields made regular trips across the Atlantic to stay with Michael's family. During the early years of their marriage, the Canfields would stay in New York with Cass Canfield and his second wife, Jane. The Canfield seniors owned a townhouse on 38th Street as well as an exquisite mock-Georgian country house in leafy Bedford in Westchester, New York. The Canfields would also stay en masse at a cottage which Cass and Jane owned on Fisher's Island, situated just off the coast of Florida.[53]

In the early 1960s, Laura and Michael routinely spent August in Martha's Vineyard, Massachusetts, with Michael's mother, Katsie, and her husband, John Churchill, who had moved there shortly after their marriage. Then, as now, Martha's Vineyard, situated off the Massachusetts coast, was a mecca for the upper crust of American society. The beautiful beaches, unspoilt landscape and sand dunes are reminiscent of the Scottish coastline which Laura had loved as a child. The quaint clapboard 'cottages' also give the island an air of history and tradition. There was also a busy social round, which the Canfields enjoyed. Laura later professed to not enjoy her summers on the Vineyard, but her family remember differently. 'She loved the holidays in America,' Sara remembers. 'And she loved spending time with the Kennedys.'[54]

The Kennedys had long been stalwarts of the island and when Laura and Michael were staying, they would be included in the social activities of Michael's ex-in-laws. Kennedy parties mainly consisted of large barbecues and rambunctious games of football or beachball, frequently resulting in injuries and broken bones. Michael and Laura did not join in with the games as they both – Michael especially – had a horror of contact sports.[55] But the Kennedy family were glamorous and engaging and the Canfields enjoyed spending time with such a dazzling family.

Having returned to England in September 1963, the Canfields were preparing to attend a dinner party on the evening of 22 November 1963, when they heard that John F. Kennedy had been shot in Dallas, Texas, and had died from his injuries. Laura heard the news on television in the kitchen of Hertfordshire House and went upstairs to tell Michael, who was dressing for dinner. Michael was devasted both by the death of his ex-brother-in-law and by the manner of his death, as was Laura. But the couple decided to continue with their dinner plans.[56]

Michael and Laura were to dine at Laura's former home, Great Westwood. The Canfields had been invited to dinner by Eric and his new wife, Grace. Born Grace Kolin, in Croatia, the daughter of a wealthy industrialist, her and her family had fled Croatia during the Second World War and moved to Lausanne in Switzerland. Here she had met Stash Radziwiłł and the couple married in 1946, moving to the Bahamas to establish British residency before settling in the United Kingdom. When Stash had fallen in love with Lee Canfield, Grace had sought revenge by fighting to keep all of their marital assets, leading to a protracted and embarrassingly public legal battle. Eventually, the couple divorced in 1959, after which Stash had married Lee Canfield. Michael had married Laura and Laura's ex-husband had married Grace. 'Quite a merry-go-round,' Laura whimsically recalled in her memoirs.[57]

Twenty-nine years younger than Eric, Grace had met the Earl of Dudley in 1960. Handsome, rather than pretty, with undeniable elegance, Grace was a snob. Unsettled by her wartime experiences as a refugee, she liked the idea of being a countess. Grace was also furious with her ex-husband for leaving her for the younger Lee Bouvier Canfield. Marrying Eric was one way for her to even the score. Grace and Eric married on 17 July 1961 and settled into Great Westwood.

On arrival on 22 November, Laura was taken aback by the champagne and huge amounts of caviar which greeted their arrival. And she was disparaging about the redecoration of her former home, causing animosity between the two Countesses of Dudley, after which Laura nicknamed her ex-husband's new wife 'the Evil Swan'.[58]

In January 1964, Paul and Peggy Munster invited the Canfields to Barbados to stay at their villa in Glitter Bay. The Caribbean weaved its magic upon Laura, just as it had done twenty years before when her sister had fallen in love with Jamaica. While Laura always enjoyed British winters and relished country pursuits like hunting, which only took place during the colder months, Michael was a sun worshipper who loved to lie in the sun and achieve a deep mahogany tan – 'the colour he liked to be,' Laura recalled.[59]

Both Michael and Laura instantly adored Barbados. The days were spent swimming, walking and sunbathing. Laura even managed to play golf – a sport that she had loved since playing as a child with her grandfather. The Munsters were plugged into the social network of Barbados, so the foursome socialised regularly with the notable residents of the island, including the ex-MP Ronald Tree, the owner of the magnificent neo-Palladian villa, Heron Bay House.

The Canfields returned to Barbados the following year to stay with the Munsters, and again in January 1965. Having fallen in love with the island, Michael and Laura decided to buy their own Bajan home – a small, unprepossessing villa in Heron Bay called Prudence. Like most buildings in the area, Prudence was made of coral stone which gave every house a light-pinkish tinge. The house had three bedrooms built around a large hall, leading into a light living room, open to the garden, giving spectacular, sun-drenched views out to the bay.[60] The house was run by Mrs Porter – a Bajan equivalent of Goldeneye's Violet.[61] The Canfields would take an annual trip to Barbados and when they were not in residence, Prudence would be leased to paying guests.

Despite their Caribbean holidays, the Canfield marriage was beginning to crack by the mid-1960s. Laura continued to be the dominant force in the relationship. Michael began to have relationships with other women, which irritated Laura, although she attempted to be sanguine about her husband's dalliances. Writing to Michael from Barbados in 1965, Laura says, 'I do realize and deeply appreciate my very "special" Crumb [Laura's nickname for

Michael]. I understand how sometimes he would like a young slip of a snail [Michael's pet name for Laura] without a long slippery past.'[62]

Michael became increasingly despondent and drank ever more heavily, which worried his wife. She pleaded, bullied and cajoled her husband to stop drinking. In a note during a holiday in Barbados in February 1965, Laura writes imploringly to Michael, 'I hate to see you "contact lensed" you have been happy and enchanting without the old escape route [...] you are far too precious to drink to get drunk, please, please don't [...] let's continue a wonderfully un-intoxicating holiday.'[63]

Michael was also bored by publishing but was unable to find another role that would challenge him. As a result of his melancholy, the Canfields' doctor, Barrington Cooper, who ran a private clinic on Devonshire Place in London, prescribed Michael the antidepressant Trimipramine. Initially, Laura described the Trimipramine as 'happy pills', but she soon became concerned about her husband's dependency.[64] When Michael travelled to New York in December 1965, Laura wrote anxiously, 'I can't bear to think of you flapping, twitching, blinking and gobbling white pills.'[65] Worryingly, Michael also began to talk routinely about dying young, which terrified his wife. In a scribbled note reminding her husband to take his medication, Laura writes, 'Be happy, forget "death wish". I love and live for you.'[66]

By the time the Canfields left for their annual trip to Barbados in early 1968, Michael was struggling emotionally. Laura was aware that her marriage was becoming unstuck and felt helpless. Travelling to Barbados ahead of her husband, she wrote imploringly to her husband, 'I love you, we have our ups and downs, but I couldn't live without you for too long.'[67] Laura adored not only Michael, but also having him by her side. 'She was in love with Michael,' her daughter continues. 'But she would lose her persona if she lost a man.'[68]

Laura was prepared to go to great lengths to make her marriage work. The Canfields considered a permanent move to the Caribbean in 1968 when Michael was offered a teaching post by the Minister for Education of Barbados.[69] But Michael turned this offer down. Laura encouraged him to look elsewhere but to no avail.

Part of the reason for Michael's reluctance to move to Barbados was the social life within the island. Bert, the Duke of Marlborough, had a house on the island, and there was always a lively crowd surrounding Heron Bay and the unofficial 'king' of the island, Ronald Tree. Michael was already exasperated by being an accoutrement to Laura. A move to Barbados would have simply continued this dynamic but in a different location.

When the Canfields returned to England in early 1968, the marriage was at breaking point. Laura herself was also affected by Michael's mood as well as the stresses within the marriage. Increasingly anxious, she was prescribed a strong sedative to help her sleep and calm her nerves. Like her sister, Laura was a casualty of the vogue for barbiturates in the mid-twentieth century. She was prescribed Mandrax, which consisted mainly of methaqualone, an incredibly strong drug which acted as a 'downer'. The drug was eventually banned in the 1980s because of the high dependency rate, as well as the high number of methaqualone-related deaths. Unfortunately, Laura quickly became dependent on Mandrax. As her daughter confirms, 'She became pill-popping dependent during her Canfield marriage.'[70]

The barbiturates also began to affect her reactions to a worrying degree. In a barely legible letter to her husband on Friday, 23 December 1968, Laura admits, 'I can't write – more drugged than you were ever drunk.'[71] Laura also increasingly began to slur her words, which led to gossip amongst her Buckinghamshire neighbours that she had become an alcoholic.[72]

During the latter years of his marriage, Michael began to take an increasing number of trips to America, ostensibly on publishing business. Initially, Laura would accompany him, but during 1968 he travelled there several times alone. Michael's mother, Katsie, had died in 1964. Without the presence of his overbearing mother, America offered Michael a means of escape from the breakdown of his marriage. Friends suspected that his business trips were really an opportunity to make plans for a life in the United States – plans which did not include Laura.[73]

In 1968, the lease on the Canfields' apartment at 15 Eaton Place expired and Laura began to look for a new base for the couple. She eventually decided on a flat, No. 58 Portman Towers, a newly constructed mansion block at 95 George Street in Marylebone.[74] The complex, which consisted of four towers, was an unusual choice for a couple who thrived on living in beautiful buildings. Practical, with porterage and parking, and in a central location, Portman Towers had little architectural merit. As Laura recalls in her memoirs, 'These modern blocks are really no more than overheated concrete squares.'[75]

Laura shipped furniture from Hertfordshire House to try and make the flat more appealing and hired a new housekeeper, Marsella Toletina.[76] Hoping that redecorating the flat would give her and Michael a shared purpose, Laura endeavoured to interest her husband in her design plans. But Michael remained unenthusiastic.

Soon, Laura was thinking about giving up the Portman Towers flat and finding something more tasteful. But the plan never materialised and Laura would end up living there for the rest of her life, looked after by Marsella.

By 1969, Michael had made the decision to leave Laura. He took his step-daughter for lunch at the Berkeley in Knightsbridge. 'He told me that he was leaving her,' Sara recalls. 'He said he was fed up with being a satellite in her firmament. It was the only time I ever saw Michael show any animation.'[77]

Michael was placing his stepdaughter in an invidious position, but he was also ensuring that her daughter would be around to support Laura when he did actually leave. 'She would be a displaced person with no Michael as a prop,' Sara concludes.[78]

But Michael did not leave Laura and remained in his marriage. And when Hugo Charteris became seriously ill, Michael abandoned any plans to leave his wife, for the moment at least. As the Canfields made plans to spend Christmas 1969 with Cass and Jane Canfield in New York, Laura received the news that her brother had been diagnosed with liver cancer.

Back in December 1962, Hugo Charteris had been diagnosed with pancreatitis after being admitted to the Royal Infirmary in Glasgow. He had been operated on and an abscess removed from his stomach. He had recovered from the operation but not before Laura had come for a visit. Marching onto the ward in floor-length mink, Laura had immediately criticised the doctors and nurses caring for her brother.

Telling all and sundry that she had been a nurse, she loudly bemoaned the hospital food before leaving the ward, only to return with some recently acquired mackerel for Hugo – a direct contradiction to his strict post-operative diet. When a doctor arrived, Laura quickly hid the illicit fish behind a radiator. Inevitably, as the fish was slowly flambéed by the radiator, a disgusting smell permeated the ward. Laura did her best to disguise the smell by repeatedly, and liberally, spraying her scent – Balenciaga's Le Dix – around the ward. She was ejected from the ward after the fish was discovered, complaining vociferously as she went.[79]

Following Hugo's recovery, the Charteris family had moved from Scotland to Elvington in north Yorkshire. Laura and Michael were frequent guests at Elvington, even staying for Christmas in 1967. Despite having a complicated relationship with his sisters, Hugo managed to remain on generally good terms with his family. Hugo and Michael liked each other, sharing a love of literature, while Hugo's wife, Virginia, was universally loved by the wider Charteris clan. 'Hugo was my favourite relation and Virginia was marvellous ... a class act,' Sara recalls.[80]

In December 1969, Hugo's doctor in York refused to operate, believing that the liver cancer was terminal. Devastated by the news, Laura was irritated to be the last to hear about it, and even more so when she discovered that Ann was staying at Elvington to support Virginia and the Charteris children. Not to be outdone by her sister, Laura immediately offered the loan of Portman Towers when Virginia managed to persuade the leading pancreaticobiliary surgeon, Sir (later Lord) Rodney Smith, to operate on her husband – the famous surgeon agreeing only on the condition that the surgery would take place at St George's Hospital on Hyde Park Corner in London.[81]

Laura immediately decided to abandon plans to travel to New York with Michael so that she could be on hand for her brother and sister-in-law. Michael flew to New York as planned on 14 December, in order to attend a Harper & Row Christmas party and to see his father and stepmother.

On Friday, 19 December, Hugo was brought to London by ambulance accompanied by Virginia. On Saturday, 20 December, Laura rang Michael to say that the prognosis for Hugo was not good. Distraught, she asked her husband to return to London. Encouraged by his father, Michael agreed to fly back to London immediately.

On the evening of 20 December, he boarded a Pan Am flight from JFK International Airport in New York, bound for London. The flight departed at 8.35 p.m. and was due to arrive at London Heathrow at 8.20 a.m.

In order to cope with his sadness about Hugo, as well as the unfolding situation with Laura, Michael had upped his dosage of antidepressants during his stay in New York. He had drunk heavily throughout the day, continuing to drink in both the airport lounge as well as on the plane.

In the early hours of Sunday, 21 December, as the Pan Am flight flew across Canada, Michael began frantically to press the call button. Grabbing at his chest and sweating profusely, he complained of intense pain. Michael was suffering a massive heart attack. Before the plane could be rerouted to a nearby airport in order to seek medical help, Michael had died. Landing at Halifax Airport in Nova Scotia just after 3 a.m. local time, a doctor declared Michael dead on arrival. The cause of death was a myocardial infarction brought on by a mixture of medication and heavy drinking.[82]

Laura was alone in the Portman Towers flat on the morning of 21 December when the phone rang at 8 a.m. London time. The call was from a doctor at the Victoria General Hospital in Halifax telling her that Michael had died from a heart attack. Rootless throughout his life, Michael had died as he had lived, halfway between America and England, his 'death wish' having come true.

Laura was completely poleaxed by Michael's death. Already worried for her brother, she now had to deal with the loss of her husband. She had known that their marriage was in trouble. But she had always assumed that she could win Michael back and the couple would find a way to continue their marriage. Now she had to deal with his permanent loss.

She immediately rang Cass and Jane Canfield, who arranged for Michael's body to be sent home from Halifax to London, accompanied by Michael's older brother, Cass Junior. And friends quickly descended on Portman Towers to support Laura. Barbie Agar arrived, as did Ivan Moffat and his wife, Kate, who took charge of the funeral arrangements.

Laura was adamant that Michael's funeral should take place as quickly as possible. A small, intimate funeral was planned for Christmas Eve at All Saints Church in Coleshill, the local church to Hertfordshire House. On 23 December, Barbie Agar drove Laura back to Hertfordshire House from London where Sara was waiting for her. Ivan and Kate Moffat travelled from their home in Buckinghamshire to talk over plans for the following day, before the group had an early supper.

Wednesday, 24 December dawned cold, breezy and damp. As the small crowd of mourners entered All Saints Church in Coleshill, a chilling wind whipped their cheeks. Michael had been a popular man but his funeral was sparsely attended due to the speed of the funeral and the proximity to Christmas.

Cass and Jane Canfield had travelled across from America. Sara and Charles Morrison attended, but their children did not. Nor did Ann, who claimed exhaustion, despite managing to find the energy to attend a Christmas party hosted by the publisher George Weidenfeld, as well as a ball at the US Embassy, in the lead-up to Christmas. The small band of mourners sang 'To Be a Pilgrim' and, fittingly, 'O Love That Will Not Let Me Go', before Michael was buried in the churchyard of All Saints, Coleshill.[83] Laura later chose the phrase coined by William Douglas-Home as an inscription on the stone – 'The Adorable Canfield', written in italic letters across a flat grave stone.[84]

The small group of mourners returned to Hertfordshire House, before Cass and Jane Canfield drove a shell-shocked Laura back to Portman Towers. She visited her brother at St George's Hospital before having dinner with the Canfields and her sister-in-law, Virginia, at the Connaught, where the Canfields were staying.

Christmas was understandably sombre. Laura spent the day with her in-laws. The trio went to St Paul's for the Christmas morning service before having lunch at the hotel. She also paid another visit to Hugo, who was in severe pain following his operation. Rather crassly, he tried to comfort his sister by saying that while he, Hugo, was in pain, Michael would never feel pain again. Laura took some comfort from this but added to her grief was real worry over her brother, who looked near death's door with tubes and drips attached to his body.[85]

Eric Dudley had called Laura the moment he had heard of Michael's death. By now living in Paris with his wife, he called Laura every day in the lead-up to the funeral but decided against attending the service itself. At 75, he felt the journey from Paris would be too much. But then, on 27 December, Laura's former stepson, Peter Ward, rang with the devastating news that Eric had died the day before.[86] Alone in Portman Towers, Laura was devastated by this second death.

A new decade meant little to Laura as she travelled to Paris in early January 1970 for Eric's funeral. Grace, now the Dowager Countess of Dudley, made it clear that Laura was not welcome at the burial at Himley.[87]

Returning wearily from Paris, there seemed little to look forward to for Laura. When Hugo was discharged from St George's, he moved into Portman Towers, where he was nursed by Virginia and Laura until he was well enough to travel back to Yorkshire. Acting as nurse did at least give Laura something to focus on but her general malaise and depression were not helped by Hugo's condition. While the operation performed by Sir Rodney Smith had been successful, the surgery had really only bought Hugo more time. He was still in constant pain and talked disconcertingly frequently of suicide.[88] When Hugo was well enough to travel, he and Virginia returned to Yorkshire and Laura was, for the first time in a long time, completely alone.

18

ANN AND IAN ...
AND THE 1960S

In early March, Ann, Caspar and the governess, Mona Potterton, flew back to London from Jamaica. Ian remained in New York to take care of some business while the rest of the family flew directly home. Ann was keen to see how work at Sevenhampton had progressed. And, more pressingly, she wanted to see Gaitskell.

While staying in New York, Ian decided to travel to Washington on 12 March to have lunch with Marion 'Oatsie' Leiter. Washington, and the whole of America, was abuzz with the upcoming Democratic National Convention where a young senator, John F. Kennedy, was hoping to secure the Democratic presidential nomination. Kennedy was the man that everybody wanted to meet. He was young, glamorous and hugely charismatic. He was also a compulsive womaniser. On the surface, he and Ian had much in common and Oatsie offered to introduce the two men. Ian was intrigued to meet Kennedy. And Kennedy, who had helped push *Dr No* up the US bestseller lists after he said publicly that he enjoyed the book, was interested to meet the creator of James Bond.[1]

Ian was invited to dinner at Kennedy's Georgetown home, where he met the senator's wife, Jackie, with whom he was particularly taken. She endeavoured to pump Ian for information about the blooming relationship between her ex-brother-in law and his sister-in-law. But Ian was more interested in talking to Kennedy about his future plans than gossiping with Jackie.

In fact, Ann and Laura were having one of their regular estrangements. Ann was furious that Laura had refused to help her tackle Mary Rose's drinking, claiming that 'the doctor advised her to keep out of it owing to their bad relationship in schoolroom days'.[2] As a result, Ann had refused to attend Laura's wedding to Michael on 13 June. But she did take great pleasure in seeing her sister 'demoted' from the Countess of Dudley to plain old

Mrs Canfield. Ann grumpily made for Chantilly in April 1960, where she poured out her woes over Mary Rose. Diana Cooper bluntly suggested that Ann just let her sister drink herself to death.[3]

Ann returned to London in late April and resumed her exhausting round of socialising. On 6 May, Ian was pressed into hosting duties when Ann held a party for fifty people to mark the wedding of Princess Margaret to Anthony Armstrong-Jones, with guests including Noël Coward and the Duke and Duchess of Devonshire.[4]

Ian then promptly bolted for a European tour as research for the next instalment of his book *Thrilling Cities*. Having hosted Hugo and Virginia Charteris and their children in Victoria Square, Ann joined Ian in Switzerland in mid-May.[5] The couple reunited at Les Avants, the Swiss home of Noël Coward, near Montreux.[6] Ann and Ian were planning to travel from Montreux to Naples, but their journey was marred by an almost comical litany of illnesses. Leaving Les Avants, the Flemings stayed for one night near Annecy in order to stay and dine at the internationally renowned Pére Bise restaurant. The food was delicious but too rich for Ian. While he vomited throughout the night, Ann was bitten on the left eyelid by a mosquito.[7] The next morning, she could hardly open her eye and by the time the Flemings reached Turin, the eyelid had become infected. She received a penicillin injection from a local nurse but she remained in pain and was unable to share the driving. Ian was exhausted from a night without sleep and the couple argued their way down through Italy.

Ann had chosen Naples as she had never visited the Italian city before. But on arrival, both Flemings were supremely disappointed. Having settled into the Hotel Excelsior, Ann immediately made for the National Museum, triggering another huge row between her and Ian. Naples was rife with crime due to the heavy mafia presence and Ian quite reasonably said that Ann should not go out alone. She ignored her husband and went to the museum anyway. Returning to the hotel, Ann found that an excited Ian had managed to arrange a meeting with the legendary and terrifying gangster Charles 'Lucky' Luciano, considered the father of modern organised crime.

Fleming met Luciano in the lounge of the hotel, where Ann joined them following a siesta. She was unimpressed by the gangster, who deftly avoided Ian's questions about drug racketeering, repeatedly saying that he had been framed in the United States by District Attorney Thomas Dewey. While Ian was riveted, Ann was bored. To enliven the conversation, she asked Luciano about the rumour that two bodies in a nearby church had been preserved by having gold pumped into their veins. The gangster denied the story, with Ann heatedly arguing that such a procedure was routine in the Middle Ages.[8]

The Flemings' mutual loathing of Naples seems to have temporarily reunited them. During their last dinner in Naples, at a harbourside restaurant on 3 June, the pair laughed and chatted together, and even wrote a joint postcard to Waugh complaining about how ghastly Naples was.[9]

But this cessation of marital hostilities was fleeting. On 4 June, the Flemings headed north, making for Monte Carlo. While Ian loved the city, especially the casino, Ann loathed the inhabitants of the principality, whom she regarded as arriviste 'eurotrash'. After two nights, the Flemings drove up to Paris, where they happily separated, albeit temporarily. Ann met Caspar and Nanny at the Gare du Nord and the trio travelled to Chantilly to spend a few relaxing days with Diana Cooper. Ian made for Le Touquet before taking the air ferry back to England.

As the Old Palace in Bekesbourne was finally sold in August 1960, and renovation work on Sevenhampton was yet to begin, the Flemings decided to rent a flat in the Whitehall building in Pegwell Bay on the Kent Coast. The flat was entirely Ian's choosing as he wanted to be close to his beloved Royal St George's golf course in Sandwich. Modern, practical and entirely unbeautiful, the flat appealed to Ian but utterly appalled Ann. Originally intended as a stopgap until Sevenhampton was ready, Ian began to talk about leasing the flat more permanently. This thought horrified Ann. As well as disliking the building, she (quite rightly) suspected that Ian wanted to keep the flat should he ever need to escape from their marriage.

As had become yearly tradition, the Flemings took separate summer holidays in 1960. Ian would be spending some time in France, Caspar was dispatched to Ireland to stay with Raymond, and Ann made for Portofino in Italy. Her hostess was Mary Herbert, the mother of Evelyn Waugh's wife, Laura, and the wife of the late explorer and MP Aubrey Herbert.

The only child of the 4th Viscount de Vesci, her mother had been Evelyn Charteris, eldest daughter of the 10th Earl of Wemyss, making her and Ann relations. Mary was known for her beauty and her fierce temper. Like Ann, she loved to create debate, and often threw a conversational bomb into a discussion to create some drama.

Ann was staying at the Villa Altachiara (the Italian for Highclere Castle) which was built in 1874 by the 4th Earl of Carnarvon. The vast, shuttered Victorian villa had been inherited by Mary Herbert after her husband's death in 1923. Mary had made the villa into a mecca for academic figures such as Evelyn Waugh, Alfred Duggan, Isaiah Berlin and Maurice Bowra.

Ann was in her element staying at the Villa Altachiara. She was surrounded by the literary and academic people whom she adored in a place that was beautiful and, as yet, unspoilt. Ann also adored Mary – even if she was critical of her as a hostess. Rather disloyally, Ann reported back to Mary's son-in-law, Evelyn Waugh, 'The rooms are spacious and could be made beautiful, it is true my bathroom lacked lavatory paper, soap and a tooth-glass, but I collected these from a neighbouring bathroom.'[10] But Ann loved the environment of the villa. She lapped up the conversation going on around her and basked in the Italian sunshine.

Returning to London for one night, Ann then travelled to Shane's Castle on 9 September to reunite with Caspar. Francis Grey joined the Flemings with sad news about his mother. Mary Rose had been due to join her son, nephew and sister in Ireland, but Francis had arrived on the train alone, confiding to his aunt that Mary Rose had spent the whole of the previous day lying on the floor. On a recent holiday with their Asquith cousin Michael and his wife, Helga, the conversation had led to childhood memories of Stanway. This had unsettled Mary Rose, who had started to drink white wine. She then drank solidly for the rest of the holiday and continued to drink once she returned to London.[11]

In September, Ann and Ian returned to England in order to take Caspar to Summer Fields to begin his first term at boarding school. Ann was not unduly upset by this separation from her son as her thoughts were taken up with worry over Sevenhampton. As the demolition of the huge original Sevenhampton house began, Ann's plans were becoming wilder and more excessive by the moment. Ian suggested that instead of replacing the old building with another enormous country house, the Flemings built a small, modern home. Writing to Evelyn Waugh from Sandwich on 22 September, Ann claimed that Ian 'wants to alter the plans and keep a flat here and build a rabbit hutch for me instead of a mansion'.[12]

Realising that the cost of the renovation of Sevenhampton was worrying her husband, Ann did momentarily consider economising. She admitted that she did enjoy aspects of life in the Whitehall building. 'It's delightful having no servants,' Ann continues to Waugh. 'I can cook and paint all day.'[13] There was an enjoyable simplicity in cooking for her husband – the idyllic, fantasy life that she and Ian had first talked of when considering marriage back in the early 1950s.

But life in Pegwell Bay was too staid for Ann. There was little social life and the flat gave her no room to entertain. She quickly became bored with life '*a deux*' with her husband and when Ian departed for Kuwait in November, she revived her grandiose plans for Sevenhampton. Ian had taken a commission from the Kuwait Oil Company to write a book which mainly served as an advertisement for the Gulf state. Increasingly worried about the Fleming outgoings, Ian had taken the assignment purely for the money. With the cost of running two houses, paying for the renovation of another, the school fees for Caspar and the high cost of Ann's entertaining, Ian was under pressure. His finances, as well as his marriage, were beginning to take a toll on his health.

With Ian in the Middle East, Ann spent a weekend with the Edens in Wiltshire, driving over to see Sevenhampton, where demolition work had started. The roof had been removed, as had the windows and all the original piping, which lay scattered across the lawn.[14] With the house now a basic shell, even the determined Ann began to waver. The scale of the project was demonstrably enormous and suddenly Ann began to appreciate why Ian was so worried. The costs of the renovation were rapidly escalating and would obviously far exceed the original budget set by her husband.

Ann remained preoccupied during a post-Christmas trip to Engadine, Switzerland, in January 1961, accompanied by Ian, Fionn, Caspar and Mona Potterton, as well as Ian's friend, Duff Dunbar. Staying at the Grand Hotel Kronenhof-Bellavista, Ian struggled to breathe at the altitude of the ski resort, a result of his heavy smoking. Ann was also irritated by the wealthy, carefree people staying at the resort – a group to whom she had once belonged while married to Esmond, when her mind had been gloriously free from money worries. Her mood was not improved when, during lunch at the Corviglia Club in Saint Moritz with the racing driver Whitney Straight and his wife, the former Daphne Finch-Hatton, she overheard a fellow patron ask who she was. 'She *was* Lady Rothermere,' Straight responded.[15]

Ann remained subdued as the family returned to London, before she and Ian left for Jamaica on 20 January 1961. The pair spent one night in New York, where Gaitskell was waiting for them. When Gaitskell asked the couple to attend a screening of an NBC television show about the Soviet Union, Ian diplomatically said he felt unwell, leaving his wife and her lover to have an evening together.[16]

But by the time the Flemings arrived in Jamaica, Ian had become genuinely unwell. He had a high temperature and was diagnosed with bronchitis by a local doctor. Ann also succumbed to a chest infection.

With both Flemings confined to bed-rest, Noël Coward became self-appointed nursemaid. Ann was half-irritated, half-amused when the majority of Coward's attention was focused on Ian, with his nursing duties consisting primarily of regularly stripping Ian in order to change his pyjamas. Seeing the couple at such a low ebb, Coward confided his thoughts on the Fleming marriage to his diary, 'Their connubial situation is rocky. Annie hates Jamaica and wants him to sell Goldeneye. It is extraordinary how many of my friends delight in torturing one another.'[17]

By early February, Ann and Ian were well enough to welcome John and Frances Donaldson to Goldeneye. John, known as Jack, was a politician who later became known for his prison reform. His wife, Frances, was a biographer, later achieving fame with her 1974 biography of Edward VIII.

The Donaldsons were easy companions, both bright and politically erudite. Their visit was a balm for the Fleming marriage: Jack shared Ian's love of underwater sea life, while Frances was happy to gossip away with Ann. The only moment of discomfort came when Ann was driving the Donaldsons back from Port Maria. As they drove through Galina, Ann pointed out Blanche Blackwell's house with the words, 'That is where Ian's Jamaican wife lives.'[18] The Donaldsons were nonplussed and uncomfortable. But Ann's breeziness was deliberate, intended to show how little a threat Blanche posed to the Fleming marriage. Her words demonstrated that while Blanche may have Ian in Jamaica, for the rest of the year, and to the rest of the world, Ann remained Ian's wife.

Leaving Ian in Jamaica, Ann returned alone to London in March. One of her first social outings was to have lunch with her former husband, Esmond, at Daylesford House – the magnificent stately home he had bought after his divorce.[19] Daylesford had become his great passion, with many believing that the renovation was an act of revenge against Ann, who would have adored to be chatelaine of such a glorious house.[20] Ann was downcast as she walked around the beautifully decorated rooms of Daylesford. As her third marriage continued to unravel, Daylesford acted as a glaring reminder of all that she had given up.

To cheer herself up, Ann travelled to France to spend a weekend with Diana Cooper at Chantilly. Diana Cooper, who had leased Château de Saint Firmin for a peppercorn rent since she left the embassy in 1948, was leaving the house and returning to England. She had bought a small townhouse on Warwick Avenue in London, in order to be close to her son.

Returning to London, Ann was not initially overly concerned when Ian was on the receiving end of a legal action. In 1958, Ivar Bryce had introduced Ian to the Irish producer Kevin McClory, who had recently produced and directed the British entry for the 1959 Venice Film Festival, *The Boy and the Bridge*. After meeting, Ian, Bryce and McClory had begun to develop a film script together which featured the character of James Bond. When *The Boy and the Bridge* was released and underperformed at the box office, Ian lost interest in the project and McClory brought in the playwright Jack Whittingham to finish the script. Unwisely, Ian had decided to base *Thunderball* – which was due for publication on 27 March 1961 – on the plot and characters from the screenplay. McClory had obtained an advance copy of the novel and he and Whittingham had issued a writ for breach of copyright, petitioning the High Court for an injunction to stop publication.

The plagiarism case was held on 24 March 1961, just four days after the issue of the writ. The presiding judge, Mr Justice Wilberforce, ruled that as the publication was so far advanced, with thousands of copies already dispatched to booksellers, he would refuse the application for an injunction. The refusal was made with the understanding that McClory and Whittingham could pursue a further action for breach of copyright.[21]

However, Ann had always disliked Ivar Bryce and was delighted to find a legitimate reason to be openly hostile, blaming him entirely for the debacle. She was unfazed by the case, but the stress became too much for Ian. Soon after the legal proceedings, and shortly after publication of *Thunderball*, Ian suffered a heart attack as he attended a Tuesday editorial meeting at *The Sunday Times* on 12 April 1961. Initially, Ian refused to leave the meeting but was eventually rushed to the London Clinic on Devonshire Place.[22]

Ann was at Victoria Square when she received a call from Ian's secretary, who explained that he had been taken to hospital after collapsing. Panicking, Ann asked the woman what was wrong, before becoming angry when the secretary was unable to give her any more details. Ann immediately set off for the London Clinic, fearing that Ian would be dead by the time she got there. When she arrived, she found him white and frail but very much alive. She was almost nonsensical with relief and only able to repeatedly tell Ian that she loved him. Although still very ill, Ian told his wife that he loved her too.[23]

The maternal instinct in Ann immediately took over and she stayed loyally by his side, doing her best to keep him amused while he was not allowed any other visitors. She also listened intently to the doctor's recommendations about changing Ian's diet and lifestyle. For the first time, Ann was forced to imagine what her life might be like without her husband. While she was far from happy in her marriage, she also realised that she would not be happy without him. And, for the first time, Ann admitted her own contribution to the stress that had brought on Ian's heart attack.

In solidarity with her husband, who had been advised to cut down on his sixty-a-day smoking habit, Ann tried unsuccessfully to stop smoking.[24] But the stress of Ian's illness soon found her reaching for the cigarettes. Ann was also sensitive enough to keep away from the London Clinic when Blanche, who was in London for the summer, came to visit Ian as he recovered. But she was spittingly furious when Blanche was dispatched by Ian to buy him some smoked salmon – a treat which was expressly forbidden by the doctors.[25]

Ian remained in the London Clinic for a month before spending a further month of convalescence at the Dudley Hotel in Hove. He kept himself busy writing a manuscript for a bedtime story he had created for Caspar, which would eventually be published in 1964 as *Chitty Chitty Bang Bang: The Magical Car*.[26] Ann resumed the peripatetic existence which always suited her best. She dashed between Hove, Pegwell Bay and London, thoroughly enjoying the role of the dutiful wife during Ian's convalescence.[27]

Ian was sufficiently recovered by the end of July to attend the wedding of his stepdaughter Fionn to John Morgan. While Ann's supercilious attitude towards Morgan had remained unchanged, she had thrown herself into the wedding preparations. The wedding was grand, taking place at St Margaret's Westminster on 26 July 1961. The wedding became one of the social events of the season. Ann even managed to secure a royal guest: Princess Alexandra, a friend of Sara and a former squeeze of Raymond O'Neill's, came to the wedding, while Cecil Beaton took the photographs.[28]

In the lead-up to the wedding, Ann and her brother had a sibling tiff when Ann asked Lord Lambton's daughters to be bridesmaids, not realising that Virginia and Hugo's daughters had already been asked. Unfortunately, Caspar let slip about the change, which upset Virginia and enraged Hugo. The row escalated quickly when Ann heard that Hugo had written to John Morgan. She was furious to discover that in the letter Hugo had said that his sister was a bad influence on her daughter. In revenge, Ann told anyone that would listen that her brother's new novel *Lifeline* was unreadable. Even as the Charteris siblings entered middle age, their squabbles still resembled those of the schoolroom.[29]

Following the wedding, Ann, Ian, Caspar and Francis Grey retreated to Pegwell Bay for August. The weather was terrible and the confines of the flat soon became claustrophobic. Despite not being allowed to play golf by his doctors, Ian managed to escape by spending the majority of his time at the clubhouse. But Ann quickly became lonely and bored. There were no like-minded people nearby and she resented the Sandwich drinks parties that Ian forced her to go to. Unsurprisingly, as the rain poured down, the Flemings began to row again.

In September, once Caspar had been returned to Summer Fields for a new term, the Flemings, craving sunshine after a sodden summer in Kent, decided to take a late summer holiday. At the end of September, they made for Provence to stay with the Australian art critic Douglas Cooper at his chateau near Avignon. Despite still not being fully recovered, Ian insisted on doing one of his beloved motor tours and drove himself and Ann to the South of France.

By the time the Flemings arrived at the Cooper house they were barely on speaking terms. The rows had begun almost as soon as they left London, with Ann accusing Ian of driving too fast. As the couple drove through northern France, Ian had accused his wife of constantly 'carping' at him.[30] As the Flemings progressed, Ian took every town at breakneck speed. He refused all entreaties from Ann to stop so that she could explore local towns or admire the scenic landscape. Ian then further irritated his wife by refusing to obey his doctor's orders and 'stuffing himself with truffles, cream, burgundy followed by smoking hundreds of cigarettes'.[31]

By the time the Flemings arrived at Château de Castille near Avignon, Ann was in tears and Ian was brooding. The couple remained on 'nonspeaks' for the remainder of their holiday, irritating their host and their fellow guests, the artist Graham Sutherland and his wife Katherine.

Returning to London, the Flemings attended a dinner at the US Embassy in Regent's Park hosted by the new American Ambassador, David Bruce and his breathtakingly glamorous wife, Evangeline. Mrs Bruce was horrified to hear Ian casually say, 'That is my wife's lover' when he was asked about fellow guest Hugh Gaitskell, who was also attending the dinner.[32] Later, when Ann and Mrs Bruce became better friends, the ambassador's wife began to understand the difficulties in the Fleming marriage, as well the British upper-class stance on infidelity.

The rows between Ann and Ian continued throughout the autumn, including a heated argument about the income from Ian's books. In the 1950s, Ian had formed a limited company, Glidrose Publications Ltd, in a bid to lower his taxes. All proceeds from his books went to Glidrose to benefit his immediate family. All film, serialisation and television rights were placed separately in a variety of trusts for Caspar. What complicated matters was that Ian had sold 51 per cent of Glidrose in 1958 to Booker Brothers, a company owned by his friend, Sir Jock Campbell, in another bid to lower his tax liability.[33] The myriad trusts confused Ann and, on the evening of 21 October, she suggested that Ian employ Arnold Goodman to streamline his financial affairs.

Aware that Goodman was Gaitskell's solicitor, Ian refused and the row escalated. He resented the intrusion of his wife in his financial and legal affairs which, understandably, rankled Ann. At the beginning of their marriage, it had been her money which had underwritten the couple and allowed Ian to write. Now that he was the breadwinner, Ann felt excluded.[34] Furious, Ann contacted Goodman, who immediately offered to help with Ian's finances. Despite Goodman's impressive reputation, Ian mulishly refused his help in a completely counterproductive move. Ann went ahead and met with Goodman anyway, inadvertently beginning a relationship which was to deepen and intensify over time.[35]

The rancour between the Flemings continued for the rest of the year. By the time Ian departed for Jamaica in January 1962, with Ann planning to travel shortly afterwards, the marriage was in a parlous state. After months of conflict over money, the renovations of Sevenhampton and Ian's health, the Flemings had argued about Caspar on their return from Christmas in Ireland. Their son had been acting up and neither Fleming seemed willing to acknowledge that Caspar's increasingly bad behaviour was linked to the obvious tensions in his parents' marriage.

Ian resented Ann's indulgent attitude towards her son, accusing her of encouraging bad behaviour and spoiling him. In response, Ann furiously accused Ian of a total lack of interest in Caspar. In a searing letter to Ann en route to Goldeneye, Ian baldly asks, 'Do we want to go on living together or not? ... In the present twilight we are hurting each other to an extent that makes life hardly bearable.'[36] He angrily explains that he is exhausted from the rows, as well as his continuous capitulations to Ann's demands, saying, 'That inhuman state of affairs has got to be ended. But it cannot be ended by my simply saying "yes" to all you think you want, whether it is a real need or a whim.'[37]

Equally embittered, Ann followed Ian to Jamaica in early February. On arrival, she was upset to discover that Ian had turned to Blanche to receive the quiet, solid support which he craved and he was demonstrably not getting within his tempestuous marriage. On her return to London in March 1962, leaving Ian alone at Goldeneye, Ann knew that her husband would once again turn to his mistress. In a letter to Ian from Victoria Square, Ann writes archly, 'now you have two weeks for adulation'.[38]

In the same letter, Ann pours out her heart to her husband. For the first time, she openly admits her resentment about Blanche, saying:

A two month's [sic] holiday for you should be made more bearable for me [...] this means that you do not telephone [your mistress] the minute we arrive [...] however much you prefer to see [...] It is a clear sign that you want to see her a great deal.[39]

She also alludes to the lack of sex in their relationship, saying, 'I beg you to cease saying I do not like sex, surely you remember our past?'[40]

The horrible truth was that Ian no longer found his wife sexually attractive. Always repulsed by any physical deformity, the scars from Ann's two caesareans had killed any desire that Ian felt for his wife. Ann knew the true reason for Ian's lack of ardour and understandably resented his reluctance to make love to her.

Answering Ian's question about whether the couple should continue to live together, Ann heartbreakingly admits, 'If you were well and we were both younger our marriage would be over.'[41] Clearly both were exhausted from their marriage; the Flemings were at breaking point. But there would be no separation or divorce. As Andrew Lycett explains, 'The relationship was turbulent at times [...] But they had waited so long to marry that they were in it for the long haul.'[42]

Back in England, Ian spent as much time as possible in Sandwich, while Ann remained in Victoria Square. But Easter 1962 was spent together at the Whitehall building. Additional tension was added by Ann inviting her father and stepmother for Easter. Guy and Vi Charteris were staying in a nearby hotel and Ann caused uproar when her father became ill while looking for nests on the local golf course. In order to attend to her father, Ann drove her car straight onto the course – an almost sacrilegious act in the eyes of golfers.[43] As a committee member of the Royal St George's, Ian was furious and embarrassed, causing yet more arguments.

Ian was also struggling with bad reviews for *The Spy Who Loved Me*, which had been published on 16 April 1962.[44] A departure from the traditional formula, Ian wrote in the first person and as a woman, with Bond only making an appearance two-thirds of the way through the story. Expecting another glamorous romp through the world of secret agents and Spectre, readers and critics were disappointed with the story of Vivienne Michel and her escape from would-be rapists, aided by James Bond.

Desperate to recreate the happiness of the Italian holiday two years before, Ann and Ian travelled to Venice in June. Staying at the Hotel Bauer Grünwald, initially the holiday was a success. Ann adored Venice and loved visiting the many beautiful churches but Ian quickly became bored.

And then Paul and Peggy Munster arrived. Ian was cheered by the arrival of Laura's great friends, primarily as he and Paul could play endless golf on the lido, but Ann resented the intrusion on her patch-up operation. Her irritation was exacerbated when the Munsters hired a speedboat, much to the delight of Ian. The party roared up and down the canals with whoops and cheers, all except for Ann who loathed getting wet – the breeze playing havoc with her hair. As Ann relayed to Evelyn Waugh, the Flemings' romantic break was reduced to 'ceaseless speedboat dashes [...] hitting the water at a vicious rate of knots and inspiring fear and boredom'.[45]

The Flemings returned to London via Chamonix, where Guy and Vi Charteris were on an alpine birdwatching holiday. A fellow guest was the naturalist Cyril Mackworth-Praed, who instantly bonded with Ian over their shared love of birds. While Ian was riveted by the conversation, Ann was bored to tears. When Ian suggested that they extend their one-night stay in Chamonix, she exploded in a rage.[46] She was bored of the holiday, bored of the conversation and bored of her husband. But she was also worried about her lover.

Gaitskell had been complaining of pain in his shoulder for some time and after appearing on a television programme in June, he had blacked out. Believing that rheumatism was the cause of his shoulder pain and the blackout a result of overwork, Gaitskell recovered and quickly resumed his hectic political schedule. He ignored the continued aches and pains, unaware that they were symptoms of lupus – the illness which would eventually kill him.[47]

Having worried constantly about Ian's health, Ann now transferred her care and attention to her lover. Ian resented this change and the couple had several barnstorming rows before Ian departed for an impromptu, and highly unusual, summer trip to Jamaica in early July 1962. The row became transatlantic as the Flemings fired letters and missives back and forth, each blaming the other for the failure of their marriage.

By the time Ian had arrived at Goldeneye, he had had enough. Worried about his health and naturally dwelling on his own mortality, he had decided that his time was too precious to be spent in arguments with Ann. He told Blanche that he had left his wife and was planning on having an extended break on the island.[48]

Back in London, Ann was frantic. Their relationship had been exhausting but Ann still loved Ian. Knowing she would never be able to win him back or even talk rationally to him while he was at Goldeneye, especially if he was spending time with Blanche, Ann resorted to devious methods. She cabled Ian and told him that she was having to undergo surgery.[49]

Ian suspected that his wife was lying but did not dare run the risk. He made plans to return to London with an overnight stopover in New York. From the Pierre Hotel, he wrote a furious letter to his wife in response to her 'cruel letters and cables'.[50] At the end of his tether, Ian writes, 'But for my love for you and Caspar I would welcome the freedom with which you threaten me with [*sic*].'[51] Then, in a final killer blow, he reveals his true frustration. 'There is no one else in my life. There is a whole cohort in yours.'[52] This may not have been strictly true on Ian's part, given that he had just left Blanche, but for the first time he revealed his exasperation with Ann's extramarital adventures.

By the time Ian landed back in London, Ann had miraculously recovered from her mysterious illness and no longer required surgery. Ian avoided a confrontation and the couple suspended hostilities long enough to attend a preview of *Dr No* at the Travellers Club, hosted by the film's director, Terence Young. Neither Ann nor Ian enjoyed the evening. Ian looked tense throughout, while Ann described the evening as 'abominable' to Evelyn Waugh, disloyally saying, 'There were howls of laughter when the tarantula walks up James Bond's body.'[53]

When Ann tentatively suggested that Ian might like to join her, Caspar and Francis Grey in Portofino in August, he wavered. He was tempted to join his family at the Herbert villa, Altachiara. But then he found out that Hugh and Dora Gaitskell would also be staying in the village, after which he flatly refused to go. Ann flew off to Italy with Caspar and Francis and enjoyed a happily social three weeks, her enjoyment hampered only slightly by the presence of a beady Dora Gaitskell.[54]

Almost as soon as Ann returned to London at the end of August, Ian departed suddenly for New York. Saying he was going on an urgent research trip; he was actually going to meet up with Blanche. Her brother Roy had died unexpectedly at the age of 52 while in New York. A grief-stricken Blanche had travelled to the city to arrange the return of her brother's body to Jamaica.[55] Ian flew straight out to offer solidarity and support.

Ann was irritated but accepting of the situation, feeling that she could not protest having just holidayed so overtly with her own lover. She was also sensitive enough to realise that Blanche needed the support of Ian during a difficult time.

Back in England by mid-September, Ian began to think ahead to the release of *Dr No* as a feature film. On 5 October, Ann and Ian attended the world premiere at the London Pavilion, followed by a party at Milroy. Produced by Albert R. 'Cubby' Broccoli and Harry Saltzman, and directed by Terence Young, *Dr No* had filmed in locations across the world the previous year, including Jamaica, where Ann and Ian had visited the set. At the première, Ian looked tired but dapper in black tie, while Ann looked absolutely radiant. Wearing a black tulle dress and fur wrap, a four-tiered pearl choker at her neck and matching pearl-drop earrings, she looked glamorous and sexy – ever the Bond girl. Even at nearly 50, Ann could radiate sex appeal. Photographs show her looking mistily into the camera, beautiful and dazzling. Looking at the photographs, she appears as the woman who has everything, with a successful husband by her side. Clearly the Flemings could still put on a show, despite a fractious year.

The James Bond film franchise has now become legendary and unstoppable. But on first release, the reviews were mixed and worried Ian. Even Ian's own family were not wholly flattering about the film. Sara remembers attending the premiere with her aunt and uncle. She asked Ann if she had enjoyed the film. 'Not a bit,' her aunt had replied. 'That Connery fellow is not at all like James Bond.'[56] Ian laughed at her criticism, before chiding his wife, 'I invented the bloody fellow.' As his niece concludes, 'The first James Bond film was a complete and utter disaster. The Goya was the only funny thing.'[57]

On 11 October, Ann became a grandmother for the first time when Fionn had a baby girl, Mary. Delighted by the birth, Ann's happiness was marred by several devastating events in the lead-up to Christmas 1962. Firstly, the Crickmeres resigned. Having loyally served Ann and Ian at Victoria Square for many years, the Crickmeres had decided to retire. After a few weeks of panic, Ann hired a Spanish couple, convincing Mrs Crickmere to return to Victoria Square for the occasional dinner party.[58]

When Hugo Charteris underwent surgery for pancreatitis in early December 1962, Ann travelled up to Yorkshire to support Virginia and the children, while her sister, Laura, inadvertently flambéed mackerel on the hospital radiator. Then, on 21 December, Mary Rose died suddenly. Heartbreakingly, she was found dead in her bed by her son, having drunk a bottle of brandy on an empty stomach.[59] Ann was obviously saddened by the death of her sister but resigned to her loss, having seen Mary Rose try and fail to stop drinking.

However, what really prayed on Ann's mind was the health of Hugh Gaitskell. Having ridden high in the latter half of 1962 with a rousing speech at the Labour Party Conference in October, Gaitskell seemed destined to be the next prime minister. But his health had been suffering, and following the party conference he made an effort to cut down on his workload. By December, his health had still not improved and he was admitted to the Manor House Hospital in north London with suspected influenza.[60] Ann exhausted herself travelling across London to spend time with her lover. She visited him on 21 December, before she heard the news of her sister's death, and was told that a check-up had revealed that Gaitskell was recovering.

Relieved, Ann, Ian and Caspar travelled to Shane's Castle for Christmas, with plans to travel to Goldeneye in the new year.[61] With his health seeming to improve, Gaitskell was able to return to his home in Hampstead for Christmas. But, on 5 January 1963, he felt unwell and was admitted to the Middlesex Hospital. The public was told that he had pleurisy.[62] Ann, who had returned to London from Ireland on 1 January, was becoming increasingly worried for her lover.

Then Ann was given further devastating news. In early January, Ian was officially told by his doctor that he had only five years to live due to his heart attack and his continued unhealthy lifestyle.[63] When Ian left for Jamaica, Ann made plans to follow him. But then, as Gaitskell became increasingly ill, she was forced to choose between husband and lover. Eventually, she made the difficult decision to travel to Goldeneye, debating the decision until the last minute. She even considered faking an illness to delay her travel plans.[64] But she knew that she could never hope to fool Ian, and in all probability, he would never forgive her for lying about a bogus illness for a second time.

However, her resolve nearly broke when she received a letter from Gaitskell telling her that she was the only person he wanted to see. On 16 January 1963, the day before she left for Jamaica, Ann went to the Middlesex Hospital to see him, but she found the ever-loyal Dora beside Gaitskell's bed. Feeling unable to force herself into the room and ask for time alone with Gaitskell, Ann instead spoke privately to Dora about the treatment that Gaitskell was receiving. Tired and emotional, Dora railed against Ann, telling her firmly that she had complete faith in the doctors. She also reminded Ann that she, Dora, was the one to make decisions about her husband's care.[65] Rebuked, Ann left the hospital without seeing Gaitskell and the following day she left for Goldeneye.

On the evening of 17 January, Gaitskell's condition deteriorated. Finally diagnosing lupus erythematosus – a disease of the immune system – the Middlesex Hospital asked Scotland Yard to help find an artificial kidney. The kidney was provided in a last-ditch attempt to cleanse Gaitskell's blood of the antibodies that were attacking his internal tissue. The attempts were unsuccessful and the following day, 18 January 1963, Gaitskell died at 9.10 p.m. with Dora by his side.[66]

Arriving in Jamaica, Ann received a cable telling her that Gaitskell was gravely ill and unlikely to survive.[67] By the time she got the cable, Gaitskell was already dead. Ann was distraught. She had made the wrong decision to leave her lover and now he was dead. While she had never loved Gaitskell with the intense passion that she had for Ian, she had loved him deeply. During the last few turbulent years, Gaitskell had given Ann unadulterated love and support. With his death, a vital cornerstone of her life had fallen away.

Conversely, Ian's health seemed to have improved during the time he had been at Goldeneye. Writing to Clarissa Eden from Goldeneye, Ann described her sadness over Gaitskell's death – 'I mind very much more than I could have imagined'[68] – before going on to describe Ian's lack of sympathy over her grief, 'When we arrived here I was far from cheerful but sharply rebuked by Ian who said he married me because I had the heart of a drum majorette!'[69]

Ann and Ian returned to London separately, with Ann arriving back at Victoria Square in early March. She was still feeling low and exhausted, not helped by her succumbing to the flu shortly after her return. Her mood was improved by the news that Raymond had become engaged to Georgina Scott.

Georgina 'Gina' Scott was the pretty and vibrant daughter of Lord George Montagu-Douglas-Scott, the brother of the 7th Duke of Buccleuch. The couple had met at South Wraxall, where they had been introduced by the Morrisons.

As part of the mighty Montagu-Douglas-Scott clan, Georgina Scott was a good match for Raymond. Ann was pleased with the pairing but was never effusive about her daughter-in-law. As Sara Morrison recalls, 'Ann was perfectly nice to Gina. But she tolerated her. She treated her like a child.'[70]

The couple married on 10 June 1963 at St Margaret's Westminster, with a reception afterwards for 1,000 people at the Orangery of Syon Park – the London home of the Duke of Northumberland. The marriage of two young, attractive aristocrats naturally became a society event. Guests included Princess Alexandra and her husband, Angus Ogilvy; the Duke and Duchess of Buccleuch; and the Earl and Countess of Dalkeith, whose son, John, was a page. Gina looked stunning in a ruffled white organdie dress, her veil secured by a diamond tiara.[71]

A few days later, on 19 June, Ann celebrated her fiftieth birthday. Despite being officially middle-aged, Ann was still beautiful, chic and, her various illnesses aside, she managed to maintain a frantic social life. Most importantly, just before her birthday, and after four years of renovation work, Sevenhampton Place was finally habitable. There was interior decoration still to be done, but Ann and Ian officially moved into their new home on 28 July.

In tearing down most of the original structure, Ann had created a beautiful and interesting home. Unusually, upon entering the house from a stone staircase leading up to the front door, guests entered a main hall, off which was Ann's bedroom and dressing room. On the ground floor were also several guest bedrooms and a main staircase, at the top of which was a portrait of Ann. The staircase led to the older, original part of the house. Halfway up the stairs was the door to the large drawing and dining rooms, which had been made from the original ballroom. The second flight of stairs led up to more guest accommodation. 'The bedrooms were a bit of a warren,' recalls Anabel Loyd. 'The passages were lined with Ian's book collection.'[72]

The drawing and dining rooms were the main focal point of the house with large, comfy yellow sofas and beautiful arrangements of flowers, giving the room a pervading fresh scent. In the dining room was a large, round table. Ann had learned from using her oval dining table at Victoria Square that circular dining tables encouraged more spirited group conversations. 'The sitting room and dining room were really lovely,' Anabel remembers. 'Aunt Ann had good taste. Sevenhampton was wonderful.'[73]

To celebrate moving into their new home, Ann and Ian hosted their first big weekend house party at Sevenhampton at the end of October. The guest list included Evelyn and Laura Waugh, Lord and Lady Avon, and Hugo and Virginia Charteris. Unusually for Ann, she complained of feeling tired and worn out before the weekend began and did not relish the prospect of entertaining. But she rallied and the guests were appropriately appreciative of the house. Unctuous to Ann's face, Evelyn Waugh was privately disparaging in a letter to Nancy Mitford in Paris. He described Sevenhampton as a 'swamp' and the bedrooms as 'tiny cubicles with paper thin walls through which every cough and snore is audible'.[74]

In the same letter, Waugh describes his alarm at Ian's appearance. 'He looks and speaks as though he may drop dead at any minute.'[75] Ian was desperately worried about another upcoming legal battle. Despite Kevin McClory not being able to stop the publication of *Thunderball*, the date had now been set for the breach of copyright action against Ian, Ivar Bryce and Jonathon Cape. The court case began on Wednesday, 20 November 1963 in the Chancery Division of the High Court.[76]

Ann continued to venomously blame Ivar Bryce for the whole legal action but loyally attended court every day. A press photo from the time shows that Ann attended resplendent in mink coat and hat, photographed beside her husband – the elegant and loyal wife. Despite Ian's smile and Ann's chic, both Flemings look tired and worried. The move to Sevenhampton, as well as the court case, had really taken their toll on Ian. Although the defence was bankrolled by Ivar Bryce, Ian worried about the financial ramifications of the court case, and the reputational implications for the James Bond brand and Ian as an author.

Ian and Bryce's defence counsel attempted to destroy McClory as a witness. But the producer refused to be cowed, knowing that the evidence backed up his claim. The court had adjourned for the weekend on Friday, 22 November when the shocking news of President Kennedy's assassination reached London. Shocked by the news, McClory used an intermediary to make an offer of settlement to Ian and Bryce. Misjudging the offer of settlement as a sign that McClory had a weak case, Ian and Bryce refused the offer. When the hearing resumed on Monday, 25 November, Ian, Bryce and their defence team realised that they had made a horrible mistake. Panicking, on Friday, 29 November, Ian and Bryce's legal counsel met privately with the judge and McClory's counsel in order to ask for an adjournment. That weekend, all the major players in the case, including Ann, met for a legal conference in the office of Ian's solicitors, Farrar & Company on Sunday, 1 December.

A settlement was offered and McClory accepted. The settlement included McClory being awarded all literary and film rights to the *Thunderball* screen-play and all film rights to the *Thunderball* novel. Ian was able to hold on to his literary rights to the original book by the skin of his teeth. But all further editions had to carry the acknowledgement that the book was 'based on a screen treatment by Kevin McClory, Jack Whittingham and the author'.[77]

The fundamental reason for the settlement was Ian's health. The stress of a long-drawn-out legal case could well have killed him and certainly contributed to his continuing bad health. Ann had put on a brave face but she was also exhausted from the legal action. Following the settlement, she spent a few days at Forest Mere health farm, before returning to Sevenhampton to plan her first family Christmas in the new house.[78] Her plans were lavish and after a shopping spree in Oxford, Ian cautioned his wife about her spending, triggering an epic row and days of tense, icy silence.

After Christmas in Wiltshire, Ann and Ian had intended to travel to Jamaica together but abandoned their plans when Ann caught bronchitis. Delighted, Ian flew off to Goldeneye alone, where he was reunited with Blanche. Ann followed on 1 February, arriving in the middle of a rainstorm.

The Flemings' guests this year were the stockbroker Hilary Bray, a golfing friend of Ian's, and his wife, Ginny.[79] Ann's arrival brought an added layer of tension to an already strained household. Ian was frustrated as he was restricted to writing for only one hour on the orders of his doctor. Matters were not helped when Ann gave her bronchitis to Ginny Bray, who coughed persistently, maddening an already highly strung Ian.[80]

The strain continued to build following the departure of the Brays. During an insufferably boring lunch with Professor Northcote Parkinson and his wife, Elizabeth, Ian had tactically excused himself. Claiming that he must rest for health reasons, he left the table, leaving a fuming Ann to amuse the Parkinsons until they finally left at 4 p.m.[81]

The pervading tension finally broke over dinner that evening. Ian told his wife that he had accepted a dinner invitation from the Parkinsons at Frenchman's Cove for the following evening. Ann was furious, having exhausted herself amusing the deadly Parkinsons. Fuelled by an evening of heavy drinking, an almighty row ensued, rivalling any tropical storm. Ian exploded, telling his wife to 'Fuck off!' and 'Go home at once!'[82] He screamed at his wife, telling her that he was fed up with looking at her face, night after night, concluding his diatribe by calling her 'a monumental bore'.[83]

A drunken and crying Ann melodramatically packed her bags and prepared to leave. But she was stymied by the fact that it was midnight and she had nowhere to go. Eventually, feeling the effects of the alcohol, she abandoned her plans to leave and went to sleep.

The next morning, both Flemings had calmed down and Ann agreed to go to Frenchman's Cove. Shown to one of the guest cottages, Ann immediately went straight to sleep. She woke to find Ian standing on the cottage balcony overlooking the sea. Unwisely, she made a crack about the next Bond girl becoming so exasperated with the secret agent that she threw herself in the sea. With arms outstretched, and leaning over the precipice, she said, 'This is the end of your next book, girl hurls herself to death sooner than succumb to old virile philistine Bond.'[84]

The simmering resentment from the previous evening flared up again and the ensuing row was brought to a swift and unsatisfactory end by the arrival of the Parkinsons with an invitation to pre-dinner cocktails. A furious and petulant Ann refused, claiming that she felt unwell. Ian gladly accepted and hotfooted out of the cottage in order to escape his wife.

After a few hours of sulking, Ann began to regret her behaviour and decided to join the party. But as she changed, Mrs Parkinson staggered into the cottage, supporting a completely inebriated Ian. Ann was mortified. She thanked a bristling Mrs Parkinson while Ian crashed around the room attempting to take his clothes off, before he passed out on the bed.

Ann was relieved to return to England on 14 March and her beloved Sevenhampton. She threw herself into the political campaign of her nephew-in-law, Charles Morrison. The incumbent member of Devizes had died suddenly and in the ensuing by-election, Morrison was standing as a Conservative candidate. Attempting to atone for his behaviour in Jamaica, Ian agreed to write an election address for Morrison.

In the staid atmosphere of a by-election, an address penned by the creator of James Bond was thrilling. The speech (which was heavily edited by the candidate's wife) was entitled 'To Westminster with Love', with the daring opening lines, 'Charles Morrison: Licensed to Kill'. The address had the desired affect and brought national attention to both the by-election and Charles Morrison, who won Devizes for the Conservatives in May 1964.[85]

Despite her energetic campaigning, Ann was seriously struggling with her health. She had increased her use of barbiturates in the tense atmosphere of Goldeneye which she unwisely mixed with alcohol. This combination had a hugely detrimental effect on her behaviour. After an evening of heavy drinking in Jamaica, Ann had climbed onto a table to replace a lightbulb. She had fallen off and badly hurt her leg.[86]

Ian was also suffering from significant health problems and had been unable to give the address to Devizes' voters himself. His heavy smoking continued to cause him problems and physical activity left him breathless. At Easter 1964, he caught a cold but still insisted on travelling to Huntercombe for a round of golf, despite Ann's protestations. The rain poured down and following the game Ian drove straight to Victoria Square in his wet golf clothes. The cold quickly developed into pleurisy and after two weeks of chest pains, Ian was admitted to the King Edward VII hospital. Here he was diagnosed as suffering with a pulmonary embolism.[87]

Ann was frantic with worry. Having lost Gaitskell in similar circumstances the previous year, she was terrified that Ian was also going to die. On her visits to hospital Ann begged her husband to stop smoking and live a healthier lifestyle. This only irritated a weakened Ian, who accused his wife of moaning. When Ian was discharged to Victoria Square in the company of a nurse, Ann chose to give her husband a wide berth and remained at Sevenhampton.

After two weeks at Victoria Square, Ian went to the Dudley Hotel in Sussex for further convalescence where he was joined by Ann on 18 June. She and Ian had lunch at English's – a seafood restaurant in Brighton. After lunch, the rain began to fall and Ann suggested that she and Ian take a taxi back to the hotel. Ian stubbornly refused and insisted on waiting in the rain at the bus stop. Ann drove furiously back to London. Nearing home, she inadvertently jumped a red light in Eaton Square and collided with a taxi. Badly shaken, Ann was unhurt, as was the taxi driver. Initially, Ann blithered apologies and admitted complete fault.[88] But later she criticised the blameless taxi driver for driving too fast – a typical reworking of the narrative by Ann.

Realising that Ian needed calm and quiet, Ann decided to give her husband space. She recognised that her presence only irritated him. Their marriage had become a battleground as they lurched from one row to the next, exacerbating Ian's poor health and causing her stress. Ann was also being diplomatic. Blanche Blackwell was in England and Ann's absence allowed her to visit Ian, which Ann knew would make her husband happy.

When Eve Fleming, who had moved back to London in 1963, had a stroke and died on 24 July 1964, Ian travelled to Oxfordshire for the funeral against the advice of his doctors.[89] Ann then drove him to Sevenhampton, where Caspar and Francis Grey had started their school holidays.

In the calm surroundings of Wiltshire, the Flemings seemed to have a rapprochement. They were happy and relaxed together, enjoying each other's company. When Dr Beal and his wife came to Sevenhampton for the bank holiday weekend, Ian persuaded Mrs Beal to take a detour en route back from lunch so that Ian could buy a picture as a present for Ann.[90]

As Ian was unable to travel abroad, the Flemings decided to spend August in Sandwich. Before they left Sevenhampton, Sara came over from her home in nearby Fyfield. She walked with Ian in the garden and recalls the chilling conversation. 'I'll never forget, he said, "I smell the undertaker's wind, darling". I was shocked, but then, a week later, he was dead.'[91]

The Flemings travelled separately to Sandwich, where they were due to stay at the Guildford Hotel. Ian travelled from Sevenhampton via London, where he saw a specialist, with Ann following shortly afterwards. She was well aware of how ill her husband was, expressing her concerns in a letter to her son-in-law. 'Ian's life now hangs on a thread. Such recovery as he could make depends on his self-control with alcohol and cigarettes.'[92]

Cooped up in the hotel and feeling increasingly unwell, Ian began to snap at both Ann and Caspar. Having contacted a local doctor after suffering bowel congestion, he then spoke to Dr Beal in London and was prescribed vitamin K.[93] On Tuesday, 11 August, Ian felt well enough to attend a lunch at the Royal St George's.[94]

That evening, he and Ann had dinner with Michael Astor at their hotel. But shortly after dinner, he suffered another heart attack. The hotel staff called an ambulance, which took Ian to the Kent and Canterbury Hospital. During the journey Ian was *compos mentis* enough to apologise to the paramedics for causing trouble and to marvel at the speed with which the ambulance got through the traffic. Arriving at the hospital at 9.30 p.m., the doctors gave Ian oxygen and stimulant injections to regulate his heartbeat.[95]

Ann, who had travelled with Ian in the ambulance, showed remarkable control. She telephoned Nanny Sillick at Victoria Square at 11 p.m. to warn her that Caspar and Francis might have to return to London. Calm and efficient, Ann talked through the possibility of Ian having a lengthy hospital stay. However, just after 1.00 a.m. on Wednesday, 12 August, Ian was pronounced dead. For three hours and forty minutes, the doctors had fought to save Ian's life, to no avail.[96] Ian had died at the age of 56.

Again, Ann calmly rang Victoria Square to tell Nanny Sillick that Ian had died. She asked Nanny to come to Canterbury later that day to collect Caspar and Francis.[97] In a horrible coincidence, Ian had died on his son's twelfth birthday.

19

ANN AFTER IAN

Like so many people hit by grief, Ann went into autopilot. Her calmness belied her total shock at Ian's death. Despite her fears for Ian's health, she was ill-prepared for his death and felt completely rudderless without him. Their romantic, passionate and bombastic relationship was over. Later, Ann would downplay the difficulties with her marriage, changing the narrative so that theirs became a great love story.

Despite her devastation, Ann forced herself into action. First, she organised for Caspar and Francis to be taken back to Victoria Square. Then she immediately began to plan the funeral. Organised for just three days after his death – Saturday, 15 August 1964 – the funeral was to be held at St James's, Sevenhampton, with only twenty family members and friends in attendance. Ian would then be buried in the surrounding graveyard.[1]

On the day of the funeral, the weather was warm and sunny. Setting out for the church, Ann took her time, walking slowly from the house. She walked around the lake and up the tree-lined path across the fields from the house to the church.

Inadvertently, her circuitous walk made her late for her own husband's funeral. The vicar had mistaken another Fleming wife for Ann and begun the service. Thus, Ann had a long, uncomfortable walk down the aisle while the clergyman gave his opening address. None of the Charteris family attended the service. Michael and Laura chose not to attend, while Hugo and Virginia were on holiday abroad. The Fleming contingent were out in force but left immediately after the service, keen to start their annual shooting holiday in Scotland.[2]

Critics and notices were generally kind about Ian. Ann was flooded with notes and letters from her friends offering sympathy and compassion. But many of Ian's friends were noticeably cool in their letters – or they did not bother to write at all. Ann was well aware that many of Ian's friends blamed her and the stress of the Fleming marriage for Ian's ill health and death.

Ann remained at Sevenhampton, increasingly numb with grief and feeling exhausted. Always happy to wallow in her feelings, she would have immersed herself in grief had it not been for her son. Caspar was now her priority and she realised that such a sad atmosphere was not good for him. She and Caspar travelled to County Durham to stay with the Lambtons at their home, Biddick Hall, where Lady Lambton planned endless trips and activities in the classic English tradition of 'keeping busy'.

On 8 September, Ann travelled to Amiens with Caspar to collect Francis Grey, who had been on holiday with his father. Planned before Ian had died, this journey to France shows Ann's determination to keep everything as normal as possible for her son. She would not have dreamed of changing her plans despite the death of her husband. As Anabel Loyd confirms, 'Aunt Ann would not have crumbled.'[3]

After a few days in Amiens, Ann, Caspar and Francis returned to Victoria Square on 11 September. Ian's memorial service was set for the 15th and Ann had last-minute arrangements to sort. Left by the Fleming family to plan the service by herself, she had chosen the twelfth-century St Bartholomew the Great in Smithfield. Ann had asked Ian's great friend Robert Harling, a noted typographer, to design an eight-page memoriam for the mourners.

Peter Fleming read the lesson and Ian's half-sister, Amaryllis, played Bach's Sarabande in C Minor on her cello. Ian's friend and the first reader of *Casino Royale*, William Plomer, delivered a heartfelt and emotional address, describing Ian's 'varied gifts and high spirits' and concluded, 'We miss him and we shall go on missing him.'[4] Plomer delicately sidestepped any awkwardness about the Fleming marriage by focusing, truthfully, on the great love that Ann and Ian had had for each other. Ann adored the address and later commissioned 300 copies for distribution. For the memorial service, Ann was chic in a black skirt suit with velvet collar, paired with a white blouse and black pillbox hat, complete with netting. Facing the press as she left the church, she looked pinched, but composed. Unsurprisingly, Blanche Blackwell was not included in the funeral or the memorial service.

With the memorial service over, Ann faced a bleak time. There was a small bright spot with the birth of Ann's second grandchild, a son called John, for the Morgans. But other than that, Ann retreated into herself, spending more time at Sevenhampton, drinking and smoking heavily, resorting to Dexedrine to help her sleep and deal with the onslaught of grief.

Ann also began to worry increasingly about money. Ian had left £289,170 in his will.[5] But having formed a limited company, Glidrose, in the 1950s, and then having sold a majority stake in the company, to Sir Jock Campbell of Booker Brothers in 1958 to minimise his tax liabilities, the tangled web of Ian's various sources of income came to the attention of the taxman after his death. Faced with inheritance taxes, Ann worried that she was broke.

As the solicitors tackled Ian's will, Ann became genuinely worried that she and Caspar would be penniless. She continually asked the executors for money. Ann testily reminded the executors that her money had funded Ian at the start of their marriage, thus she felt that she had a right to his money now. In desperation, she turned to Arnold Goodman again, who was only too happy to untangle the complicated skeins of the Fleming estate.[6]

Her worries were not eased when she joined the Fleming family in London at the end of November 1964 to sort out the remaining valuable belongings of Eve Fleming. The group went to Tooths – an art dealer on Bond Street – to divide up the art collection. Eve had willed that her children should choose pictures by order of age. As Ian was now dead, legally Ann was not entitled to anything, but the Fleming brothers insisted that she be included. However, she was the last to choose, taking her turn after Peter, Richard, Amaryllis and Michael's widow, Letitia – missing out on her preferred choice of a rendition of a magnolia.

Then the group trooped to the solicitor's office for the division of Eve's jewellery. Here, a shamefaced solicitor admitted that there had been a mistake. As the wife of the second son, Ann was second in the line of seniority and should have been the second person to choose from the pictures. The solicitor asked if Ann was satisfied with her choice of pictures. Put on the spot, Ann pretended that she was satisfied. She was further irritated to find that all the jewels and furs belonging to Eve had been left to Amaryllis, with the understanding that the Fleming daughters-in-law could buy anything Amaryllis did not want.[7] Already irritated that the Fleming clan had left her to plan Ian's memorial alone, Ann resented another discourtesy. She gradually wound down her relationship with the Fleming clan after Ian's death, except for Peter, who became a pseudo-father figure to Caspar.

Her first Christmas as a widow was spent at Shane's Castle with her two sons and her daughter-in-law. Still feeling lethargic and miserable, Ann dreaded Christmas. She also saw no point in travelling to Jamaica: for her, the island and Goldeneye had been Ian's domain. She worried that being in a place that was so uniquely Ian, she would feel even more wretched. She never visited Goldeneye, or Jamaica, again. The house would eventually be inherited by Caspar and sold in 1976.

Ann was jolted out of her lethargy when she saw an article in the December issue of *Esquire* magazine. Penned by Malcolm Muggeridge, the article claimed, inaccurately, that Ian had smoked a pipe. The article had also gone on to misquote Ian and criticise the sadistic qualities of James Bond. Ann was furious, conveniently forgetting her own less than charitable views about the secret agent. Writing furiously to Evelyn Waugh, she claimed that 'Muggeridge has shat upon Ian.'[8] But with her anger came a new purpose. Perhaps because she had failed to defend either Ian or his novels during their marriage, she now took on the mantle of Ian's protector.

In this new self-appointed role, Ann agreed to speak to *The Sunday Times* journalist John Pearson in early 1965. Pearson had been commissioned to write the first official biography of Ian, and Ann was initially enthusiastic, happily talking about her late husband and their relationship. For Ann, the interviews with Pearson were therapeutic and cathartic: she had an excuse to talk about Ian without ceasing. But the sessions were also understandably emotional. For someone who was publicly, rather than privately, very controlled, Ann frequently found herself reduced to tears as she talked about her early relationship with Ian.

Later Ann would regret her decision to talk to Pearson. During the interviews she had been wildly indiscreet and she was unhappy with how she came across in the book. After the publication she was hugely critical of the author and bad-mouthed him across London. She even went so far as to claim that Ian and Pearson had never even met, when, in fact, Pearson had worked as Ian's assistant for many years at *The Sunday Times*.[9]

Apart from gilding and protecting her late husband's reputation, Ann's main focus became Caspar. 'She dedicated herself to his best interests,' Sara Morrison recalls.[10] As her son had developed a keen interest in Egyptology, Ann took Caspar to Egypt during the Easter break of 1965. Staying at the New Winter Palace in Luxor, Ann marvelled at the Victorian elegance of the hotel but was disappointed with everything else. The heat and the noise drove her mad and she soon tired of sightseeing, writing gloomily to Evelyn Waugh:

> I do not like Egyptian art, it seems monotonous. Neither youth, nor age, nor love, nor fun is depicted [...] this afternoon we drive two hours into the desert to see a temple. I bet it's as dull as the others.[11]

She goes on to say, 'Caspar is awfully happy.'[12] Her determination to make her son happy became all-encompassing, which had the inadvertent effect of stifling Caspar. As Sara concludes, 'The weight of that love. The aunt's adoration of him [...] I almost pitied him for that reason.'[13]

With the spring of 1965, Ann began to resume her role as hostess at Victoria Square. Still miserable without her husband, she was at least able to invite all of her 'boobies' without having to consider Ian. Slowly, she began to find her feet as a single woman. For the first time since the age of 19, Ann found herself without a husband. Having moved from Shane to Esmond and then from Esmond to Ian, Ann was now her own mistress. She would never marry again but she did form intense, platonic bonds with men. Where formerly she had had lovers, now Ann preferred friendship.

One of these intense friendships was with the Labour politician Roy Jenkins. The son and grandson of a miner, Jenkins had grown up in south Wales. Socially, he was the polar opposite of Ann. While he was proud of his roots and would play the working-class card whenever required, his upbringing had actually been fairly suburban. By the time Jenkins was born in 1920, his father had left the mines in order to become a full-time union official and would later become MP for Pontypool.

After state school in Wales, Jenkins read PPE at Balliol College, Oxford. Here, he was a contemporary of Ted Heath and Dennis Healey. He also developed an intense bond with future Foreign Secretary Anthony Crosland, which was rumoured to have bordered on the sexual.

Jenkins gained a first-class degree but with the Second World War still raging, he joined the 55th West Somerset Yeomanry, before working at Bletchley as a codebreaker. Immediately after the war, Jenkins unsuccessfully stood in the 1945 election as MP for Solihull, before joining the Industrial & Commercial Finance Corporation. In 1948, he was elected as MP for Southwark Central, becoming the youngest MP at that time.

The archetypal *bon viveur*, Jenkins was a magnetic combination of immense charm and wit. And, despite his Labour credentials, he adored the finer things in life, such as fine wine, enormous cigars and good food (his parliamentary diary was always kept clear at lunchtime so that he could have a three-course lunch). While he was not a snob, Jenkins enjoyed the company of the traditional upper-class elite. This predilection even extended to his mistresses. In 1945 he had married Mary Morris, always known as Jennifer, a determined, attractive and clever woman who would eventually become chair of the National Trust. Jennifer took an incredibly accepting view of her husband's prolific extramarital affairs, which included Caroline Gilmour, the daughter of the 8th Duke of Buccleuch, and Leslie Bonham Carter, the daughter of publishing magnate Condé Nast.[14]

Jenkins and Ann had met through Gaitskell, whom they had both adored, and their relationship intensified after his death. Each had what the other loved. Jenkins had real political power. He was a rising star of the Labour Party and was poised to become Home Secretary. Ann was a beautiful, well-born, elegant woman. And both were habitually promiscuous. But unaccountably, the relationship between Jenkins and Ann was never sexual. 'Ann was one of the few whom Roy missed out on,' Jennifer Jenkins later told Sara Morrison. When questioned about the relationship after Ann's death, Sara had asked Jenkins if he had ever been tempted to sleep with her aunt. 'The relationship was never of that kind,' Jenkins responded.[15]

Like Gaitskell before him, Jenkins thrived within Ann's milieu. Always happiest in company, he relished the endless socialising at Victoria Square, as well as the weekend house parties at Sevenhampton. As Sara laconically concludes, 'The aunt fanned Roy's love for useless society.'[16] Influenced by Ann, Roy and Jennifer even began to look for a country house in the Cotswolds, eventually purchasing St Amands, in East Hendred, Oxfordshire, in late 1965.

The other man who was to become a firm fixture in Ann's life was, like Jenkins, a powerful political player. Described as a 'fixer to the Upper Classes',[17] Arnold Goodman had come into Ann's life through her friend Clarissa Eden.

Having already helped Ann with Ian's estate, in 1965 Goodman morphed from acquaintance to friend, 'much to the irritation of Clarissa Eden,' Sara notes wryly.[18] Like Jenkins, Goodman was from a working-class background. His Jewish parents had owned a drapery business and he had been brought up in Hackney. Clever, ambitious and ruthless, Goodman had attended University College London, before studying law at Downing College, Cambridge. He eventually became solicitor to Prime Minister Harold Wilson, who made him a life peer as Baron Goodman of the City of Westminster on 20 July 1965.[19]

Goodman was far from attractive. A political acquaintance, David Edington, recalls of him, 'Extraordinary hair, like a brillo pad.'[20] Even Ann herself was less than charitable when she routinely described Goodman as 'a very large Jew'.[21] But he provided Ann with exactly what she needed – solidity and adoration. Over the course of their relationship, he untangled Ian's estate and placed Ann on a surer financial footing. Later, Ann would use Goodman's flat at 79 Portland Place as her London base after she had sold Victoria Square. But, like Jenkins, the relationship was believed to be platonic. 'I don't think they were lovers,' Sara recalls.[22] Edington agrees, 'I think it was companionship.'[23]

Like Jenkins, the attraction of Goodman for Ann was power. During a dinner party at Victoria Square, Anthony Crosland, who was then Secretary of State for Education and Science, arrived to speak to Goodman about urgent and very secret political business. This was exactly the sort of political intrigue which delighted Ann and made Goodman so attractive. His

importance, influence and being at the epicentre of events made him completely irresistible. All the guests at the dinner had ears on elastic, finding a
variety of excuses to leave the table and walk slowly past the library door
where the urgent discussions were being held. There was much disappoint-
ment when Goodman later revealed that he and Crosland had only been
discussing a proposed nationwide 70mph speed limit.[24]

Goodman continued to be a steadying influence as Ann's pathological
worry about money began to affect the Bond franchise during late 1965.
Ann was unaware – or refused to understand – that when Ian had sold 51 per
cent of Glidrose to Booker McConnell Ltd, he had reduced his tax liabilities
substantially, allowing the Flemings a higher income. Now that Ian was
dead, Ann resented Booker McConnell's influence over Ian's work. She also
resented that she and Caspar had to share Bond royalties with the company
and was overtly hostile to the chairman, Sir Jock Campbell.

When Glidrose decided to commission Kingsley Amis to write a new
James Bond book – to be called *Colonel Sun* – Ann was irate.[25] As well
as being the self-appointed protector of Ian's reputation, she thought
Campbell, Booker McConnell and Glidrose were money-grabbing. She was
particularly furious with her brother-in-law, Peter, who sat on the board
of Glidrose and had actively promoted the idea of a new book. What Ann
could not, or would not, understand was that Peter, Glidrose and Booker
McConnell were all attempting to keep the Bond franchise going, rather
than let it die with Ian. It was in her financial interest for the Bond franchise
to be expanded, but she stubbornly viewed any discussion about James Bond
as vulgar and sacrilegious to the memory of her husband.

To her fury with Glidrose was added her renewed venom with John
Pearson, whose *The Life of Ian Fleming* was due to published in 1966. The
book was largely inoffensive and Ann had happily given interviews to
Pearson. But now she decided that she hated both the manuscript and the
author. She backtracked on her interviews, claiming that she had been
stricken with grief and pressured into talking. And when she was given a
manuscript of the book, she demanded endless changes, jeopardising the
publication date. Pearson and *The Sunday Times* were genuinely surprised
at Ann's volte-face, as well as her anger. But eventually an agreement was
reached and the book was published, accompanied by much chuntering
from Ann.[26]

On a brighter note, Ann also received her first proposal of marriage
since the death of Ian in January 1966. Still beautiful, inevitably Ann
would attract the attention of eligible men. This first offer came from a
bright, engaging (and young) Oxford don. Marcus Dick was a professor

of philosophy at Balliol, who had moved to Oxford from the University of East Anglia. He was newly separated from his wife, Cecilia – a historian – and had three young children (his daughter, Cressida, would eventually become Commissioner of the Metropolitan Police).[27]

Ann and Dick had been introduced by their mutual acquaintance Isaiah Berlin, and Ann had adopted him into her donnish Sevenhampton circle. She was flattered and charmed by his attention – he was 44 to her 52 when he proposed. But she did not take the proposal seriously. She was still grieving for Ian and Dick was newly separated from his wife. Gently, Ann turned down his proposal and the pair remained friends until his death in 1971. But the news reverberated around the world. Even Lady Avon wrote from Barbados to ask if the story were true.[28]

While Ann was given a much-needed ego boost by the marriage proposal, her health continued to plague her. She had what she felt was her customary winter cold in early 1966 which then developed into a fever. By March, when she was still feeling ill, she underwent several X-rays which revealed a sinus infection. A hospital stay was required while Ann had her sinuses drained.[29] Her heavy drinking and smoking were blamed for her sinus infection, as well as her wider health problems, and her doctors advised her to limit both. Assuring the medical staff that she would endeavour to cut down on smoking and drinking, when she returned to Sevenhampton to convalesce she blithely continued to do both.

Recovered, she hosted a house party for the Easter weekend on 10 April. Her guests included Peter and Sonia Quennell, Roy Jenkins (without his wife) and Diana Cooper. However, the jollities were harshly interrupted by the news that Evelyn Waugh had died suddenly on 12 April.[30] Ann was dismayed by the death of a close friend and the loss of her primary pen pal. She enjoyed his humour and caustic wit, which was much like her own. But more than missing a correspondent, Waugh's death meant that yet another of Ann's coterie of adoring men had fallen away.

Ann continued to recover physically during the summer months of 1966, making the most of the warm weather and the beautiful surroundings by entertaining at Sevenhampton. During the weekend of 30 and 31 July 1966, Ann hosted some real political heavyweights, including the ever-present Roy Jenkins (without his wife), the Home Secretary James Callaghan, the MP and diarist Richard Crossman, as well as her close friends, the diplomat Nicholas Henderson and his wife, Mary.[31] To Ann, the weekend was a huge pleasure, representing nothing more than the sort of entertaining that she adored. She thrived in the role of political hostess, catering to the needs of the power brokers of the day.

But the weekend would take on a more sinister sheen later in the year. In the lead-up to the Labour Party Conference, which began on 3 October 1966, Prime Minister Harold Wilson heard about the July weekend at Sevenhampton. Always paranoid, Wilson was perturbed that so many of his Cabinet were together. He immediately suspected a plot to overthrow him.[32] The press soon got hold of the story and began to hassle Ann.

Initially rather pleased to be seen as a political hostess at the very epicentre of political intrigue, Ann was tempted to gossip. But she was wise enough to realise that she would quickly lose her privileged position if she was indiscreet. Advised by the ever-faithful Goodman, she quickly and repeatedly denied the story. Her denial meant that Jenkins was able to remain in his role as Home Secretary. Lauded as a popular and successful politician, Jenkins was viewed as a natural successor to Wilson and, threatened by his popularity, the prime minister was looking for any excuse to get rid of Jenkins. Plotting to overthrow the government was undeniably a valid reason. Inadvertently, Ann was largely responsible for maintaining the political status quo.[33] Her rebuttal of the story convinced the prime minister that Jenkins had not been plotting and allowed the Home Secretary to keep his job.

Jenkins remained grateful to Ann and the relationship became even stronger. In August 1967, the Jenkins family holidayed with Ann at her rented villa in Sardinia, along with Maurice Bowra and Cyril Connolly. The press hounded the MP, with two photographers even surprising Ann in bed. Luckily, she was alone and doing nothing worse than drinking coffee.[34]

Ann returned to London and Victoria Square on 2 September. Already in a post-holiday funk, Ann received the news that her father had died at the age of 82 on 21 September.[35] Ann naturally grieved for the loss of her father, but the death also triggered her enduring grief for Ian, as well as her more recent grief over the loss of Evelyn Waugh. In the space of three years, she had lost the three most important men in her life – her husband, her best friend and now her father.

Despite her grief – or more likely, because of it – Ann threw herself into a manic social and travel schedule. She was unable to remain still, refusing to give herself time to be bored or even think. When in London she was never alone, permanently hosting drinks and dinner parties at Victoria Square. And during long weekends at Sevenhampton, Ann had a roster of friends staying.

She travelled to Ireland for Christmas 1967. Then to Italy in March with Caspar, staying with the Hendersons in Naples, and then Rome, where she and Caspar stayed with her friend Judy and her husband, the photographer Milton Gendel. Returning Caspar to school for the summer term, Ann immediately departed for Lismore in Ireland to stay with the Devonshires, travelling via Wales with the painter John Craxton. She made a brief pit-stop back at Victoria Square before departing for Paris in May with Diana Cooper, to attend several fashion shows and buy some new clothes.

Unsurprisingly, given her globe-trotting and socialising, Ann began to complain of exhaustion and her health began to suffer again. But she was buoyed by the attention of a new man in the summer of 1968. At a dinner party in Surrey, she had met Leslie O'Brien, the Governor of the Bank of England. O'Brien was just the sort of man whom Ann admired. Despite her arch snobbery at times, Ann had a sneaking admiration for self-made men. Like Goodman, O'Brien was a grammar school boy who joined the Bank of England in 1927. O'Brien had the admirable distinction of being the first Governor of the Bank of England not to have gone to Oxbridge, as well as being the first governor not to have a university degree. He had got to the top through hard work, becoming chief cashier in 1955, before taking over as Governor of the Bank of England from Lord Cromer, the husband of Ann's former stepdaughter Esme, in 1966.[36]

Despite being married, O'Brien admitted to friends that he had 'fallen heavily for Ann'.[37] He gently but purposefully pursued her, inviting her to dinner at the governor's flat in October of 1968. Sadly, this visit seems to have put the kibosh on any budding relationship. While Ann admired O'Brien, her innate snobbishness came into play when she saw the way he had decorated the governor's grace-and-favour flat. She was appalled with the municipal art on the walls, which were on loan from the Ministry of Works, as well as O'Brien's choice of wall paper.[38]

Having been drawn to the banker because of his power, Ann was disappointed to find that he was a timid host. Worse, he was genuinely shocked when Ann attempted to rev up the stilted conversation. Seated next to Ian's old boss, Lord Thomson, Ann encouraged him into making bitchy comments about Arnold Goodman. (Thomson fast regretted his indiscretions. The very next day, he asked Goodman for lunch and apologised, knowing full well that Ann would have funnelled all of his bitchiness back to Goodman.)[39] The cautious O'Brien was shocked by Ann's outré behaviour but he remained sweet on her nonetheless, and he remained part of Ann's social circle.

As Ann began to recover from the death of Ian, Caspar became an increasing concern. The death of his father on his twelfth birthday in 1964 precipitated the beginning of a downwards spiral. Already damaged by the intensity and drama of his parents' relationship, by the late 1960s, Caspar's problems were becoming evident. 'He was angry,' Sara remembers.[40]

Carrying the name of Fleming and dealing with the death of his father, Caspar grew up quickly. As Sara says, 'He was very clever and much too grown up from a very young age.'[41]

Ann was a practical mother. She always ensured that her children went to the dentists, saw doctors and were properly cared for. As her niece recalls, 'Her children's lives were much more ordered than my own [...] there was a maternal streak in Ann that had been left out of the other sisters.'[42] But she was not an overtly loving mother. 'She didn't come across as particularly warm,' Anabel Loyd recalls. 'We knew that Ann adored him [...] but she wasn't fussing over him.'[43]

The general consensus was that Ann was not a good mother. 'I remember Caspar falling about laughing, saying [sarcastically] "Ann is such a good mother",' Anabel continues.[44] Years later, at Laura's funeral, the journalist Alastair Forbes was equally critical, 'He said Aunt Ann was a terrible mother.'[45]

After prep school at Summer Fields, Caspar attended Eton like his grandfather and father. Here he developed a love of history and archaeology and was a popular student. 'He was very funny,' Hugo Vickers, a contemporary of Caspar's at Eton, remembers. 'He looked exactly like Dennis the Menace.'[46]

But with his dark hair and pale face, there was also something sinister about Caspar. 'He didn't smile an awful lot and had a very white face,' Anabel remembers.[47] Sara thought the boy was 'a little bit sadistic',[48] as did her mother. 'Laura always thought Caspar was round the bend. Caspar threatened to break Laura's dog's neck if she told Ann something.'[49]

Caspar's behaviour became more outrageous during his time at Eton. Hugo Vickers recalls shopping with him one day during term time. The boys entered a book shop and Caspar complained about having only enough money to buy one of the two books he wanted. After leaving the bookshop, Caspar produced the two books: 'He had bought one and stolen the other.'[50]

While teenage shoplifting is far from unusual, Caspar's growing obsession with guns was far more alarming. 'I knew that he liked to shoot things,' his cousin recalls.[51] Boys having a passion for guns is common, especially for a boy of Caspar's class and background, where shooting is a social staple. But Caspar rapidly built up an illicit collection of weaponry.

On Sunday, 16 February 1969, Caspar's housemaster found a loaded Luger revolver in the boy's study. Caspar was reported to the headmaster, Anthony Chenevix-Trench, who in turn reported the find to the police. Caspar, terrified, ran away from Eton and disappeared. Ann was frantic and, spitting venom, she blamed the headmaster for her son's disappearance.

Twelve hours later, Caspar turned up at Sevenhampton. His illegal collection of guns was turned over to Peter Fleming, who had a gun licence and immediately locked the collection away.[52]

Before the school could decide Caspar's fate, another Etonian was arrested on Saturday, 22 February in possession of cannabis and a firearm. The boy told the police that Caspar had sold him the gun. The following Tuesday, 25 February, the police arrived at Sevenhampton to interview Caspar, Ann and Peter. Ann was upset by the police visit, during which Peter Fleming admitted that he had locked up the majority of Caspar's guns, except for a Browning automatic which, inexplicably, he had thrown down a well in his garden.[53]

Peter was fined £30 for illegally possessing firearms and ammunition. As Caspar was only 16, he came before the juvenile court and was fined £25 for illegal possession of firearms and ammunition.[54] Unable to blame her son, or herself, for any of the disgrace, Ann furiously blamed everyone else. She continued to badmouth Chenevix-Trench for calling the police, and described the local magistrates as 'Bond villains'.[55]

Caspar did not return to Eton. 'He didn't come back, so I imagine he was expelled,' Hugo Vickers recalls.[56] He returned to Sevenhampton while Ann and Peter talked through options, eventually deciding on a tutorial college in Oxford so Caspar could take his A levels and apply for Oxbridge.

But Ann was distracted in the winter of 1969 when news came that her brother, Hugo, had been diagnosed with pancreatic cancer. She immediately travelled to the Charteris family home in Elvington in Yorkshire. Showing her capacity for kindness, Ann stayed for three weeks. She took charge of the house and Charteris children, so that Virginia could be with Hugo while he underwent treatment in York Hospital.

Mainly due to their precarious financial situation, the Charterises lived in a house with no staff and no central heating. Ann spent her time cooking and cleaning, throwing herself into whatever task was needed.[57] She returned to London exhausted and emotionally drained. She spent Christmas 1969 at Sevenhampton with Caspar and prepared for the end of a decade which had not been kind to her.

20

LAURA AND BERT ...
AND THE 1970S

Laura was left reeling by the death of Michael. But, like her sister, she quickly transformed the narrative about their relationship. Her husband had died rather than leave her, as he had planned to do. As a result, Laura was allowed to be the grieving widow, devastated by the loss of her husband and their supposedly perfect relationship. As she later wrote about Michael in a private memo on her sixtieth birthday in 1975, 'a beloved young husband who loved me as much as I loved him, I think it was the perfect marriage'.[1]

Throughout the rest of her life, this portrayal of the Canfield marriage became so oft repeated that Laura herself began to believe it. As her granddaughter, Anabel Loyd, recalls, 'I don't know whether he was the love of her life. After his death he took on that status.'[2] But Laura was genuinely devastated by his death. 'She was like a displaced person. She lost her persona,' her daughter remembers.[3] And within a few days of Michael's death, she had the added sadness of the death of her ex-husband, Eric. In an effort to distract herself, she travelled to New York in early 1970 to stay with Michael's father and stepmother, before the trio spent several weeks in La Jolla in California.

On her return to Buckinghamshire, Laura found Hertfordshire House lonely. Having begun to use barbiturates during her marriage to Michael, Laura resorted to heavy use of Dexedrine and Mandrax. Her dependency affected both her character and her appearance. Friends and near neighbours, the Guthrie Moirs had been regular visitors to Hertfordshire House during Laura's marriage to Michael. Suzy Guthrie Moir recalls Laura as 'one of mother's best friends. Although they had a love/hate relationship. They could be vitriolic to each other.'[4] Suzy, who was a teenager at the time of

Michael's death, remembers Laura in early 1970: 'She just looked a mess, pale and puffy, drawn. She looked very gaunt.'[5] Laura was clearly not taking care of herself; she was eating very little and her already thin frame became skeletal. As Suzy ponders, 'I would wonder now if she was anorexic.'[6]

And her heavy dependency on barbiturates often gave the appearance of drunkenness. As Suzy recalls of one particular visit in the summer of 1970, when she arrived with her parents to see Laura:

> She barely spoke. She was obviously, what we thought, drunk. She was dishevelled, slurring her words and she could barely stand up right. It seemed odd to be so drunk so early in the day. Looking back, I would be very concerned about her.[7]

Essentially, Laura was lonely without Michael. 'She was always happy if someone was around,' her granddaughter recalls.[8] Terrified of being alone, Laura once again worked through an impressively stellar cast of male admirers. One of her many fawning admirers was local antiques dealer Frank Wigram, whom she and Michael had known well. Laura considered marrying him purely for companionship, but any chance of a serious romance with Wigram was remote. 'He was very nice,' Anabel recalls. 'But very wet and very boring. We all assumed he was gay.'[9]

The tremendously glamorous and good-looking film producer and screenwriter Ivan Moffat became a paramour of Laura's in 1970. He was coming to the end of his second marriage to Katherine Smith, the daughter of Lord Hambleden and an heiress to the W.H. Smith fortune. The couple had a dalliance which lasted for much of 1970 before he returned to Los Angeles at the end of 1970, although the pair remained friends for the rest of Laura's life.[10]

And in August 1970, Laura travelled to Venice with Barbara and Herbert Agar. Here, she met Colonel Alexander 'Alex' Young, a former solider and managing director of a construction company. The pair started a romance which was decidedly one-sided. 'He was a slave,' Sara recalls.[11] Like her sister, Laura loved having adoring men around her, and 'the colonel' would be kept dangling for the rest of his life, pressed into service whenever Laura was lonely. Laura's friend, Hugo Vickers, is more generous about the relationship: 'He was perfectly nice … But she teased him mercilessly.'[12] The couple would holiday together several times over the coming years and Laura would liberally make use of his chauffeur-driven Rolls-Royce. But the relationship was never serious on her part as 'the colonel' bored her. As her daughter recalls, 'He was deadly.'[13]

Another contender was her old flame, the 73-year-old Duke of Marlborough. 'Bert had been around all the time,' Sara Morrison remembers. 'He was like an oversized terrier.'[14] He crassly proposed only a few weeks after Michael had died. As Hugo Vickers explains, 'The duke had been in love with her for ages.'[15] The proposal fell flat but did not adversely affect the friendship between Bert and Laura.

But her love affairs took a backseat as Hugo Charteris became increasingly ill throughout 1970. His cancer had returned and he died on 20 December 1970, aged 48. Laura and Ann had frequently met in York, where they had both been constant visitors during their brother's final days.

Laura was devastated by the death of her brother, coming less than a year since the death of Michael. After Hugo's funeral in Skipton, Laura accepted an invitation from Bert Marlborough to stay with his daughter Sarah and her third husband, Theodoros Roubanis, at their holiday home near Montego Bay in Jamaica.

For three weeks, Laura enjoyed sunbathing, swimming and an endless round of lunch and dinner parties. But two days before she was due to leave, Sarah asked Laura to come with her to view some farms which were for sale and she was thinking about buying. While exploring one of the vacant farm buildings, Laura walked straight into a concrete beam, giving herself concussion.[16] She was patched up by a local doctor and, against medical advice, travelled to New York before flying back to London. Returning to Hertfordshire House, still suffering from a concussion and feeling jet-lagged, Laura unwisely mixed her Dexedrine with sleeping pills. Having slept for a few hours, she awoke and went down to the kitchen. In her stupor she slipped on the back stairs, falling and breaking her jaw.[17]

After a few days in Stoke Mandeville Hospital, Laura returned home. In pain, feeling vulnerable and lonely, she began to think seriously about Bert as a potential husband. Encouraged, he began to propose repeatedly. In August 1971, Laura finally accepted over dinner at Mirabelle when Bert proposed with a diamond and sapphire ring. 'She wanted to belong again. There was stability with Bert,' her daughter remembers.[18] 'She was bored,' Hugo Vickers explains of Laura's decision to marry.[19] And the magnificent Blenheim Palace would provide her with much-needed activity and purpose. 'I could do something about Blenheim', Hugo Vickers recalls being told by Laura.[20]

In preparation for her marriage, Laura placed Hertfordshire House on the market, accepting an offer in October 1971, before spending Christmas with Bert and his family at Blenheim. Laura and Bert had not publicly announced their engagement, but when close friends and family were told, there was incredulity all round. 'The idea that Mummy was ever going to marry Bert was ridiculous,' Sara says. 'Of all her link ups, Bert was my least favourite.'[21] And Bert's son and heir, John (always known as 'Sunny' because of his courtesy title of the Earl of Sunderland), was far from happy. 'Sunny resented Laura as she tried to reorganise Blenheim,' Sara recalls. 'I was on Sunny's side over that. She was unnecessarily officious.'[22] Relations were not improved when Bert presented the Marlborough pearls to his bride-to-be at a family Christmas dinner in the banqueting hall at Blenheim.

At 12 p.m. on Saturday, 26 January 1972, at Caxton Hall in London, Laura became the 15th Duchess of Marlborough. She wore a simple, elegant red dress from Hardy Amies, complete with belted fur coat and a fur pillbox hat. She accompanied the outfit with some impressive jewellery – large pearl earrings, as well as the Marlborough pearls as a choker. Laura looked radiant, clear eyed and glamorous. Bert looked Victorian in a dark three-piece suit – complete with watch chain – and a dark winter coat, looking elderly in comparison to his beaming new wife.[23]

The short official ceremony was followed by celebratory drinks at the flat of Bert's daughter, Rosemary, followed by a lunch for fourteen family members and friends at the Connaught.[24] After lunch, Bert and Laura travelled to Hertfordshire House, where they spent their wedding night – the last night that Laura would ever spend there. The following day, 27 January 1972, the Duke and the new Duchess of Marlborough arrived back at Blenheim Palace, accompanied by Pat and Jenny Duncan, who would continue to work for Laura.

That evening, Bert rather ham-fistedly gave his new bride her wedding present. He presented her with two gold boxes decorated with tiny jewels which had originally belonged to his first wife. Continuing awkwardly, Bert explained to Laura that these two boxes would be hers to keep, whereas the Marlborough pearls would only be hers for her lifetime. Laura professed to be delighted with her husband's first wife's belongings as a wedding present and used the boxes for the rest of her marriage – one for cigarettes and the other for make-up.[25]

The Marlboroughs eschewed a honeymoon and chose to remain at Blenheim, with Bert spending the first two days of his marriage shooting on the estate. Laura attempted to dissuade her new husband because of the freezing conditions, but he was adamant. On the morning of Wednesday, 30 January, he complained of feeling unwell. Laura was immediately concerned. Following gastro-intestinal surgery in 1967 as a result of diverticulitis – an inflammation of the walls of the large intestine – Bert had been advised by his doctors to avoid rich food and alcohol, advice which he had largely ignored. The duke had also been cautioned to avoid catching cold. Laura's nursing instincts came to the fore and she convinced her new husband to abandon a third day of shooting and remain in bed instead. When Bert still complained of feeling unwell, Laura persuaded him to have a check-up with his consultant, John Dawson, the eminent surgeon, which Bert duly booked for Monday, 7 February.[26]

On Saturday, 5 February, a party had been arranged in the old riding school for all of the Blenheim staff to celebrate Bert and Laura's marriage. At the last moment, Bert ducked out, saying that he did not feel well enough to attend.[27] Sunny was pressed into service and accompanied his new stepmother to the party. The pair were photographed reading a book of congratulation from the staff, a rictus smile on Sunny's face.

Laura looked every inch the duchess in her red wedding dress. She made a speech in which she gently but firmly let the staff know that she was now the boss. There had been a change of guard at the palace and Laura was not going to be a second Mrs de Winter. She asked the staff to come directly to her if there were issues or problems within the estate.[28] Subtly – and with typically steely determination – Laura had placed herself at the very epicentre of Blenheim life, further irritating her new stepson.

The next day there was another party. This time the guests were the Blenheim tenants and this warranted a party within the palace.[29] Bert felt well enough to attend and made a speech introducing his second wife. Laura remained quiet. The tenants were not her responsibility, whereas the Blenheim staff were. Although still worried about her husband, Laura admits in her memoirs that the weekend of socialising gave her a new lease of life. Being in charge of Blenheim gave her a purpose. Once again, she had a large house to run and a staff to manage. And she relished the prospect of large-scale redecoration of Blenheim.[30]

On Monday, 7 February, Bert and Laura drove to London for Bert's check-up. The doctors were to undertake tests which would involve a two-night stay at the Edward VII Hospital. Clearly nervous, Bert asked Laura if they could have tea at Portman Towers before he went to the hospital. At 6 p.m., Bert and Laura arrived at the Edward VII, where he checked into a private room.[31] Laura planned to stay at the Portman Towers flat for the next couple of nights before she and Bert would return to Blenheim once the tests had been completed. That night Bert's condition deteriorated. While still at Blenheim he had complained of stomach pain – a symptom of diverticulitis – but once in hospital he suffered from nausea and diarrhoea. Unsure of what was causing his stomach problems, the doctors continued to test Bert for various different illnesses to no avail.[32]

His stay at the hospital was extended and Laura remained at Portman Towers. With no sign of improvement, Bert remained in hospital for the whole of February. While Laura did not have to nurse him, she was attentive. She would spend most mornings with him at the hospital before leaving him to sleep in the afternoon. She would return in the early evening and insisted on making Bert walk up and down the corridors to keep him active.

But his continued illness worried both his medical team and his wife. After several weeks at the Edward VII, Bert was well enough to attend a lunch party with Laura in Eaton Place on Sunday, 27 February. Returning to the hospital late that afternoon, he and Laura had an early supper before Laura left for Portman Towers. Later that evening, Bert became seriously unwell again, resulting in a diagnosis of Crohn's disease. On 2 March, Laura was told that the diagnosis meant that Bert would require more surgery.[33]

On 4 March, Bert was operated on by the renowned intestinal surgeon Oswald Lloyd David – the surgeon who had operated on him five years before. As the previous surgery had been successful there was no undue cause for concern, but naturally Laura was anxious. Bert entered surgery at 9 a.m. and Laura returned to wait at Portman Towers. At 3 p.m. she received a phone call to say that the operation had been a success but had taken longer than expected.[34]

That evening, Laura went to the Edward VII Hospital to find Bert still very groggy from the anaesthetic. Believing that her husband was lying too flat, which she knew could cause pneumonia, Laura began to complain vociferously to the hospital staff, loudly reminding the medical team that she had been a nurse. She then made herself more unpopular by demanding an outside nurse be brought in to care for Bert at all times, despite the hospital being incredibly well staffed.

On 5 March, Bert seemed better and was able to talk with Laura. But over the next few days there seemed to be worryingly little improvement. On Friday, 10 March, Bert was well enough to be moved from his bed to a chair in his room and to receive a visit from his daughter, Rosemary.[35] That evening, Laura returned to the hospital and again complained to the ward staff that Bert was lying too flat on his bed. She finally left the ward at 1 a.m. on Saturday, 11 March.[36]

At 9 a.m., having had a few hours' sleep, Laura was just preparing to leave the flat for the hospital when her phone rang. It was Mr Dawson, who told her that Bert had died a few minutes before. Laura had been married for a total of forty-six days – just over six weeks.[37]

Sunny arrived at Portman Towers to drive a distraught Laura back to Blenheim, where she was joined by Barbie Agar the following day. On Tuesday, 14 March, Bert's body was returned to Blenheim and laid in the chapel. The staff arranged flowers and dressed the coffin in a mauve covering, as was the tradition. Then Laura stormed in and rearranged the flowers, demanding that the coffin be covered with the standard which always flew atop Blenheim whenever Bert was in residence.[38]

On Wednesday, 15 March, Bert's funeral took place at St Mary Magdalene Church in Woodstock. He was then buried next to his first wife, Mary, in the churchyard of St Martin's Church in Bladon. As well as tenants and staff, Laura was joined by Bert's family. Ann travelled with Sara and Charles Morrison and later bitchily, but wittily, described the day in a letter to Nicholas Henderson, 'My sister had taken to be a duchess and living in a palace, and to be deposed after six weeks is not to her liking [...] She gazes towards Woodstock and murmurs about "my people"!'[39]

In the same letter, Ann writes, 'The new Duke will have great difficulty in deposing her.'[40] In a way, Ann was right about her sister. 'She liked being a Duchess,' Hugo Vickers recalls, and she would remain the Dowager Duchess of Marlborough for the remainder of her life.[41] But Bert's status as a duke and her status as a duchess had not been the primary attraction for Laura. Her marriage to Bert and her role as chatelaine of a grand house had given her a much-needed purpose. She had been excited at the thought of redecorating Blenheim and had begun an ambitious overhaul. Now, with the death of Bert, there would be no place for her at the palace and her plans would come to nothing. She was bereft and purposeless again.

Bert had made over his London home in Shepherd's Close, Mayfair, to Laura when they married, and had intimated that she would also be given a property on the Blenheim Estate.[42] But relations with her stepson had broken down so irretrievably that during a tense discussion a few days after the funeral, Sunny made it clear that his stepmother would not be welcome on the estate. 'Sunny and Mummy never liked each other,' Sara remembers. 'She loathed Sunny.'[43]

As a quid pro quo, Sunny agreed that the Marlborough estate would purchase a suitable country house for Laura. He also agreed that his stepmother could stay at Blenheim Estate until such a house was found. Laura returned the Marlborough pearls to Sunny, but was peeved when he also asked for the return of the bejewelled boxes which Bert had given her as a wedding present. The boxes were encrusted with small jewels which had been given to the Spencer-Churchill family over the years, and constituted a valuable asset of the Blenheim collection. But their return left Laura seething as she believed Sunny only asked for their return out of spite.[44]

Laura remained at Blenheim, half-heartedly looking for a house, blaming the property boom of 1972 for a lack of available, or suitable, properties.

She also decided to sell Bert's house in Mayfair, feeling that she had no need of a townhouse when she had Portman Towers – a decision which she was later to regret.

Her stepson soon began to make it clear that Laura had outstayed her welcome. Following Bert's memorial service on 28 March 1972 at the Guards Chapel, Laura travelled to Greece to stay with Bert's daughter, Sarah, and her husband, Theo Roubanis, at their home in Athens.[45] On her return in early May, she found that there was no car to collect her from London Airport. When she finally reached Blenheim, she found that her rooms had not been prepared, nor was there any tea on offer, and the staff had made no preparations for dinner.[46]

Laura knew that she was beaten. She stayed the night at Blenheim before heading back to Portman Towers the very next day. She retreated to Beechwood House, the Sussex home of Barbara and Herbert Agar, for a few days of sympathy and care. The Agars encouraged Laura to look at a house which was on the market in Sussex, and she was later shown a house near Salisbury which had been suggested by Robert Heber-Percy. But again, Laura's heart was not in her property search.

Out of desperation, Laura eventually rented a house – Cranbourne Grange in Winkfield, near Windsor. She took the furnished house for six months and immediately regretted the decision. On 9 June 1972, Laura returned to Blenheim to collect the last of her things, aided by Pat and Jenny Duncan, and left the palace for the last time.[47] Cranbourne Grange (now demolished) was a cavernous, pseudo-Victorian house, with large, draughty rooms. Always sensitive to her surroundings, Laura hated the dark furniture as well as the general layout of the house. The large front garden which led onto a busy road was also unfenced, and Laura worried continuously that one of her beloved dogs would run out onto the road.

For the first time in her life, Laura felt unable to bounce back. Having lost Michael and then Bert, she felt aimless. She was also exhausted from the arguments with Sunny as well as the move from Blenheim. She felt crippled with inertia, which was not helped by her heavily self-medicating with barbiturates.

On 13 June 1972 – the day that would have been her wedding anniversary to Michael – Laura went to her bedroom and took a deliberate overdose of the barbiturate Nembutal with whisky.[48] Later that evening, Jenny Duncan found Laura unconscious. An ambulance was called and Laura was rushed to the Edward VII Hospital in Windsor. She recovered consciousness in the ambulance and complained of a headache. By the time she reached the hospital she was in a stable condition and able to speak. Her daughter was leaving her London home to take her children to see *The Mousetrap* when she received the call that her mother had taken an overdose. She immediately travelled to Windsor, where she was met by Ann.[49]

On 14 June, Laura was moved from the Edward VII Hospital to a private psychiatric unit near Ascot. She was appalled by the place and furious that Sara had left instructions for her mother to be referred to as 'Mrs Spencer' in an attempt to avoid the attention of the press.[50] Regretting her suicide attempt, and hating to be treated as a psychiatric patient, Laura quickly recovered and left the nursing home for Cranbourne Grange in early July. In a personal memo written three years later, while staying at the Cipriani in Venice, Laura referred to her suicide attempt, writing, 'Life teaches many things, one being that come what may you have to live to the end. Once I attempted a way out. It was a foolish failure.'[51]

Soon after her return to the Grange, Laura saw an advert for a small country house, Gellibrands, on Old Shire Lane, near Chalfont St Peter on the border of Hertfordshire and Buckinghamshire. The building was sixteenth century with modern additions, and Laura was not immediately taken with the house. The first time she viewed the property she was aghast at the amount of work needed before she could move in. There was a modern staff cottage on the 30-acre grounds, which the ever-loyal Duncans could live in, and a long drive that gave the house a secluded feel, despite being so close to London. The main attraction for Laura was that Gellibrands was close to Hertfordshire House – so she would be in a familiar area and would have friends close by. Laura made an offer of £110,000 and it was accepted.[52]

Daunted by the renovation work to be done on Gellibrands, Laura sold Prudence in Barbados to free up some cash, before work began in earnest. Lanning Roper arrived to redecorate the gardens, creating a sprawling terrace along one side of the house, as well as different garden 'areas', a tennis court and swimming pool. Unlike her other houses, Laura took no great pleasure in renovating Gellibrands. Having always had a flair for interior design, she struggled with this new country home. Her granddaughter recalls the home as 'bijoux' rather than grand.[53] And Laura would always refer to the house as 'the cottage'.[54] The house took three years to renovate, with Laura moving in mid-renovation to keep a beady eye on the workmen. 'It was very nice. Very comfortable. With very steep stairs,' Anabel Loyd recalls.[55] But by the time the house was finished in 1975, Laura was unenthusiastic: 'She always maintained that it was haunted.'[56]

By Christmas 1975, Laura was again showing worrying signs of depression. Dr Barrington Cooper arranged for her to be admitted to the

Springfield University Hospital in Tooting, in south London, where she was prescribed lithium and monitored for three weeks.[57]

By the summer of 1976, Laura was sufficiently recovered to enjoy the intense heat of the summer, grateful that Lanning Roper had convinced her to install a swimming pool at Gellibrands. But in July 1976 Laura tripped down the steep main stairs, resulting in a broken foot and cracked ribs. The fall may well have been caused by the mixing of lithium and Dexedrine, but Laura preferred to blame the house. 'She said she was pushed by a ghost,' her granddaughter remembers.[58]

Despite her injuries, Laura was determined to go on holiday to Venice with 20-year-old Anabel. Laura claimed that she wanted to spend time with her granddaughter, but Anabel suspects that she was only invited because many of the regular Venice crowd were absent that year. Originally planned for two weeks, the pair had a shorter holiday due to Laura's injuries but still had a whale of a time. The pair stayed at the Cipriani, with regular trips to Harry's Bar. However Laura's health was plaguing her during her holiday. 'She was not terribly well,' Anabel recalls. 'She had to give herself injections [...] But I had enormous fun staying with her.'[59]

As Laura turned 60 in 1975, her health continued to plague her. As well as her fall, she had continual stomach problems and migraines, which may well have been linked to her use of barbiturates. Irrationally, she continued to blame Gellibrands, a home that she could not bring herself to love. In November 1977, she had her gallbladder removed at the London Clinic. The surgery seemed to have a remarkably beneficial impact on Laura. Her migraines decreased and she felt like she had more energy. Friends noticed that she seemed more alert, while Laura herself happily declared that her gallbladder had 'poisoned' her.[60]

By the time her granddaughter Anabel married Michael Stapleton in May 1979 at Tisbury Church, followed by a reception at Wardour Castle in Wiltshire, Laura was back on form. She thoroughly approved of Michael as a grandson-in-law. 'Laura liked Michael and Michael liked her,' Anabel recalls.[61]

Ann and Laura were together at the wedding and Anabel remembers being slightly bemused by both her grandmother and her great-aunt. At 22, Anabel was nearly twenty years younger than her husband, an age difference which Ann and Laura both thoroughly approved of. 'They were both, "Oh wonderful darling, we were married to men twenty years older than us",' Anabel remembers. 'And I thought, yes, but you were both divorced!'[62]

21

ANN AND THE LAST YEARS

Ann entered the 1970s irrationally worried about her finances. She rushed into a decision to sell Ian's book collection to the Lilly Library of Indiana University. Unlike any British collections or universities, the Lilly Library was able to offer $150,000 (far and away the most commercially respectable offer) for Ian's collection of rare books, as well as his manuscripts and first editions of the Bond novels.[1] The deal was agreed in early 1970 and almost straight away, Ann regretted her decision. While the money certainly eased her fears about penury, she mourned the loss of the 1,000-strong collection, which had formerly lined the walls of Sevenhampton, and their connection to Ian.

But by 1971, Ann had more than money to worry about. Her drinking had become a real cause for concern. While Ann and Ian had enjoyed heavy drinking sessions and booze-fuelled rows, there had never been any suggestion of an addiction or alcoholism. But at a weekend in Gloucestershire, a fellow guest was stunned to see Ann slowly work her way through a bottle of whisky during the course of an evening.[2] The problem became evident when Ann was told to stop drinking while taking antibiotics for a fever in early 1971. 'Gloom drove me to swilling down the pills with more and more alc[ohol].'[3] In an effort to disguise her drinking, she continued an endless round of socialising where she could justifiably have a drink in hand.

Her increasingly fraught relationship with her son also contributed to Ann's increasing dependency on alcohol. Caspar had studied hard after his expulsion from Eton and won a place to study Egyptology at Merton College, Oxford. But his studies were not a success. There were very few people on the same course and Caspar eventually dropped out after two years. Pursuing his interest in archaeology, he took part in several excavations and developed a relationship with Rachel Toynbee, a fellow student from Oxford. The relationship seemed to ground him and Ann approved of this bright, pretty girl. In August 1972, she took both Caspar and Rachel to Mani in Greece to stay with the Leigh Fermors.[4]

But Ann did not realise that her troubled son was becoming increasingly dependent on drugs. Caspar had started to use illegal drugs recreationally, which was not untypical of the era. As Anabel Loyd recalls, 'Everyone was taking things.'[5] She remembers a weekend in Sevenhampton when she was a teenager. Caspar rifled through his mother's bathroom cupboards in search of pills: 'The whole search was a bit of a laugh,' with Caspar trying to amuse his cousin during a wet weekend in Wiltshire.[6] But Caspar's intermittent usage did eventually develop into full-scale addiction. As Anabel, who was at Marlborough College, says, 'I was aware that Caspar was taking drugs. But I didn't know when it got bad.'[7]

While he was limited by his budget, Caspar's drug use remained in check. But in 1973 he reached the age of 21 and was given access to the trust fund established by Ian before his death. He also inherited Goldeneye, which had been rented out ever since his father's death. Suddenly Caspar had the resources to do whatever he wanted and his drug use escalated.

Ann seems to have either ignored Caspar's growing addiction or was too preoccupied to notice that her son was struggling. Continually worried about money, Ann sold Victoria Square in early 1973, believing that maintaining both a large London house and Sevenhampton was beyond her budget. The sale netted her £50,000 and temporarily allayed her money worries. While she considered a future London base, she rented 10 Holland Park, a large four-storey Victorian villa, before settling more permanently in a flat on Royal Hospital Road in Chelsea.[8]

Matters finally came to a head when Caspar decided to travel to Jamaica in August 1974 with his cousin Frances Charteris, the daughter of Hugo and Virginia Charteris. For the first time since Ian's death, he stayed at Goldeneye. Here he met with Blanche Blackwell who, rather crassly, showed Caspar love letters to her from his father.[9] At Goldeneye, in the house so loved by his father, Caspar made his first suicide attempt. Taking an overdose of pills, Caspar then swam out to sea. He was rescued by a local fisherman and a helicopter was summoned by Blanche to take him to Port Maria Hospital, where he had his stomach pumped. Ann was at Sevenhampton when she heard the horrific news. Desperate to take care of her son, she arranged for Caspar to be flown back to Britain, intending to nurse him back in Wiltshire.[10]

Only a select few were made aware of Caspar's suicide attempt. Ann did not care about public judgement or opinion (the attempt came only thirteen years after suicide had been legalised) but more to protect her son. There had always been enormous press interest in the only son of the creator of James Bond. Ann wanted Caspar to have the space and freedom to be himself, without constant comparisons to his famous father. As Ann said during a rare interview, 'I think all father images shouldn't overshadow a child's life. I think he'd better make his own life.'[11]

Ann attempted to help her son privately at Sevenhampton, but the scale of the problem soon became evident as Caspar struggled with both his depression and withdrawal from drugs. Occasionally, he would return to his rented one-room flat on Old Church Street in Chelsea.[12] By November 1974, Ann realised that Caspar needed proper care and she arranged for her son to enter Swindon Psychiatric Unit.[13]

While Ann was relieved that Caspar would finally receive the care he so desperately needed, she felt intensely guilty that she could not care for her son. After three months looking after him, Ann was chronically exhausted and on the verge of depression herself. Once again, she used alcohol as a way of coping with her problems. She started to drink throughout the day, starting with a brandy straight after breakfast. After visiting Caspar in the psychiatric unit at Swindon Hospital, she would always take a solitary trip to the pub for another brandy or two before making the journey back to Sevenhampton.[14]

Caspar had three extended stays in Swindon Psychiatric Unit in 1975. During these stays he was medicated and was given electric shock therapy. By the late summer, he seemed to be showing signs of improvement and was judged well enough to visit Shane's Castle for a holiday in September. In Ireland, a place that he had always loved, and cared for by Raymond and Gina O'Neill, Caspar seemed much better. He laughed and talked, spending hours walking and searching for ancient arrowheads.

Returning to London at the end of September, he stayed at Ann's flat while his mother remained at Sevenhampton. Back in London, Caspar's depression returned and he rapidly declined. 'He hadn't slept for days,' Anabel recalls.[15] On the evening of 1 October, Fionn travelled to the flat on Royal Hospital Road to check on her brother. Finding him asleep after days of insomnia, she left him to rest.[16]

The following day, a neighbour of Ann's returned to his own flat and noticed that the curtains of the neighbouring flat had not been opened. Aware of Caspar's history, the neighbour let himself in and found Caspar dead in one of the bedrooms. Caspar had changed into his pyjamas and written a suicide note, before taking three bottles of barbiturates and climbing into bed. The suicide note, which was found in his pyjama pocket, demonstrated Caspar's tragic desperation, reading simply, 'If not this time it will be next.'[17]

Ann was at Sevenhampton when she heard the horrific news that her son had taken his own life at the age of 23. Devastated and hysterical, she had to be sedated for several days. In this final, appalling blow, everything she had created with Ian was gone. Her husband was dead and now, the beloved son – the most tangible sign of their intense love affair – was also dead. Added to her utter desolation was the chronic guilt that inevitably accompanies suicide.

Ann remained in Wiltshire following Caspar's death. She was too grief-stricken to attend the inquest on 12 October at the Westminster Coroner's Court, where a verdict of suicide was duly recorded.

The small funeral was held at St James's in Sevenhampton, with only family and a few of Caspar's close friends attending. Rachel Toynbee attended. Having formed an uneasy alliance with Ann during her relationship with Caspar, she now had no time for the grieving mother. 'Rachel blamed Aunt Ann for everything,' Anabel concludes.[18]

Despite the tragedy of Caspar's suicide, Ann attempted to alter the narrative around her son's death. In her correspondence following his suicide, she began to talk of Caspar's illness and depression affecting only the last fifteen months of his life, conveniently ignoring the troubles that he had endured during his teenage years. She recalled their relationship as uncomplicated and described Caspar as a 'marvellous companion', which was far from the truth.[19] The relationship between Ann and her son had broken down to such an extent that he had even been physically violent, knocking Ann to the floor on one occasion.[20] 'He was oppressed by his mother,' Hugo Vickers concludes.[21]

Ostensibly, Ann and the wider family professed that the motivations for Caspar's suicide remained a mystery. As Anabel recalls, 'I don't know why Caspar was so screwed up.'[22] But Sara Morrison is more candid in her explanation of the suicide, 'We knew that he was an emotional mess. With parents like that what do you expect?'[23]

Ann could be forgiven for drinking herself to death after the suicide of her youngest son. Instead, she admirably chose to combat her alcoholism and entered a nursing home in July 1976. Publicly, she was seeking help for exhaustion. Privately, she was undergoing intense rehabilitation, mindful of how addiction had contributed to her son's death. The routine response to alcoholism is to give up alcohol entirely. Typically, Ann charted her own course and only gave up drinking during the day. She continued to drink wine with meals and would frequently enjoy a gin and tonic in the evenings, freely admitting that she often counted down the minutes until 6 p.m., when she could legitimately have a drink.[24] The approach was idiosyncratic, demonstrating Ann's steely determination to fight alcoholism her own, individual way. She was also prescribed Heminevrin, a barbiturate more commonly known as clomethiazole, which is used to treat and prevent withdrawal symptoms from alcohol.[25]

Having been expected to fester in Wiltshire, friends of Ann were amazed that, as 1977 dawned, she began to resume a full social life. In November 1977, at the age of 64, Ann marked a return to form with a house party at Sevenhampton. The group was a perfect mix made up of old friends and handsome young men. Included in the group were Peggy Munster and Mary 'Midi' Gascoigne, as well as the writer Raymond Mortimer. There was also a new, young friend, the cartoonist and journalist Mark Boxer.[26] A dynamic, attractive and engaging young journalist with *The Sunday Times*, Boxer was known as a man about town with immense charm. He had spent the majority of his career with the Thomson Group and would later edit the rehabilitated society magazine *Tatler*. With his engaging manner, his humour and his dark good looks, Boxer reminded Ann of Ian, and the pair established a flirtatious but platonic friendship.

The success of the house party, and the reminder of her glory days of entertaining, gave Ann her social confidence back. In December, she threw a grand party at the Ritz to mark the publication of Paddy Leigh Fermor's book *A Time of Gifts*.[27] Wearing a black cocktail dress, with her hair coiffured, Ann arrived at the Ritz in an elegant fur.

Ann Fleming, the hostess, was back and she was in her element. Just a stone's throw from Warwick House – the location of her former successes – Ann welcomed guests to a private room overlooking Green Park. By her side that evening, as well as in life more generally, was the large presence of Arnold Goodman, providing quiet, solid support during the last few turbulent years of Ann's life.

In July 1978, Ann hosted Goodman and a crowd of people to Sevenhampton for the coming-out ball of Elizabeth Phipps at nearby Buscot Parsonage. The theme was 'opera' and all the guests went to town with their costumes. Goodman went as Friar Tuck, while Ann's friend from Farringdon, Robert Heber-Percy, dressed as Mephistopheles in eye-catching scarlet. But Ann stole the show as 'The Ghost of Opera' in a gold and peach dress, complete with headdress of ostrich feathers and matching fan. She oozed radiance as she drank champagne and danced among the other 500 guests, finally leaving to return to Sevenhampton at 3 a.m.[28]

Ann's ill health continued to plague her. She frequently had a persistent cough – not helped by her smoking habit. She also had constant stomach problems, which were occasionally so painful that she would have to go to bed. Ann's use of the barbiturate Heminevrin, prescribed to help with her withdrawal from alcohol, is commonly linked to cold-like symptoms and nasal congestion, and Ann complained of suffering near-constant colds in the winter of 1978.[29]

Despite her discomfort, Ann resumed her hectic travelling schedule. She spent the Christmas of 1978 in Ireland, before travelling to Scotland and Greece in 1979. Becoming more adventurous, Ann also travelled to Israel for the first time in early 1980, as well as Morocco in March with Patrick Trevor-Roper.[30] Having always used travel as a means to avoid boredom, Ann now used travel to deal with her grief. Her later travels frequently focused on places with a rich, archaeological history – a tragic nod to the interests of her youngest son.

Back at Sevenhampton with Goodman in January 1981, the pain in her stomach became so bad that Ann was admitted to Swindon General Hospital. Initially, she was diagnosed with having a twisted intestine which the doctors believed an operation would cure. Ann returned to Sevenhampton but the pain continued and intensified.[31] She was readmitted to hospital for further tests which revealed a malignant tumour in Ann's stomach.

Ann was told that she had cancer in April 1981. While her family were informed that she only had three months to live, Ann herself was not told the truth.[32] She reacted stoically to the diagnosis, realising that she was ill but not knowing that the disease would be terminal. Publicly, she seemed more inconvenienced by an accompanying dose of laryngitis, making light of the cancer diagnosis to friends in letters. In a letter to Deborah, Duchess of Devonshire, she pithily says, 'I have laryngitis and cancer, the former is the most immediately depressing – voiceless.'[33]

Initially, she spent time at Portland Place before retreating permanently to Sevenhampton. Here she was looked after by a nurse who had been hired by her sister Laura, despite the difficulties within their sisterly relationship. Ann's health rapidly deteriorated and she continued to lose weight. 'Ann was given a cocktail of drugs,' Anabel recalls. 'I remember thinking that the drugs will kill her.'[34]

Ever the hostess, as Ann lay in bed, she received a roster of visitors. Debo Devonshire had lunch with Ann on 4 June and Patrick Trevor-Roper visited almost daily.[35] Fionn returned to Sevenhampton to be with her mother and Goodman remained a constant presence. Sara, who lived in nearby Fyfield, also spent time with her aunt. Even towards the end, Ann remained witty, saying to her niece, 'Now I know I am dying because Arnold has asked me to marry him.'[36]

On Saturday, 11 July, Ann slipped into a coma, dying in the early hours of Sunday, 12 July 1981. Her funeral was held a week later at St James's Church in Sevenhampton on Friday, 17 July. As well as a reading of Psalm 23, the congregation sang two hymns, 'O God, our help in ages past' and 'Praise, my soul, the King of heaven'.[37] After the service, the small group of mourners, including her sister Laura, trooped outside to the churchyard, where Ann was laid to rest beside her two great loves. On one side was her son, Caspar. On the other was her beloved Ian – a man who had driven her mad with love, lust and frustration. Their great, complicated love story finally at an end.

A memorial service was held for Ann on Friday, 20 November 1981 at St James's Church, Piccadilly. As a woman who had made her mark as a hostess, the memorial service was no exception. St James's was crowded with a blend of politicians from across the political spectrum, aristocrats, actors, journalists, writers and television stars. All had come from far and wide to celebrate a woman who had packed a riotous life into sixty-eight years. And had been the most consummate and extraordinary hostess.

Speaking at the memorial service, the author and academic Lord Noel Annan recounted Ann's life. He described her love of literature, her wit and her reputation as a remarkably bombastic hostess. 'In naval terms she was something of a privateer,' Annan remembered. 'She would move into a calm lagoon where barques and frigates were careening peacefully and suddenly let off a broadside. The calm vanished, ripples spread across the waters, the whole harbour became animated, galvanized, expectant.'[38] Bizarrely, while Annan made reference to Ann's marriages to Shane and Esmond, there was no mention of Ian.

Paddy Leigh Fermor read *The Garden of Cyrus* by Thomas Browne, introducing the passage 'The Mystic as Gardener' with the words, 'There is something reminiscent of Sir Thomas Browne in the scenery at Sevenhampton [...] the passage is apt, too, because it was one of Ann's favourites, and she often asked her friends to read it aloud.'[39]

Nicholas Henderson was unable to attend the service as he was serving as the British Ambassador in Washington, but he sent a tribute which was read during the service. He remembered Ann as 'consistently, indeed uncompromisingly and often courageously, herself'. And he described her qualities as a hostess: 'I cannot forbear to stress that giving pleasure to others was part of her being, part maybe of the way of enjoying it herself.'[40]

The party was finally over for Ann. In the small, sleepy, country churchyard of Sevenhampton in Wiltshire, the Fleming family remain together. A surprisingly quiet and unremarkable place for such a volatile family, their grave marked by an imposing, lichen-covered obelisk. People from across the world come to this Wiltshire churchyard to pay homage to the famed creator of James Bond. How galling for Ann that her husband's 'vulgar creation' is the reason that people still visit the gravesite.[41]

22

LAURA AND THE 1980S

As Ann's life drew to a close, Laura seemed to be having a renaissance. As well as the beneficial impact to her health after the removal of her gallbladder, Laura had been approached by the publisher Lord Weidenfeld to write her memoirs. In 1978, she was introduced to the biographer Hugo Vickers, who would edit the memoirs and become a close friend during the last decade of her life.[1]

Laura relished rewriting the narrative of her life in her memoirs, *Laughter from a Cloud*. As well as describing her epic success with, and attraction for, an endless roster of men, she placed the blame for the breakdown of her myriad marriages firmly on the shoulders of her ex-husbands. But the book was searingly honest and frank about her other relationships, including the breakdown of communication with both her daughter and her sister.

Laura's immediate family were, understandably, unenthusiastic. '[The memoirs] were definitely a topic of conversation – generally we all thought "oh for goodness sakes",' her granddaughter remembers. 'The general feeling was "ho ho how ridiculous".'[2] But the book sold well, although not well enough for Weidenfeld. 'Laura was furious that there wasn't a second edition,' Hugo Vickers remembers.[3]

The publication of *Laughter from a Cloud* on 10 April 1980 had an unexpected consequence for Laura. The bookseller Christina Foyle threw a celebratory lunch for her at the Dorchester on Wednesday, 16 April. The guests included Barbara Cartland and Margaret, Duchess of Argyll, as well as the historian and columnist, Sir Arthur Bryant, who had been asked to chair the lunch. He had initially refused, worried that Laura's memoir would be too salacious for his weighty reputation. But when Bryant arrived at the Crystal Room of the Dorchester he was, like so many men before him, bowled over by Laura.

Even at nearly 65, Laura clearly still had a raw appeal. Bryant made a beeline for her despite being accompanied to lunch by a girlfriend. He generously and untruthfully compared Laura's memoirs to the writing of Dr Johnson, which failed to impress her. His next subject matter had more impact: their mutual love of dogs. Bryant had written a book called *Jimmy: The Dog in My Life* – an ode to his beloved terrier, whom he had rescued in 1942. Laura, who loved dogs almost as much as she loved men, was charmed.

The following day, Bryant dropped a signed copy of *Jimmy* at Portman Towers with a letter making his feelings clear. 'I owe you an apology for yesterday. I enjoyed your company so much that I forgot all about my speech,' adding, 'It is not the business of a chairman to fall in love with his introducee [...] but then I don't see how anyone could help doing so with you.'[4] This was just the sort of romantic overture which Laura adored. The pair enjoyed a rapid exchange of letters in which Bryant, nauseatingly, began to refer to Laura as 'Jimmy' after she compared herself to his late pet.

★ ★ ★

Born in 1899, Arthur Bryant had grown up near Buckingham Palace, where his father worked within the Royal Household. After Harrow, he obtained a scholarship to Pembroke College in Oxford but instead elected to join the Royal Flying Corps in 1917. After the end of the First World War, he read modern history at Queen's College, Oxford. After a short-lived stint as a barrister at the Inner Temple, in 1923 he became headmaster of the Cambridge School of Arts, Craft and Technology. A magnetic and dynamic speaker, he vastly improved enrolment numbers at the school before becoming a lecturer in history for the Oxford University delegacy for extramural studies.

In 1929 he published his first book *The Spirit of Conservatism*, before going on to publish notable biographies on Samuel Pepys and Charles II. A popular figure, Bryant became somewhat of a 'celebrity academic', regularly contributing to newspapers and magazines, as well as appearing on television and radio broadcasts.

His stellar professional reputation was matched by his equally stellar reputation with women. Tall, dark and handsome, Bryant had been a hit in the debutante ballrooms of the interwar years. In 1926 he had married Sylvia Shakerley, daughter of Sir Walter Shakerley. This marriage ended in divorce, and in 1941, he had married Anne Brooke. This marriage would also end in divorce in 1975.[5]

An unlikely lothario, Bryant adored the company of pretty women. As well as his two marriages, Bryant managed a veritable menagerie of ladies, including a long-standing affair with his secretary, Pamela McCormick, as well as his 'muse', Alwynne Bardsley, and a Salisbury neighbour, Lorelei Robinson. Despite his promise to marry Pamela McCormick following his divorce from Anne in 1975, by 1980 the couple had still not married and Bryant continued to energetically, and seemingly indiscriminately, pursue women.

After his divorce from Anne, Bryant divided his time between a beautiful eighteenth-century house, Myles Place, in the close of Salisbury Cathedral, and Pamela's London flat. Bryant had been staying with Pamela and taken her as his date to the Foyle lunch on 16 April, when he had met Laura.[6]

Returning to Gellibrands after a publicity tour in Yorkshire, Laura extended an invitation to Bryant to visit. In late May 1980, Bryant travelled to Gellibrands for a weekend with his new beau. The pair enjoyed a romantic meal in the dining room before Bryant read aloud to Laura from *The Happy Hypocrite* by Max Beerbohm. However, Bryant was disappointed when he was shown to his room, which was on the other side of the house from Laura. The pair retired to their separate rooms where, after an abortive attempt to talk via the internal telephone, Laura and Bryant curiously decided to exchange letters. While he rambled on about 'the destruction and shame of all the things we both feel about the England we were brought up to love',[7] Laura was at her flattering, coquettish best, writing, 'If I could but find the words at this late hour to tell you how you enchanted me yesterday – you are the only real GENTLEMAN in my sad befuddled eyes since Michael died.'[8]

Back at Myles Place, Bryant wrote a long letter in which he proposed to Laura, describing her as the type of woman who had 'all the qualities I need to complement and mend my own character [...] whose own experience in life has fitted her to give me everything I so sorely need to help me in my tasks, life and work'.[9]

Despite this remarkably egotistical proposal, three days later, Laura accepted. Less than two months after meeting, Laura and Bryant were engaged. For Bryant, Laura was a catch. At 64, she was seventeen years younger than the 81-year-old academic. She still had allure – the sex appeal which had defined her life had not faded. But more importantly, she had status – and money. 'He thought he was getting a rich duchess,' Hugo Vickers concludes.[10] To Bryant, the combination was irresistible.

For Laura, the attraction to Bryant was a little more complicated. He was dynamic and attractive in his own way, with enormous charm. But Bryant also provided the adoration which Laura craved. 'He worshipped at her feet,' her daughter recalls. 'It was an ego trip for her.'[11] And, like her marriage to Bert Marlborough, Bryant offered security and company; an antidote to the loneliness which so terrified her. Like Bryant, Laura loved the idea of love.

Carried away with the romance of the situation, Laura had found a way to finish her life story with one last, lasting, romance.

However, her family were less than enthusiastic about the romance. 'The engagement was a complete joke. A complete non-event,' Sara recalls.[12] 'I think she loved his dogs,' Laura's granddaughter Anabel accurately surmises.[13]

But before the couple could get too carried away, there were some practicalities to be taken care of. Bryant had to quickly extricate himself from an informal engagement to Pamela McCormick. With an upcoming literary lunch at which both Laura and Pamela would be in attendance, Bryant wrote to Pamela explaining the situation, devastating his former lover.

Although the engagement between Laura and Bryant had not been officially announced, several newspapers began to devote column inches to the budding romance. Finally, on Tuesday, 1 July, the announcement of their upcoming marriage appeared in *The Sunday Times*. A neighbour in Salisbury Close, David Reindorp, the son of the bishop, remembers Bryant putting his back out soon after the engagement was announced. As the neighbour recalls, 'For about a week afterwards, Sir Arthur could be seen walking around the close like an awkward crab. Clearly the result of an energetic celebration of the engagement between him and the duchess.'[14]

But their energetic happiness was short-lived. As the couple spent more time together, moving between Myles Place, Gellibrands and Portman Towers, their breathless initial romance faded. Laura began to complain about Myles Place, claiming that she did not want to run such a large, unwieldy home after they were married without adequate staff.

There was also a bigger problem. 'Arthur was very middle class,' Hugo Vickers remembers. 'And Laura hated anything middle class. Washing cars and twitching curtains, she hated that.'[15] When he entertained, Bryant would bring the silver down in a great sack, 'then he would carry it all up to the attic after dinner', a habit which horrified Laura.[16]

As well as her disparagement of his middle-class habits, Bryant also discovered that Laura could be incredibly tough and dismissive. 'She could be sharp,' Hugo Vickers explains.[17] Used to having his ego flattered, this treatment did not sit well with him. Bryant chastised Laura for her behaviour, describing her in a letter as 'a Duchess but one who so disappointingly turned out to lack all the proper and enobling [*sic*] physical attributes and amplitudes of true Duchesshood'.[18]

More worryingly for Bryant, he also discovered that while Laura had been left well off through her marriages, she had made several unsuccessful investments. In 1976, Laura had guaranteed a loan of £15,000 from Coutts

& Co. for an American friend of Michael Canfield's, who needed the money to fund the education of his two sons. The man had defaulted on the loan and, threatened with legal action by the bank, Laura had paid the guarantee from her own pocket. Egged on by Bryant, Laura employed the legal firm, Coles & Stevenson to file a lawsuit against Coutts & Co. for negligence in allowing Laura to stand as guarantor, as well as malpractice for making her pay the outstanding loan of £15,000.[19]

Initially delighted to have a man on her side, Laura quickly became irritated as Bryant fired off letters to her solicitors, as well as A.E. Hamlin, the legal representative of Coutts & Co. Bryant crassly suggested a meeting between the two legal counsels to resolve the matter. This earned a sharp response from the Coutts' legal counsel, who wrote to Laura's lawyers, saying, 'We really do not quite know what it is that you are proposing as the only proposal, as far as we are concerned [...] is that your client should withdraw her claim.'[20]

He also encouraged Laura to threaten legal action against her former solicitor, Mr Mills, for failing to warn her of a proposed extension to the M25 when she purchased Gellibrands in 1972. Finally, Laura snapped when Bryant made an offhand comment about her financial management, triggering a blazing row. Bryant backed off and Laura dropped the case against Coutts & Co., later settling out of court with Mr Mills for £75,000.[21]

In September 1980, Bryant once again suffered a back injury and was forced to take to his bed. Always at her best when acting as nurse, Laura proved to be a conscientious carer. She stayed with him at Myles Place, happily administering daily morphine injections. Unfortunately, Laura was a little too overzealous with the injections. While giving a talk in Salisbury Cathedral, Bryant collapsed as a result of a near overdose of morphine.[22]

As Bryant got better, the relationship seemed to get worse. Laura finally left Myles Place after she found out that Bryant had been writing to Pamela and had even had dinner with his ex-squeeze. In a retaliatory gesture, Laura travelled to Portugal with Colonel Alex Young in October. The holiday had the desired effect. Bryant came running back and the couple were reunited in November, making plans to spend Christmas together.

Unfortunately, the festive period did not begin well. Arriving at Myles Place at the beginning of December, the couple had a row almost immediately after Laura made them late for dinner with the bishop and dean of Salisbury Cathedral. Laura returned to Gellibrands, writing to Bryant on 5 December, accusing him of behaving like an 'adolescent'.[23]

Always better in correspondence and in long, late-night telephone calls, Bryant apologised to Laura, swearing to her that he would change his

ways. She relented and agreed that Bryant could come to Portman Towers
for Christmas. While staying, Bryant went for a walk in Green Park on
23 December and slipped on some ice, cracking several vertebrae in his back.

This time, injury did not bring out the caring side in Laura. Once again,
she administered morphine injections, but by Boxing Day the strain had
become too much. The couple rowed after Laura announced her intention
to see a friend, and Bryant threatened to leave despite his injuries.

He returned to Salisbury chastened, writing to Laura on 28 December
1980, 'My Darling love, The world doesn't make much sense for me without
you.'[24] But Laura remained unmollified, writing on the 29th, 'I have tried to
forget Christmas – you know my reasons', before continuing:

> Why on Boxing Day after you had slept for some five hours, and I told
> you I had to visit a sick aged friend, did you turn on me like some reincar-
> nation of Mr Barrat [sic] to his daughter Elizabeth.[25]

The relationship limped on into 1981. In a last attempt at reconciliation,
Bryant planned a trip for him and Laura to Madeira. Instead, Laura chose
to take another holiday to Portugal with the colonel, after which the proposed Madeira trip was cancelled. Publicly, the couple remained engaged
and attended events together. Laura accompanied Bryant to several literary
dinners, as well as when he spoke at Harrow – his old school. But these
events were punctuated with ever more frequent rows, which took on an
almost comical quality. After a row about the cost of oil central heating on
Tuesday, 13 October 1981, Bryant rang Laura at Gellibrands simply to slam
the phone down on her. A bemused Laura wrote to him the following day,
'Darling Cross Patch [...] I don't think anyone has ever telephoned me ever
in order to slam down the instrument.'[26]

The year 1981 was one of upheaval for Laura. In June, Barbie Agar
died at the age of 82, and in July, Ann died from cancer. The death of her
last remaining sister was complex for Laura, as she and Ann had become
increasingly estranged. Bryant was surprisingly concise when he wrote to
Laura the day before Ann's funeral, 'I know that, despite her alienation from
you, you loved your sister and that the thought of that early companionship
and the love that bound that brilliant family made that alienation an aching
grief for you.'[27] Having once been close, the relationship became, as
Anabel Loyd recalls, defined by 'rivalry and jealousy. Aunt Ann somehow
disapproved of grandma.'[28] Their divergent paths had caused friction to
such an extent that, by the end of Ann's life, the sisters were barely on
speaking terms.

The death of Ann also prompted the end of another relationship. During her engagement to Bryant, Laura had also been encouraging the attentions of a Swiss yachtsman and writer, Hans de Meiss-Teuffen. This handsome, swashbuckling, 70-year-old adventurer had fallen for Laura after the pair met in Venice at the tail end of the 1970s.

With a playboy reputation, de Meiss-Teuffen had a chequered past. Born on the Austrian-Hungarian border in 1911, de Meiss-Teuffen had initially started work in London as a banker, before beginning a peripatetic life of adventuring and sailing. When war broke out in 1939, he joined the Swiss military before leaving to become a freelance war correspondent. Among his more outlandish and unsubstantiated claims were that he had been both a spy and a double agent.[29]

In 1946, he sailed his boat, *Speranza* across the Atlantic in a record of fifty-eight days, after which he developed a reputation as a public speaker. He also published two moderately successful memoir-cum-travel books, *Destination in the Wind* in 1951 and *Winds of Adventure* in 1953. Charming and fun, de Meiss-Teuffen was fascinated by European history. Knowing of Laura's relationship with Bryant, de Meiss-Teuffen frequently peppered his paramour with questions about the other man in her life. Aware of Bryant's near hatred of anyone who was not part of the Allied effort during the Second World War, and de Meiss-Teuffen's claims of being a double agent, Laura kept the two men very separate.

But the men did have their adoration of Laura in common. De Meiss-Teuffen was besotted with Laura. In a letter in late 1980, he wrote, 'Oh Laura! There is the moment when realization hits you like a ton of bricks – you *très chérie* being the ton of bricks […] who has turned me over like soil.'[30] Initially, de Meiss-Teuffen wrote adoring letters from his Palazzo in Salerno, before renting a farmhouse near Stroud, Gloucestershire, in 1981.

But the romance came to an abrupt end when de Meiss-Teuffen tactlessly wrote to Laura, two days after her sister's funeral, to ask a favour about Ann's former home:

> The reason for this letter […] to ask you, if I did something very wrong […] or very not-done […] by writing to Anne [*sic*] Fleming's solicitors. I asked them if they might need and want a responsible person (me!) to baby-sit the house […] Yousee [*sic*] my lease here comes to an end by Sept. 30th.[31]

Laura was furious and her ardour instantly cooled. She backed off, causing de Meiss-Teuffen to write desperate letters. On 9 November 1981, he wrote plaintively, 'Your letters began to a) peter out […] b) belittle --- criticize […] condemn […] and I couldn't believe it?? WHY.'[32]

These letters coincided neatly with a rapprochement between Laura and Bryant, which may explain why Laura was so quick to drop de Meiss-Teuffen. In November, Laura introduced Bryant to Diana Cooper, and by Christmas the relationship seemed to be back on an even keel. Bryant had committed to writing the last part of his volumes of the history of England, which kept him busy and, crucially, separate from Laura. Once again, being physically apart drew the couple closer together emotionally, despite the odd fractious exchange. On Friday, 13 November 1981, Laura wrote testily, 'Why do you call me little barker? Most people think I've rather a nice voice, it must be the telephone',[33] to which Bryant responded soothingly, 'Your little gruff voice going straight to one's heart.'[34]

Bryant's commitment to the book kept the couple separate for much of 1982, with the pair exchanging warm, loving letters and telephone calls. Writing on 3 August from Gellibrands, Laura sounds caring and affectionate. 'You don't have to spend the rest of your life writing – but it is your choice – others [sic] pleasure.'[35]

In October, the couple were together at Gellibrands when they inadvertently featured in a fly-on-the wall documentary series about the police. Having received a tip-off that Gellibrands was to be burgled, police surrounded the property, only to discover Laura and Bryant very much at home. Bryant was furious to be disturbed. Laura was amused until Gellibrands was burgled a few days later while she was staying in London.[36]

The burglary, as well as the extension of the M25 motorway, which would come within 2 miles of Gellibrands, prompted Laura to move again. She made plans to sell the house and relocate permanently to London. She decided to auction off much of the furniture at Christie's auction house. With only Portman Towers as her base in future, Laura culled much of the beautiful furniture collection that she had built up during her lifetime. The sale at Christies on Tuesday, 19 April 1983 featured a total of 244 items.[37] Her granddaughter, Anabel, visited two days before the sale and was 'staggered by what she was getting rid of'.[38]

By 1983, the relationship between Bryant and Laura had cooled again. A Salisbury neighbour remembers seeing them together at an event in the cathedral. 'They barely spoke to each other,' he recalls. 'I remember doubting the marriage would ever happen.'[39] Bryant was also perceptive enough to realise that the relationship was over, writing to Laura on 18 June 1983, 'My lost but dearly loved Darling'.[40]

In September 1983, Laura accompanied the colonel to Frankfurt for a business trip where she dazzled at a series of official dinners. Alex Young remained a firm, but much derided part of Laura's life. He would take her to regular lunches at the Ritz, as well lavish trips abroad, including Germany, Portugal and Paris. 'He was good to her,' Hugo Vickers recalls.[41] When he splashed out on a lavish suite for Laura at the George V Hotel in Paris, he asked her what she thought of the drawing room as they travelled back to London. 'Was there a drawing room?' Laura had replied loftily, not having bothered to look during her stay.[42]

By the time Bryant published his final book, *Set in a Silver Sea*, in February 1984, the relationship between him and Laura was well and truly over, although the pair continued to exchange letters. When Sir Arthur Bryant died on 22 January 1985, Laura regretted not seeing her former beau. In a letter to Hugo Vickers, she admits, 'I feel awful not to have gone for a visit to the Close', adding, 'I have felt much sadder than I expected by Arthur's departure from this rather grim earth [...] I was often infuriated by his late night calls but I shall certainly miss them.'[43] She attended his funeral service at Salisbury Cathedral on Monday, 28 January 1985, accompanied by Hugo Vickers, as well as the memorial service, held at Westminster Abbey on Friday, 15 March.

Laura's great friends, and her admirers, began to slip away during the last decade of her life. Lanning Roper died in London on 22 March 1983. De Meiss-Teuffen, who had continued to send energetic love letters to Laura, died suddenly from heart failure in Zürich on 9 October 1984. Diana Cooper died in June 1986, and the Duchess of Windsor died at her home in Paris on 24 April 1986. Laura was among the small number of people invited to attend the duchess' funeral, which was held at St George's Chapel, Windsor, on Tuesday, 29 April 1986. Finally, the ever-adoring colonel died at his home in Reigate on 7 March 1989.

But Laura remained active, spending regular weekends in Surrey with Loelia Lindsay and her husband, Martin. She also enjoyed annual summer visits to Venice, frequently accompanied by Hugo Vickers, who became something of a surrogate son. When at home, Laura read a lot and enjoyed watching television. And there were epic telephone conversations. 'She was a tremendous telephoner,' Hugo remembers. 'On one occasion when I had the flu she called me on-and-off for about eight hours.'[44]

She also, wisely, gave up driving, surrendering 'my faithful car', her silver Mercedes SL sports car which she had bought in 1971.[45] Hugo Vickers recalls a last journey with Laura. 'She smacked into a parked car and immediately said, "Oh, I didn't see that". I never let her drive again.'[46] Laura had been a terrible driver for all of her life. When asked who was the worst driver, Laura or the terrifying Diana Cooper, who drove as if in a demolition derby, Laura's daughter thought for a moment before saying, 'Diana. But only by a fraction.'[47]

And there was still a faithful stream of visitors to Portman Towers. Her former Hertfordshire House neighbour, Suzy Guthrie Moir, remembers visiting with her children. 'Laura adored children. As long as they weren't her own.'[48] And her granddaughter agrees, 'She revved up small children to do the worst possible things.'[49] Ivan Moffat was also a frequent visitor to Portman Towers for energetic games of bridge, which often went on into the early hours.

Friendship became increasingly important to Laura as she entered her seventies. 'In her old age she became better at having friends,' Sara remembers. 'She knew about having friends latterly.'[50]

Laura also began to suffer from serious ill health. 'There were several flirtations with cancer,' her granddaughter remembers, after which Laura gave up smoking.[51] In August 1988, Laura developed breast cancer and had a tumour removed from her left breast at St Bartholomew's Hospital in London. She chose not to receive radiotherapy and was prescribed Tamoxifen, a drug used to prevent breast cancer.[52] The cancer returned in 1989 and she was admitted to the London Clinic.

Her family was told that she was likely to die, but Laura rallied and during her convalescence greatly enjoyed surprising her fellow patients.[53] 'She would walk up and down the corridor, opening all the doors,' Hugo Vickers recalls. 'She said all the other patients were like mummies – they were all bandaged up after facelifts.'[54]

Laura returned to Portman Towers, where she would still receive visitors in a 'chiffon dressing gown and pearls'.[55] Dr Cooper had continued to prescribe a high level of barbiturates to her, which began to affect her speech and reactions in the last year before her death. 'Towards the end of her life she was groggy,' Anabel says.[56]

On the morning of 19 February 1990, Laura was found dead in her bed at her Portman Towers flat by her faithful housekeeper Marsella, who had worked for Laura since 1968. She had died in her sleep at the age of 74. Barrington Cooper signed the death certificate, saying to Sara, 'Your mother was at peace with her life for the very first time.'[57]

There was some speculation that Laura's death might not have been entirely natural. Her granddaughter, Anabel, recalls, 'This is conjecture, but when she died, she hadn't been feeling great. She might have accidentally overdosed.'[58] Sara agrees, recalling that Barrington Cooper blamed her mother's death on 'too many sleeping pills'.[59] The night before she died, she had telephoned her granddaughter, Anabel; her daughter, Sara; and Hugo Vickers; 'All of her favourite people,' Hugo concludes.[60]

The funeral at All Saint's Church, Coleshill, was well attended but muted. 'It was pretty grim, that funeral,' Anabel remembers. 'There was a ghastly purple velvet thing over the coffin which Laura would have hated.'[61] Following the service, the mourners gathered outside the church as Laura was buried beside Michael Canfield.

For a woman who had been successively the Viscountess Long, the Countess of Dudley, Mrs Canfield, the Duchess of Marlborough and the Dowager Duchess of Marlborough, her gravestone is engraved simply with only her name 'Laura'. As Hugo Vickers wryly comments, 'Only the very grand would do that.'[62] As per Laura's instructions, she was buried next to her third husband, Michael. His equally simple stone bears the words, 'The Adorable Canfield'.

Throughout her life, Laura had preferred to turn away from any of life's unpleasantness, determinedly rewriting her own narrative with regards to her numerous love affairs. Buried next to the husband who had been planning to leave her, in a quiet, leafy churchyard, Laura had finally written her own happy ending.

ACKNOWLEDGEMENTS

I didn't realise until I came to write this book that writing is very much a team effort. Without the help and support of so very many people, this book would never have happened. So, thank you to the whole of the below team:

Above all, I want to extend a very special thank you to Sara Morrison and Anabel Loyd, who patiently put up with my exhausting questions about their family, as well as providing me with photographs of Ann and Laura. Not only that, they were also kind enough to give me endless lunches, coffees and, absolutely vital to any biographer, delicious banoffee pie. I am so grateful to them both.

Thank you also to Andrew Lycett, who was kind enough to share his thoughts on Ann and Ian with me, and to Phoenix/Orion Books for allowing me to quote from Andrew's definitive biography of Ian Fleming.

Hugo Vickers has been unfailingly generous with his time, sharing his memories of Laura, as well as allowing me access to his extensive archive.

I am hugely grateful to the following people, organisations and institutions who have generously helped me with interviews, memories, letters and archives, as well as their time:

David Loyd, Alexandra Randall, Matthew Parker, Suzy Guthrie Moir, David Edington, April Ashley, Mary Coad, the Duke and Duchess of Buccleuch, Kathryn Price, Crispin Powell, the Lord and Lady Edward Manners, Suzy Reindorp, David Reindorp, Alexa Frost and the Blenheim Estate, the Ian Fleming Estate and the Ian Fleming Publications Limited Team, the Estate of Robert Harling and Biteback Publishing, John Morrell, Karen Morrell, Helen Morrell, Mark Baker, Elouise Carden, Pamela Tansey, Mark Beynon, Jess Jordan, Peter Hill, the Coffey family, Sophy Welch, Zoe Dhami, Kumal Dhami, Donna Trim, Becky Morrison, Claire Pritchard, Stephanie King, David King, Fiona Simons, Mark Amory, Gerald Sangster, John Pearson, the Countess of Avon, Lady Ashburton, the Hon. Fionn Morgan, Chris Bamber, Alex Boulton and Lana Salah.

And my personal thanks to Danny and Lavinia Richardson and Tom Reindorp.

Lastly, but by no means least, thank you to Sarah Coffey, who has been unfailingly generous with her time and unstinting in her patience when listening to me endlessly talk through this project and always provided gentle and helpful advice.

NOTES

Chapter 1: Introduction and the Beginning

1 Sara Morrison, interview.
2 *Ibid.*
3 *Ibid.*
4 Anabel Loyd, interview.
5 David Edington, interview.
6 Sara Morrison, interview.
7 *Ibid.*
8 *Ibid.*
9 Hugo Vickers, interview (attrib.).
10 Sara Morrison, interview.
11 David Reindorp, interview.
12 Letters belonging to the author's family.
13 Sara Morrison, interview.
14 Amory, Mark (ed.), *The Letters of Ann Fleming* (London: Collins Harvill, 1985), p.25.
15 Sara Morrison, interview.
16 *Ibid.*
17 *Ibid.*
18 *Ibid.*
19 *Ibid.*

Chapter 2: Childhood

1 Marlborough, Laura, *Laughter from a Cloud* (London: Weidenfeld and Nicolson, 1980), p.4.
2 *Ibid.*, p.15.
3 *Ibid.,* p.3.
4 *Ibid.*
5 *Ibid.*, p.12.
6 *Ibid.*, p.5.
7 Sara Morrison, interview.
8 *Ibid.*
9 Marlborough, *Laughter from a Cloud*, p.3.

10   Amory, *The Letters of Ann Fleming*, p.21.
11   Sara Morrison, interview.
12   Amory, *The Letters of Ann Fleming*, p.27.
13   Sara Morrison, interview.

Chapter 3: Teenage Years

1   Marlborough, *Laughter from a Cloud*, p.13.
2   Amory, *The Letters of Ann Fleming*, p.30.
3   Mary Coad, interview.
4   *Ibid.*
5   Amory, *The Letters of Ann Fleming*, p.32.
6   *Ibid.*, p.33.
7   *Ibid.*

Chapter 4: First Marriages

1   Amory, *The Letters of Ann Fleming*, p.34.
2   *Ibid.*
3   *Ibid.*, p.33.
4   David Edington, interview.
5   Marlborough, *Laughter from a Cloud,* p.21.
6   *Daily Mirror*, 7 October 1932.
7   Marlborough, *Laughter from a Cloud,* p.21.
8   Sara Morrison, interview.
9   Suzy Guthrie Moir, interview.
10   Anabel Loyd, interview.
11   Marlborough, *Laughter from a Cloud*, p.20.
12   Sara Morrison, interview.
13   *Ibid.*
14   *Ibid.*
15   *Ibid.*
16   *Star* (Christchurch), 21 December 1933.
17   Marlborough, *Laughter from a Cloud*, p.22.
18   *Ibid.*
19   Marshall, Russell, *Dictionary of New Zealand Biography* (New Zealand: Bridget Williams Books, 1998) p.8.
20   Marlborough, *Laughter from a Cloud*, p.21.
21   Sara Morrison, interview.
22   *Ibid.*
23   Marlborough, *Laughter from a Cloud*, p.28.
24   Hugo Vickers, interview.
25   Sara Morrison, interview.
26   Marlborough, *Laughter from a Cloud*, p.30.
27   Sara Morrison, interview.
28   *Ibid.*
29   *Ibid.*

Chapter 5: Ann Meets Ian ... and Esmond

1   Lycett, Andrew, *Ian Fleming* (London: Phoenix, 1995) p.93.
2   *Ibid.*
3   *Ibid.*, p.96.
4   Sara Morrison, interview (attrib.)
5   *Ibid.*
6   Lycett, *Ian Fleming* p.69.
7   Amory, *The Letters of Ann Fleming*, p.35.
8   Andrew Lycett, interview.
9   Amory, *The Letters of Ann Fleming*, p.36.
10 Bourne, Richard, *The Lords of Fleet Street* (London: Unwin Hyman, 1990) p.134.
11 *Ibid.*
12 *Ibid.*, p.137.
13 *Ibid.*
14 *Ibid.*
15 *Ibid.*, p.139.
16 Mary Coad, interview.
17 Bourne, *The Lords of Fleet Street*, p.146.
18 *Ibid.*, p.145.
19 *Ibid.*, p.146.
20 Sara Morrison, interview.
21 *Ibid.*
22 *Ibid.*
23 Amory, *The Letters of Ann Fleming*, p.36.
24 Lycett, *Ian Fleming*, p.93.
25 *Ibid.*, p.79.
26 Amory, *The Letters of Ann Fleming*, p.37.
27 *Ibid.*, p.32.
28 Anabel Loyd, interview.

Chapter 6: Laura Meets Eric ... and Randolph

1   Sara Morrison, interview.
2   Marlborough, *Laughter from a Cloud*, p.32.
3   Sara Morrison, interview.
4   White, Roger, *Witley Court and Gardens* (London: English Heritage, 2006).
5   Cunneen, Chris, *Australian Dictionary of Biography, Volume 8* (Carlton: Melbourne University Press, 1981) pp.347–48.
6   Obituary, Lord Dudley, *The Times*, 30 June 1932.
7   19 February 1919, *Tatler*.
8   Marlborough, *Laughter from a Cloud*, p.33.
9   Sara Morrison, interview.
10 *Ibid.*
11 'Tragic Death of Viscount's Son', 11 December 1929, *Nottingham Evening Post*.
12 'Air Disaster', 25 July 1930, *Gloucester Citizen*.
13 Marlborough, *Laughter from a Cloud*, p.34.
14 *Ibid.*, p.35.

15 Suzy Guthrie Moir, interview.

16 Osbourne, Frances, *The Bolter* (London: Virago Press, 2008) p.43.

17 Marlborough, *Laughter from a Cloud*, p.36.

18 *Ibid.*, p.66.

19 Letter, Randolph Churchill to Laura, 28 January 1943.

20 Leslie, Anita, *Cousin Randolph: The Life of Randolph Churchill* (London: Hutchinson, 1985).

21 Marlborough, *Laughter from a Cloud*, p.66.

22 Sara Morrison, interview.

23 *Ibid.*

24 Taylor, A.J.P., *Churchill: Four Faces and the Man* (London: Allen Lane, 1969).

25 Soames, M., *Clementine Churchill* (London: Doubleday, 2002).

26 Sara Morrison, interview.

27 Private memorandum from the collection of Laura, Duchess of Marlborough (undated).

28 Letter, Randolph Churchill to Laura, 24 October 1942.

29 Letter, Virginia Cowles to Laura, undated.

30 Letter, Randolph Churchill to Laura, 28 January 1943.

31 Letter, Randolph Churchill to Laura, 25 December 1944.

32 Letter, Laura to Michael Canfield, undated.

Chapter 7: The War

1 Speech by Neville Chamberlain, 30 September 1938.

2 Marlborough, *Laughter from a Cloud*, p.40.

3 *Ibid.*, p.43.

4 *Ibid.*, p.44.

5 Sara Morrison, interview.

6 *Ibid.*

7 Amory, *The Letters of Ann Fleming*, p.38.

8 *Ibid.*

9 Mary Coad, interview.

10 Sara Morrison, interview.

11 *Ibid.*

12 Amory, *The Letters of Ann Fleming*, p.39.

13 Sara Morrison, interview.

14 *Ibid.*

15 Obituary, Roddy Thesiger, *The Times*, 6 April 2005.

16 21 September 1940, *Country Life*.

17 Bourne, *The Lords of Fleet Street*, p.130.

18 *Ibid.*, p.155.

19 Amory, *The Letters of Ann Fleming*, p.41.

20 *Ibid.*, p.39.

21 *Ibid.*, p.41.

22 *Ibid.*

23 'Honeymoon at Himley Hall', 29 November 1934, *The Times*.

24 Marlborough, *Laughter from a Cloud*, p.46.

25 *Ibid.*, p.48.

26 *Ibid.*

27 Sara Morrison, interview.

28 Suzy Guthrie Moir, interview.

29 15 November 1940, BBC.

30 Letter, Matron O.M. Snowden, correspondence of Laura, Duchess of Marlborough.

31 Sara Morrison, interview.

32 *Ibid.*

33 *Ibid.*

34 Marlborough, *Laughter from a Cloud*, p.58.

35 *Ibid.*

36 Private memorandum from the collection of Laura, Duchess of Marlborough, 10 August 1975.

37 Statement to the High Court of Frances Laura, Countess of Dudley, the petitioner, *Dudley vs Dudley*, February 1954, p.1.

38 Sara Morrison, interview.

39 Marlborough, *Laughter from a Cloud*, p.71.

40 Statement to the High Court of Frances Laura, Countess of Dudley, the petitioner, *Dudley vs Dudley*, February 1954, p.2.

41 Sara Morrison, interview.

42 *Ibid.*

43 Marlborough, *Laughter from a Cloud*, p.79.

44 Statement to the High Court of Frances Laura, Countess of Dudley, the petitioner, *Dudley vs Dudley*, February 1954, p.3.

45 Marlborough, *Laughter from a Cloud*, p.81.

46 *Ibid.*, p.51.

47 Sara Morrison, interview.

48 *Ibid.*

49 Amory, *The Letters of Ann Fleming*, p.42.

50 *Ibid.*

Chapter 8: Post-War

1 Sara Morrison, interview.

2 Lycett, *Ian Fleming*, p.79.

3 Amory, *The Letters of Ann Fleming*, p.42.

4 Andrew Lycett, interview.

5 Sara Morrison, interview.

6 Amory, *The Letters of Ann Fleming*, p.42.

7 Mary Coad, interview.

8 Bourne, *The Lords of Fleet Street*, p.156.

9 *Ibid.*

10 Sara Morrison, interview.

11 *Ibid.*

12 Amory, *The Letters of Ann Fleming*, p.103.

13 *Ibid.*, p.44.

14 Sara Morrison, interview.

15 Statement to the High Court of Frances Laura, Countess of Dudley, the petitioner, *Dudley vs Dudley*, February 1954, p.3.

16 *Ibid.*

17 Sara Morrison, interview.

18 Amory, *The Letters of Ann Fleming*, p.44.

19 *Ibid.*

Chapter 9: Laura and Eric

1   Statement to the High Court of Frances Laura, Countess of Dudley, the petitioner, *Dudley vs Dudley*, February 1954, p.1.

2   *Coal Industry Nationalisation Act 1946*, Chapter 59.

3   Private memorandum from the collection of Laura, Duchess of Marlborough, undated.

4   *Ibid.*

5   Sara Morrison, interview.

6   15 January 1947, *The Times*, 'Himley Hall Sold to Coal Board'.

7   Marlborough, *Laughter from a Cloud*, p.101.

8   Ziegler, Philip, *King Edward VIII* (New York: Alfred A. Knopf, 1991) pp.306–40.

9   Vickers, Hugo, *Behind Closed Doors* (London: Hutchison, 2011) p.339.

10 Marlborough, *Laughter from a Cloud*, p.101.

11 *Ibid.*

12 Suzy Guthrie Moir, interview.

13 Sara Morrison, interview.

14 Vickers, *Behind Closed Doors*, p.339.

15 *Ibid.*

16 *Ibid.*, pp.339–40.

17 Sara Morrison, interview.

18 Marlborough, *Laughter from a Cloud*, p.105.

19 Letter from the Duchess of Windsor to the Countess of Dudley, from RMS *Queen Elizabeth*, dated 1946.

20 Vickers, *Behind Closed Doors*, p.339.

21 'Windsor Jewels Bring an Auction Record', *The New York Times*, 3 April 1987.

22 Private memorandum from the collection of Laura, Duchess of Marlborough, undated.

23 Sara Morrison, interview.

24 *Ibid.*

25 *Ibid.*

26 *Ibid.*

27 *Ibid.*

28 *Ibid.*

29 *Ibid.*

30 Statement to the High Court of Frances Laura, Countess of Dudley, the petitioner, *Dudley vs Dudley*, February 1954, p.3.

31 *Ibid.*, p.6.

32 Marlborough, *Laughter from a Cloud*, p.91.

33 *Ibid.*, p.92.

34 *Ibid.*

35 *Ibid.*

36 *Ibid.*, p.93.

37 *Ibid.*

38   *Ibid.*
39   Statement to the High Court of Frances Laura, Countess of Dudley, the petitioner, *Dudley vs Dudley*, February 1954, p.4.
40   *Ibid.*
41   Letter from Randolph Churchill to Laura, 11 May 1946.
42   Statement to the High Court of Frances Laura, Countess of Dudley, the petitioner, *Dudley vs Dudley*, February 1954, p.4.
43   Sara Morrison, interview.
44   Statement to the High Court of Frances Laura, Countess of Dudley, the petitioner, *Dudley vs Dudley*, February 1954, p.6.

Chapter 10: Ann and Esmond ... and the *Daily Mail*

1   Bourne, *The Lords of Fleet Street*, p.155.
2   Anabel Loyd, interview.
3   Lycett, *Ian Fleming*, p.163.
4   *Ibid.*
5   *Ibid.*, p.159.
6   Sara Morrison, interview.
7   Amory, *The Letters of Ann Fleming*, p.31.
8   Sara Morrison, interview.
9   Amory, *The Letters of Ann Fleming*, p.241.
10   22 June 1946, *Daily Mail*.
11   *Daily Mail* Ideal Home Exhibition Records, 1910–90, Victoria & Albert Museum, catalogue 1947.
12   Interview, Sara Morrison.
13   Amory, *The Letters of Ann Fleming*, p.43.
14   Memoriam, Ann Fleming 1913–1981 (Order of Service), 20 November 1981.
15   Sara Morrison, interview.
16   Memoriam, Ann Fleming 1913–1981 (Order of Service), 20 November 1981.
17   Anabel Loyd, interview.
18   Sara Morrison, interview.
19   Amory, *The Letters of Ann Fleming*, p.44.
20   Sara Morrison, interview.
21   Amory, *The Letters of Ann Fleming*, p.53.
22   Lycett, *Ian Fleming*, p.172.
23   *Ibid.*
24   *Ibid.*
25   Sara Morrison, interview.
26   Amory, *The Letters of Ann Fleming*, p.56.
27   *Ibid.*, p.58.

Chapter 11: Laura and Eric, *Deuxième Partie*

1   Statement to the High Court of Frances Laura, Countess of Dudley, the petitioner, *Dudley vs Dudley*, February 1954, p.6.
2   *Ibid.*

3   *Ibid.*
4   Sara Morrison, interview.
5   Marlborough, *Laughter from a Cloud*, p.107.
6   *Ibid.*
7   Sara Morrison, interview.
8   Marlborough, *Laughter from a Cloud*, p.108.
9   *Ibid.*
10 *Ibid.*
11 Sara Morrison, interview.
12 *Ibid.*
13 Marlborough, *Laughter from a Cloud*, p.126.
14 *Ibid.,* p.127.
15 *Ibid.,* p.129.
16 Sara Morrison, interview.
17 Marlborough, *Laughter from a Cloud*, p.108.
18 Sara Morrison, interview.
19 Marlborough, *Laughter from a Cloud*, p.103.
20 Sara Morrison, interview.
21 Marlborough, *Laughter from a Cloud*, p.109.
22 Amory, *The Letters of Ann Fleming*, p.59.
23 Marlborough, *Laughter from a Cloud*, p.109.
24 *Ibid.*
25 Private memorandum from the collection of Laura, Duchess of Marlborough, undated.
26 Sara Morrison, interview.
27 Osbourne, *The Bolter*, p.244.
28 Statement to the High Court of Frances Laura, Countess of Dudley, the petitioner, *Dudley vs Dudley*, February 1954, p.7.
29 Marlborough, *Laughter from a Cloud*, p.109.
30 Statement to the High Court of Frances Laura, Countess of Dudley, the petitioner, *Dudley vs Dudley*, February 1954, p.7.
31 Hugo Vickers, interview.
32 Amory, *The Letters of Ann Fleming*, p.59.
33 Statement to the High Court of Frances Laura, Countess of Dudley, the petitioner, *Dudley vs Dudley*, February 1954, p.7.
34 *Ibid.*

Chapter 12: Pregnancies

1   Andrew Lycett, interview.
2   Lindsay, Loelia, *Cocktails and Laughter* (London: Hamish Hamilton, 1983) p.99.
3   Lycett, *Ian Fleming*, p.180.
4   *Ibid.*
5   Amory, *The Letters of Ann Fleming*, p.62.
6   *Ibid.*
7   *Ibid.*
8   *Ibid.,* p.56.
9   *Ibid.,* p.66.

10 *Ibid.*

11 *Ibid.*

12 Lycett, *Ian Fleming*, p.182.

13 Amory, *The Letters of Ann Fleming*, p.68.

14 Lycett, *Ian Fleming*, p.186.

15 Marlborough, *Laughter from a Cloud*, p.112.

16 Sara Morrison, interview.

17 *Ibid.*

18 Letter from Gerry Koch de Gooreynd to Laura, 27 May 1948.

19 Letter from Gerry Koch de Gooreynd to Laura, 4 June 1948.

20 Sara Morrison, interview.

21 Marlborough, *Laughter from a Cloud*, p.114.

22 Statement to the High Court of Frances Laura, Countess of Dudley, the petitioner, *Dudley vs Dudley*, February 1954, p.8.

23 Amory, *The Letters of Ann Fleming*, p.69.

24 Lycett, *Ian Fleming*, p.187.

25 Amory, *The Letters of Ann Fleming*, p.70.

26 *Ibid.*, p.71.

27 Lycett, *Ian Fleming*, p.188.

28 *Ibid.*, p.192.

29 Amory, *The Letters of Ann Fleming*, p.76.

30 Lycett, *Ian Fleming*, p.193.

31 Amory, *The Letters of Ann Fleming*, p.77.

32 *Ibid.*, p.78.

33 Lycett, *Ian Fleming*, p.195.

34 *Ibid.*

35 Amory, *The Letters of Ann Fleming*, p.79.

36 Sara Morrison, interview.

37 Amory, *The Letters of Ann Fleming*, p.80.

38 Lycett, *Ian Fleming*, p.208.

39 *Ibid.*, p 207.

40 Bourne, *The Lords of Fleet Street*, p.158.

41 Lycett, *Ian Fleming*, p.200.

42 Bourne, *The Lords of Fleet Street*, p.158.

43 Amory, *The Letters of Ann Fleming*, p.93.

44 *Ibid.*, p.94.

45 *Ibid.*, p.97.

46 *Ibid.*

47 *Ibid.*

48 *Ibid.*

49 Lycett, *Ian Fleming*, p.211.

50 *Ibid.*, p.210.

51 *Ibid.*, p.211.

52 Amory, *The Letters of Ann Fleming*, p.98.

53 *Ibid.*

54 *Ibid.*

55 *Ibid.*, p.99.

56 Statement to the High Court of Frances Laura, Countess of Dudley, the petitioner, *Dudley vs Dudley*, February 1954, p.17.

57   Amory, *The Letters of Ann Fleming*, p.100.
58   *Ibid.*, p.101.
59   Lycett, *Ian Fleming*, p.214.
60   Amory, *The Letters of Ann Fleming*, p.103.
61   *Ibid.*, p.102.

Chapter 13: Ann and Ian ... and James Bond

1   Sara Morrison, interview.
2   *Ibid.*
3   *Ibid.*
4   *Ibid.*
5   Harling, Robert, *Ian Fleming* (London: Biteback Publishing, 2015), p.260. Reproduced by kind permission of Biteback Publishing.
6   Amory, *The Letters of Ann Fleming*, p.103.
7   Payn, Graham, and Sheridan Morley (eds), *The Noël Coward Diaries* (London: Phoenix, 1982) p.142.
8   Amory, *The Letters of Ann Fleming*, p.110.
9   Lycett, *Ian Fleming*, p.144.
10   Sara Morrison, interview.
11   John Pearson, interview.
12   Amory, *The Letters of Ann Fleming*, p.108.
13   Lycett, *Ian Fleming*, p.218.
14   *Ibid.*
15   *Ibid.*
16   Amory, *The Letters of Ann Fleming*, p.108.

Chapter 14: Laura and the 1950s

1   Statement to the High Court of Frances Laura, Countess of Dudley, the petitioner, *Dudley vs Dudley*, February 1954, p.19.
2   *Ibid.*
3   *Ibid.*, p.19.
4   *Ibid.*, p.20.
5   *Ibid.*
6   *Ibid.*, p.21.
7   Sara Morrison, interview.
8   *Ibid.*
9   Marlborough, *Laughter from a Cloud*, p.135.
10   Sara Morrison, interview.
11   Marlborough, *Laughter from a Cloud*, p.141.
12   Sara Morrison, interview.
13   *Ibid.*
14   Obituary, Anthony Pelissier, *The New York Times*, 7 April 1988.
15   Sara Morrison, interview.
16   *Ibid.*
17   *Ibid.*

18 Hugo Vickers, interview.
19 Letter, Anthony Pelissier to Laura (date unknown).
20 Sara Morrison, interview.
21 Letter, Anthony Pelissier to Laura, Saturday, 11 April (year unknown).
22 *Ibid.*
23 *Ibid.*, 17 September 1957.
24 Sara Morrison, interview.
25 Statement to the High Court of Frances Laura, Countess of Dudley, the petitioner, *Dudley vs Dudley*, February 1954.
26 Marlborough, *Laughter from a Cloud*, p.134.
27 Lee, Sidney, *Dictionary of National Biography* (London: Smith, Elder and Co., 1894).
28 Sara Morrison, interview.
29 *Ibid.*
30 *Ibid.*
31 *Ibid.*
32 Marlborough, *Laughter from a Cloud*, p.146.
33 *Ibid.*
34 Sara Morrison, interview.
35 Marlborough, *Laughter from a Cloud*, p.146.
36 Sara Morrison, interview.
37 Letter, Anthony Pelissier to Laura, 17 September 1957.
38 Marlborough, *Laughter from a Cloud*, p.148.
39 Suzy Guthrie Moir, interview.
40 Marlborough, *Laughter from a Cloud*, p.149.
41 Letter, Anthony Pelissier to Laura (undated: Tuesday evening).
42 Sara Morrison, interview.
43 *Ibid.*
44 Marlborough, *Laughter from a Cloud*, p.151.

Chapter 15: Ann and Ian ... and Family Life

1   Amory, *The Letters of Ann Fleming*, p.99.
2   *Ibid.*, p.111.
3   Marlborough, *Laughter from a Cloud*, p.121.
4   Amory, *The Letters of Ann Fleming*, p.117.
5   *Ibid.*, p.120.
6   *Ibid.*, p.119.
7   *Ibid.*, p.301.
8   *Ibid.*, p.121.
9   *Ibid.*
10 *Ibid.*, p.120.
11 *Ibid.*, p.301.
12 Lycett, *Ian Fleming*, p.226.
13 *Ibid.*, p.227.
14 Sara Morrison, interview.
15 Amory, *The Letters of Ann Fleming*, p.119.
16 Harling, *Ian Fleming*, p.273.
17 Amory, *The Letters of Ann Fleming*, p.125.

18 *Ibid.*, p.122.
19 Lycett, *Ian Fleming*, p.237.
20 Amory, *The Letters of Ann Fleming*, p.123.
21 *Ibid.*, p.124.
22 Lycett, *Ian Fleming*, p.239.
23 Amory, *The Letters of Ann Fleming*, p.126.
24 Harling, *Ian Fleming*, p.27.
25 John Pearson, interview.
26 *Ibid.*
27 *Ibid.*
28 Amory, *The Letters of Ann Fleming*, p.129.
29 Lycett, *Ian Fleming*, p.241.
30 *Ibid.*, p.243.
31 Amory, *The Letters of Ann Fleming*, p.127.
32 John Pearson, interview.
33 Amory, *The Letters of Ann Fleming*, p.134.
34 'Death at Sea of Lord Norwich', *The Times*, 2 January 1954.
35 Amory, *The Letters of Ann Fleming*, p.135.
36 *Ibid.*, p.136.
37 *Ibid.*
38 Mosley, Charlotte (ed.), *The Letters of Nancy Mitford and Evelyn Waugh* (London: Hodder and Stoughton, 1996) p.341.
39 *Ibid.*
40 Sara Morrison, interview.
41 Amory, *The Letters of Ann Fleming*, p.139.
42 *Ibid.*, p.140.
43 *Ibid.*
44 *Ibid.*
45 *Ibid.*, p.58.
46 Sara Morrison, interview.
47 Amory, *The Letters of Ann Fleming*, p.144.
48 Lycett, *Ian Fleming*, p.234.
49 Amory, *The Letters of Ann Fleming*, p.146.
50 Sara Morrison, interview.
51 Amory, *The Letters of Ann Fleming*, p.149.
52 *Ibid.*
53 *Ibid.*, p.150.
54 *Ibid.*
55 *Ibid.*
56 *Ibid.*, p.151.
57 *Ibid.*, p.156.
58 *Ibid.*, p.161.
59 Lycett, *Ian Fleming*, p.274.
60 Amory, *The Letters of Ann Fleming*, p.165.
61 *Ibid.*
62 Lycett, *Ian Fleming*, p.282.
63 *Ibid.*
64 Amory, *The Letters of Ann Fleming*, p.170.
65 Sara Morrison, interview.

66   Amory, *The Letters of Ann Fleming*, p.170.
67   *Ibid.*, p.171
68   Lycett, *Ian Fleming*, p.382.

Chapter 16: Ian and Blanche – Ann and Gaitskell

1   Lycett, *Ian Fleming*, p.279.
2   *Ibid.*
3   Sara Morrison, interview.
4   Lycett, *Ian Fleming*, p.279.
5   Amory, *The Letters of Ann Fleming*, p.179.
6   Sara Morrison, interview.
7   Brivati, Brian, *Hugh Gaitskell* (London: Richard Cohen Books, 1996).
8   *Ibid.*
9   David Edington, interview.
10   Brivati, *Hugh Gaitskell*, p.143.
11   *Ibid.*
12   Williams, Phillip Maynard, *Hugh Gaitskell* (London: Jonathon Cape, 1985) p.151.
13   Sara Morrison, interview.
14   *Ibid.*
15   *Ibid.*
16   *Ibid.*
17   Amory, *The Letters of Ann Fleming*, p.184.
18   *Ibid.*, p.189.
19   *Ibid.*
20   *Ibid.*
21   Lycett, *Ian Fleming*, p.308.
22   *Ibid.*
23   Sara Morrison, interview.
24   *Ibid.*
25   *Ibid.*
26   Lycett, *Ian Fleming*, p.308.
27   Amory, *The Letters of Ann Fleming*, p.195.
28   Lycett, *Ian Fleming*, p.314.
29   *Ibid.*, p.315.
30   Amory, *The Letters of Ann Fleming*, p.210.
31   *Ibid.*
32   *Ibid.*, p.213.
33   Lycett, *Ian Fleming*, p.319.
34   Amory, *The Letters of Ann Fleming*, p.209.
35   Lycett, *Ian Fleming*, p.323.
36   Amory, *The Letters of Ann Fleming*, p.214.
37   *Ibid.*, p.213.
38   *Ibid.*
39   *Ibid.*
40   Lycett, *Ian Fleming*, p.330.
41   Amory, *The Letters of Ann Fleming*, pp.218–19.
42   *Ibid.*

43 *Ibid.*
44 Lycett, *Ian Fleming*, p.337.
45 Amory, *The Letters of Ann Fleming*, p.219.
46 *Ibid.*, p.221.
47 Sara Morrison, interview.
48 *Ibid.*
49 *Ibid.*
50 *Ibid.*
51 Amory, *The Letters of Ann Fleming*, p.222.
52 *Ibid.*, p.227.
53 *Ibid.*
54 *Ibid.*
55 Sara Morrison, interview.
56 Amory, *The Letters of Ann Fleming*, p.213.
57 Lycett, *Ian Fleming*, p.346.
58 Amory, *The Letters of Ann Fleming*, p.229.
59 *Ibid.*
60 Sara Morrison, interview.
61 Obituary, Sir John Morgan, *The Times*, 3 July 2012.
62 Amory, *The Letters of Ann Fleming*, p.283.
63 *Ibid.*, p.229.
64 *Ibid.*, p.283.
65 Lycett, *Ian Fleming*, p.374.
66 Amory, *The Letters of Ann Fleming*, p.233.
67 *Ibid.*, p.237.
68 *Ibid.*, p.213.
69 Harling, *Ian Fleming*, p.321. Reproduced by kind permission of Biteback Publishing.
70 *Ibid.*, p.325.
71 *Ibid.*
72 Amory, *The Letters of Ann Fleming*, p.242.
73 *Ibid.*, p.243.
74 *Ibid.*
75 *Ibid.*, p.250.
76 *Ibid.*
77 *Ibid.*
78 Lycett, *Ian Fleming*, p.363.
79 *Ibid.*
80 *Ibid.*

Chapter 17: Laura and 'The Adorable Canfield'

1 David Edington, interview.
2 *Ibid.*
3 'Michael Temple Canfield: US Army Enlistment Document', 23 January 1944.
4 Marlborough, *Laughter from a Cloud*, p.157.
5 Sara Morrison, interview.
6 Letter, Laura to Michael Canfield (undated).
7 Sara Morrison, interview.

8   *Ibid.*
9   'Michael Temple Canfield: US Army Enlistment Document', 23 January 1944.
10 Sara Morrison, interview.
11 Dubois, Diana, *In Her Sister's Shadow: An Intimate Biography of Lee Radziwill* (New York: Little Brown and Company, 1995) p.65.
12 *Ibid.*
13 *Ibid.*, p.60.
14 *Ibid.*
15 Letter, Michael Canfield to Laura, 14 December 1959.
16 David Edington, interview (attributed).
17 *Ibid.*
18 Marlborough, *Laughter from a Cloud*, p.152.
19 *Ibid.*
20 Anabel Loyd, interview.
21 Marlborough, *Laughter from a Cloud*, p.152.
22 *Ibid.*, p.151
23 Private memorandum from the collection of Laura, Duchess of Marlborough, undated.
24 Marlborough, *Laughter from a Cloud*, p.153.
25 *Ibid.*
26 *Ibid.*, p.154.
27 Letter, Anthony Pelissier to Laura (undated).
28 Letter, Laura to Michael Canfield, 3 September 1959.
29 Marlborough, *Laughter from a Cloud*, p.155.
30 Sara Morrison, interview.
31 Letter, Laura to Michael Canfield, 3 September 1959.
32 Sara Morrison, interview.
33 Anabel Loyd, interview.
34 *Ibid.*
35 Sara Morrison, interview.
36 Personal photograph album of Laura, Duchess of Marlborough.
37 Anabel Loyd, interview.
38 Hugo Vickers, interview.
39 David Reindorp, interview.
40 Letters to the author's family.
41 Suzy Guthrie Moir, interview.
42 Letter, Michael Canfield to Laura, 11 February 1960.
43 Sara Morrison, interview.
44 Hugo Vickers, interview.
45 Letter, Laura to Michael Canfield (undated).
46 Suzy Guthrie Moir, interview.
47 Letter, Laura to Michael Canfield (undated).
48 Letter, Laura to Michael Canfield, May 1962 (day unknown).
49 Amory, *The Letters of Ann Fleming*, p.320.
50 Sara Morrison, interview.
51 Anabel Loyd, interview.
52 *Ibid.*
53 Letter, Laura to Michael Canfield (undated).
54 Sara Morrison, interview.

55 Marlborough, *Laughter from a Cloud*, p.172.
56 *Ibid.*, p.173.
57 *Ibid.*, p.177.
58 Letter, Laura to Michael Canfield (undated).
59 Written in a personal photograph album of Laura, Duchess of Marlborough.
60 Marlborough, *Laughter from a Cloud*, p.177.
61 *Ibid.*
62 Letter, Laura to Michael Canfield (dated December 1965).
63 Letter, Laura to Michael Canfield (dated 'Tuesday Night').
64 Letter, Laura to Michael Canfield (undated).
65 Letter, Laura to Michael Canfield, 11 December 1965.
66 Letter, Laura to Michael Canfield (undated).
67 Letter, Laura to Michael Canfield, 18 November 1969.
68 Sara Morrison, interview.
69 Marlborough, *Laughter from a Cloud*, p.193.
70 Sara Morrison, interview.
71 Letter, Laura to Michael Canfield, 23 December 1968.
72 Suzy Guthrie Moir, interview.
73 *Ibid.*
74 Letter, Michael Canfield to Laura, 14 November 1968.
75 Marlborough, *Laughter from a Cloud*, p.197.
76 Sara Morrison, interview.
77 *Ibid.*
78 *Ibid.*
79 Marlborough, *Laughter from a Cloud*, p.201.
80 Sara Morrison, interview.
81 Marlborough, *Laughter from a Cloud*, p.203.
82 Obituary, Michael Temple Canfield, *The New York Times*, 22 December 1969.
83 Order of Service, funeral of Michael Canfield, 24 December 1969.
84 Parish Church of All Saints, Coleshill.
85 Marlborough, *Laughter from a Cloud*, p.206.
86 'Lord Dudley Dies; Industrialist', *The New York Times*, 27 December 1969.
87 Hugo Vickers, interview.
88 Marlborough, *Laughter from a Cloud*, p.205.

Chapter 18: Ann and Ian … and the 1960s

1 Lycett, *Ian Fleming*, p.367.
2 Amory, *The Letters of Ann Fleming*, p.251.
3 *Ibid.*, p.259.
4 *Ibid.*
5 *Ibid.*, p.254.
6 Lycett, *Ian Fleming*, p.372.
7 *Ibid.*
8 Amory, *The Letters of Ann Fleming*, p.256.
9 *Ibid.*, p.258
10 Amory, *The Letters of Ann Fleming*, p.267.
11 *Ibid.*, p.269.

12 *Ibid.*, p.270.
13 *Ibid.*, p.271.
14 *Ibid.*, p.274.
15 *Ibid.*, p.276.
16 *Ibid.*, p.278.
17 Payn and Morley (eds), *The Noël Coward Diaries*, p.464.
18 Lycett, *Ian Fleming*, p.382.
19 Bourne, *The Lords of Fleet Street*, p.158.
20 Amory, *The Letters of Ann Fleming*, p.280.
21 Lycett, *Ian Fleming*, p.384.
22 *Ibid.*
23 Amory, *The Letters of Ann Fleming*, p.282.
24 *Ibid.*
25 Lycett, *Ian Fleming*, p.384.
26 *Ibid.*
27 Amory, *The Letters of Ann Fleming*, p.282.
28 Sara Morrison, interview.
29 Amory, *The Letters of Ann Fleming*, p.283–85.
30 Lycett, *Ian Fleming*, p.392.
31 Amory, *The Letters of Ann Fleming*, p.290.
32 Lycett, *Ian Fleming*, p.392.
33 *Ibid.*, p.428.
34 Amory, *The Letters of Ann Fleming*, p.293.
35 Sara Morrison, interview.
36 Amory, *The Letters of Ann Fleming*, p.296.
37 *Ibid.*, p.297.
38 *Ibid.*, p.302.
39 *Ibid.*, p.301.
40 *Ibid.*
41 *Ibid.*, p.302.
42 Andrew Lycett, interview.
43 Amory, *The Letters of Ann Fleming*, p.305.
44 *Ibid.*, p.306.
45 *Ibid.*, p.308.
46 *Ibid.*, p.310.
47 Williams, *Gaitskell*.
48 Lycett, *Ian Fleming*, p.407.
49 *Ibid.*
50 Amory, *The Letters of Ann Fleming*, p.303.
51 *Ibid.*, p.304.
52 *Ibid.*
53 *Ibid.*, p.315.
54 *Ibid.*, p.316.
55 Lycett, *Ian Fleming*, p.410.
56 Sara Morrison, interview.
57 *Ibid.*
58 Amory, *The Letters of Ann Fleming*, p.318.
59 *Ibid.*, pp.320–21.
60 Brivati, *Hugh Gaitskell*, p.426.

61   Amory, *The Letters of Ann Fleming*, pp.320–21.

62   Brivati, *Hugh Gaitskell*, p.426.

63   Lycett, *Ian Fleming*, p.414.

64   *Ibid.*

65   Amory, *The Letters of Ann Fleming*, p.321.

66   Brivati, *Hugh Gaitskell*, p.427.

67   Amory, *The Letters of Ann Fleming*, p.321.

68   *Ibid.*

69   *Ibid.*

70   Sara Morrison, interview.

71   The archives of the Duke of Buccleuch.

72   Anabel Loyd, interview.

73   *Ibid.*

74   Mosley, *The Letters of Nancy Mitford and Evelyn Waugh*, p.488.

75   *Ibid.*

76   Pearson, John, *The Life of Ian Fleming* (London: Jonathon Cape, 1966) p.363.

77   Lycett, *Ian Fleming*, p.432.

78   Amory, *The Letters of Ann Fleming*, p.331.

79   *Ibid.*, p.335.

80   *Ibid.*

81   *Ibid.*, p.339.

82   *Ibid.*, p.340.

83   *Ibid.*

84   *Ibid.*

85   Sara Morrison, interview.

86   Amory, *The Letters of Ann Fleming*, p.340.

87   Lycett, *Ian Fleming*, p.438.

88   Amory, *The Letters of Ann Fleming*, p.342

89   *Ibid.*, p.348

90   Lycett, *Ian Fleming*, p.441.

91   Sara Morrison, interview.

92   Amory, *The Letters of Ann Fleming*, p.349

93   Lycett, *Ian Fleming*, p.443.

94   Pearson, *The Life of Ian Fleming*, p.368.

95   Lycett, *Ian Fleming*, p.443.

96   *Ibid.*

97   *Ibid.*

Chapter 19: Ann After Ian

1   Lycett, *Ian Fleming*, p.443.

2   Sara Morrison, interview.

3   Anabel Loyd, interview.

4   Harling, *Ian Fleming*, p.359. Reproduced by kind permission of Biteback Publishing.

5   Lycett, *Ian Fleming*, p.446.

6   Sara Morrison, interview.

7   Amory, *The Letters of Ann Fleming*, p.362.

8   *Ibid.*, p.363.

9   John Pearson, interview.
10 Sara Morrison, interview.
11 Amory, *The Letters of Ann Fleming*, p.366.
12 *Ibid.*
13 Sara Morrison, interview.
14 Campbell, John, *Roy Jenkins: A Well-Rounded Life* (London: Vintage, 2015).
15 Sara Morrison, interview.
16 *Ibid.*
17 David Edington, interview.
18 Sara Morrison, interview.
19 Brivati, Brian, *Lord Goodman* (London: Richard Cohen Books, 1999).
20 David Edington, interview.
21 Amory, *The Letters of Ann Fleming*, p.354.
22 Sara Morrison, interview.
23 David Edington, interview.
24 Amory, *The Letters of Ann Fleming*, p.380.
25 *Ibid.*, p.383.
26 John Pearson, interview.
27 Amory, *The Letters of Ann Fleming*, pp.374–76.
28 *Ibid.*, p.376.
29 *Ibid.*, p.377.
30 *Ibid.*, p.353.
31 *Ibid.*, p.381.
32 David Edington, interview.
33 Sara Morrison, interview.
34 Amory, *The Letters of Ann Fleming*, p.385.
35 *Ibid.*, p.386.
36 Obituary, Leslie O'Brien, *The Independent*, 27 November 1995.
37 David Reindorp, interview.
38 Amory, *The Letters of Ann Fleming*, p.391.
39 *Ibid.*
40 Sara Morrison, interview.
41 Anabel Loyd, interview.
42 Sara Morrison, interview.
43 Anabel Loyd, interview.
44 *Ibid.*
45 *Ibid.*
46 Hugo Vickers, interview.
47 Anabel Loyd, interview.
48 Sara Morrison, interview.
49 *Ibid.*
50 Hugo Vickers, interview.
51 Anabel Loyd, interview.
52 Amory, *The Letters of Ann Fleming*, p.393.
53 *Ibid.*
54 *Ibid.*
55 *Ibid.*
56 Hugo Vickers, interview.
57 Amory, *The Letters of Ann Fleming*, p.401.

Chapter 20: Laura and Bert ... and the 1970s

1   Private memorandum from the collection of Laura, Duchess of Marlborough, 10 August 1975.
2   Anabel Loyd, interview.
3   Sara Morrison, interview.
4   Suzy Guthrie Moir, interview.
5   *Ibid.*
6   *Ibid.*
7   *Ibid.*
8   Anabel Loyd, interview.
9   *Ibid.*
10 Letters of Laura, Duchess of Marlborough.
11 Sara Morrison, interview.
12 Hugo Vickers, interview.
13 Sara Morrison, interview.
14 *Ibid.*
15 Hugo Vickers, interview.
16 Marlborough, *Laughter from a Cloud*, p.219.
17 *Ibid.*, p.220.
18 Sara Morrison, interview.
19 Hugo Vickers, interview.
20 *Ibid.*
21 Sara Morrison, interview.
22 *Ibid.*
23 'Marlborough Marries Mrs Canfield', *The New York Times*, 27 January 1972.
24 Sara Morrison, interview.
25 Marlborough, *Laughter from a Cloud*, p.225.
26 *Ibid.*
27 *Ibid.*, p.226.
28 *Ibid.*
29 *Ibid.*
30 *Ibid.*, p.227.
31 *Ibid.*
32 *Ibid.*, p.228.
33 *Ibid.*
34 *Ibid.*, p.229.
35 *Ibid.*
36 *Ibid.*
37 *Ibid.*
38 Sara Morrison, interview.
39 Amory, *The Letters of Ann Fleming*, p.407.
40 *Ibid.*
41 Hugo Vickers, interview.
42 Marlborough, *Laughter from a Cloud*, p.231.
43 Sara Morrison, interview.
44 Marlborough, *Laughter from a Cloud*, p.231.
45 *Ibid.*, p.232.
46 *Ibid.*, p.233.

47   *Ibid.*
48   *Ibid.*, p.235.
49   Sara Morrison, interview.
50   *Ibid.*
51   Private memorandum from the collection of Laura, Duchess of Marlborough, 10 August 1975.
52   Marlborough, *Laughter from a Cloud*, p.240.
53   Anabel Loyd, interview.
54   Letter, Laura to Sir Arthur Bryant, 28 December 1982.
55   Anabel Loyd, interview.
56   *Ibid.*
57   Marlborough, *Laughter from a Cloud*, p.245.
58   Anabel Loyd, interview.
59   *Ibid.*
60   Marlborough, *Laughter from a Cloud*, p.246.
61   Anabel Loyd, interview.
62   *Ibid.*

Chapter 21: Ann and the Last Years

1   Lycett, *Ian Fleming*, p.450.
2   David Edington, interview.
3   Amory, *The Letters of Ann Fleming*, p.402.
4   *Ibid.*, p.406.
5   Anabel Loyd, interview.
6   *Ibid.*
7   *Ibid.*
8   Amory, *The Letters of Ann Fleming*, p.409.
9   Hugo Vickers, interview.
10   Lycett, *Ian Fleming*, p.451.
11   Berton, Pierre, *The Cool Crazy Committed World of the Sixties: Twenty-One Television Encounters* (Canada: McClelland and Stewart, 1966).
12   Anabel Loyd, interview.
13   Amory, *The Letters of Ann Fleming*, p.413.
14   *Ibid.*, p.415.
15   Anabel Loyd, interview.
16   *Ibid.*
17   Amory, *The Letters of Ann Fleming*, p.414.
18   Anabel Loyd, interview.
19   Amory, *The Letters of Ann Fleming*, p.414.
20   Lycett, *Ian Fleming*, p.451.
21   Hugo Vickers, interview.
22   Anabel Loyd, interview.
23   Sara Morrison, interview.
24   Amory, *The Letters of Ann Fleming*, p.415.
25   *Ibid.*, p.418.
26   *Ibid.*, p.416.

27 Mosley, Charlotte (ed.), *In Tearing Haste: Letters Between Deborah Devonshire and Patrick Leigh Fermor* (London: John Murray, 2008).
28 Amory, *The Letters of Ann Fleming*, p.419.
29 *Ibid.*, p.418.
30 *Ibid.*, pp.424–25.
31 *Ibid.*, p.426.
32 *Ibid.*, p.428.
33 *Ibid.*, p.426.
34 Anabel Loyd, interview.
35 Amory, *The Letters of Ann Fleming*, p.427.
36 Sara Morrison, interview.
37 Order of Service, the funeral of Ann Fleming, 17 July 1981.
38 Memoriam, Ann Fleming 1913–1981 (Order of Service), 20 November 1981.
39 *Ibid.*
40 *Ibid.*
41 Sara Morrison, interview.

Chapter 22: Laura and the 1980s

1   Hugo Vickers, interview.
2   Anabel Loyd, interview.
3   Hugo Vickers, interview.
4   Letter, Sir Arthur Bryant to Laura, 17 April 1980.
5   Robinson, William Sydney, *Historic Affairs* (London: Zuleika, 2021).
6   Letter, Sir Arthur Bryant to Laura, 17 April 1980.
7   Letter, Sir Arthur Bryant to Laura (undated).
8   Letter, Laura to Sir Arthur Bryant (undated).
9   Letter, Sir Arthur Bryant to Laura (undated).
10 Hugo Vickers, interview.
11 Sara Morrison, interview.
12 *Ibid.*
13 Anabel Loyd, interview.
14 David Reindorp, interview.
15 Hugo Vickers, interview.
16 *Ibid.*
17 *Ibid.*
18 Letter, Sir Arthur Bryant to Laura, 28 December 1980.
19 Letter, A.E. Hamlin & Co. to Messrs Coles and Stevenson, 8 December 1980.
20 *Ibid.*
21 Letter, Sir Arthur Bryant to Peter Egerton-Warburton, 18 November 1980.
22 David Reindorp, interview.
23 Letter, Laura to Sir Arthur Bryant, 5 December 1980.
24 Letter, Sir Arthur Bryant to Laura, 28 December 1980.
25 Letter, Laura to Sir Arthur Bryant, 29 December 1980.
26 Letter, Laura to Sir Arthur Bryant, 14 October 1981.
27 Letter, Sir Arthur Bryant to Laura, 21 July 1981.
28 Anabel Loyd, interview.
29 'Zionist Speaker', *The Jewish Chronicle*, 13 December 1946.

30 Letter, Hans de Meiss-Teuffen to Laura, July 1980.
31 Letter, Hans de Meiss-Teuffen to Laura, 19 July 1981.
32 Letter, Hans de Meiss-Teuffen to Laura, 9 November 1981.
33 Letter, Laura to Sir Arthur Bryant, 13 November 1981.
34 Letter, Sir Arthur Bryant to Laura, 14 November 1981.
35 Letter, Laura to Sir Arthur Bryant, 3 August 1982.
36 'The duchess has copped out', *Daily Mail*, 12 October 1982.
37 'The remaining contents of Gellibrands, Chalfont St Peter, Buckinghamshire removed to Christies's South Kensington', Christie's Catalogue, 19 April 1983.
38 Anabel Loyd, interview.
39 David Reindorp, interview.
40 Letter, Sir Arthur Bryant to Laura, 18 June 1983.
41 Hugo Vickers, interview.
42 *Ibid.*
43 Letter, Laura to Hugo Vickers.
44 Hugo Vickers, interview.
45 Personal photograph album of Laura, Duchess of Marlborough. Reproduced by kind permission of the Morrison family.
46 Hugo Vickers, interview.
47 Sara Morrison, interview.
48 Suzy Guthrie Moir, interview.
49 Anabel Loyd, interview.
50 Sara Morrison, interview.
51 Anabel Loyd, interview.
52 Letter, O.J.A. Gilmour to Dr Barrington Cooper, 11 August 1988.
53 Anabel Loyd, interview.
54 Hugo Vickers, interview.
55 *Ibid.*
56 Anabel Loyd, interview.
57 Sara Morrison, interview.
58 Anabel Loyd, interview.
59 Sara Morrison, interview.
60 Hugo Vickers, interview.
61 Anabel Loyd, interview.
62 Hugo Vickers, interview.

BIBLIOGRAPHY

Amory, Mark (ed.), *The Letters of Ann Fleming* (London: Collins Harvill, 1985).

Bedell Smith, Sally, *Reflected Glory: The Life of Pamela Churchill Harriman* (New York: Touchstone, 1996).

Berton, Pierre, *The Cool Crazy Committed World of the Sixties: Twenty-One Television Encounters* (Canada: McClelland and Stewart, 1966).

Bloch, Michael (ed.), *James Lees Milne Diaries 1942–1954* (London: John Murray, 2007).

Bourne, Richard, *The Lords of Fleet Street* (London: Unwin Hyman, 1990).

Brivati, Brian, *Hugh Gaitskell* (London: Richard Cohen Books, 1996).

Brivati, Brian, *Lord Goodman* (London: Richard Cohen Books, 1999).

Campbell, John, *Roy Jenkins: A Well-Rounded Life* (London: Vintage, 2015).

Cooper, Artemis, *Patrick Leigh Fermor: An Adventure* (London: John Murray, 2012).

Cromer, Esme, *From this Day Forward* (Stoke Abbott: Thomas Harmsworth Publishing Company, 1991).

Davie, Michael (ed.), *The Diaries of Evelyn Waugh* (London: Weidenfeld and Nicolson, 1976).

De Courcy, Anne, *Debs at War* (London: Phoenix, 2005).

De Courcy, Anne, *The Husband Hunters* (London: Orion, 2017).

Dubois, Diana, *In Her Sister's Shadow: An Intimate Biography of Lee Radziwill* (New York: Little Brown and Company, 1995).

Eden, Sir Anthony, *Full Circle* (London: Cassell and Company, 1960).

Eden, Clarissa, *A Memoir: From Churchill to Eden* (London: Weidenfeld and Nicolson, 2007).

Evans, Sian, *Queen Bees* (London: Two Roads, 2016).

Fenwick, Simon, *Joan: The Remarkable Life of Joan Leigh Fermor* (London: Macmillan, 2017).

Harling, Robert, *Ian Fleming* (London: Biteback Publishing, 2015).

Leslie, Anita, *Cousin Randolph* (London: Hutchinson, 1985).

Lindsay, Lady Loelia, *Cocktails and Laughter* (London: Hamish Hamilton, 1983).

Lycett, Andrew, *Ian Fleming* (London: Phoenix, 1995).

Marlborough, Laura, *Laughter from a Cloud* (London: Weidenfeld and Nicolson, 1980).

Mosley, Charlotte (ed.), *In Tearing Haste: Letters Between Deborah Devonshire and Patrick Leigh Fermor* (London: John Murray, 2008).

Mosley, Charlotte (ed.), *The Letters of Nancy Mitford and Evelyn Waugh* (London: Hodder and Stoughton, 1996).

Mosley, Charlotte (ed.), *The Mitfords: Letters Between Six Sisters* (London: Harper Perennial, 2007).

Norwich, John Julius (ed.), *Darling Monster: The Letters of Lady Diana Cooper to her Son John Julius Norwich 1939–1952* (London: Chatto and Windus, 2013).

Osbourne, Francis, *The Bolter* (London: Virago, 2008).

Parker, Matthew, *Goldeneye* (London: Windmill Books, 2014).

Payn, Graham, and Sheridan Morley (eds), *The Noël Coward Diaries* (London: Phoenix, 1982).

Pearson, John, *The Life of Ian Fleming* (London: Jonathon Cape, 1966).

Robinson, William Sydney, *Historic Affairs* (London: Zuleika, 2021).

Trethewey, Rachel, *Before Wallis* (Stroud: The History Press, 2018).

Vickers, Hugo, *Behind Closed Doors* (London: Hutchison, 2011).

Vickers, Hugo, *Cecil Beaton: The Authorised Biography* (London: Weidenfeld and Nicolson, 1985).

Wainwright, Robert, *Sheila* (London: Allen and Unwin, 2014).

Weidenfeld, George, *Remembering My Good Friends* (London: Harper Collins, 1994).

Williams, Phillip Maynard, *Hugh Gaitskell* (London: Jonathon Cape, 1985).

Ziegler, Philip, *Diana Cooper: The Biography of Lady Diana Cooper* (London: Penguin, 1983).

Zinovieff, Sofka, *The Mad Boy, Lord Berners, My Grandmother and Me* (London: Jonathan Cape, 2014).

INDEX